Outlier States

Outlier States

American Strategies to Change, Contain, or Engage Regimes

Robert S. Litwak

Woodrow Wilson Center Press
Washington, D.C.

The Johns Hopkins University Press
Baltimore

EDITORIAL OFFICES

Woodrow Wilson Center Press
Woodrow Wilson International Center for Scholars
One Woodrow Wilson Plaza
1300 Pennsylvania Avenue NW
Washington, D.C. 20004-3027
www.wilsoncenter.org

ORDER FROM

The Johns Hopkins University Press
Hampden Station
P.O. Box 50370
Baltimore, Maryland 20211
Telephone 1-800-527-5487
www.press.jhu.edu/books/

2 4 6 8 9 7 5 3 1

Library of Congress Cataloging-in-Publication Data is available.

ISBN-13: 978-1-4214-0811-8 (hardcover : alk. paper)
ISBN-13: 978-1-4214-0812-5 (pbk. : alk. paper)
ISBN-10: 1-4214-0811-2 (hardcover : alk. paper)
ISBN-10: 1-4214-0812-0 (pbk. : alk. paper)

Woodrow Wilson International Center for Scholars

The Woodrow Wilson International Center for Scholars is the national, living U.S. memorial honoring President Woodrow Wilson. In providing an essential link between the worlds of ideas and public policy, the Center addresses current and emerging challenges confronting the United States and the world. The Center promotes policy-relevant research and dialogue to increase understanding and enhance the capabilities and knowledge of leaders, citizens, and institutions worldwide. Created by an act of Congress in 1968, the Center is a nonpartisan institution headquartered in Washington, D.C., and supported by both public and private funds.

Conclusions or opinions expressed in Center publications and programs are those of the authors and speakers and do not necessarily reflect the views of the Center staff, fellows, trustees, advisory groups, or any individuals or organizations that provide financial support to the Center.

The Center is the publisher of *The Wilson Quarterly* and home of Woodrow Wilson Center Press and dialogue television and radio. For more information about the Center's activities and publications, please visit us on the Web at www.wilsoncenter.org.

To Liz,

and to my father and the memory of my late mother

Contents

Abbreviations

BRICs	Brazil, Russia, India, and China
CCP	Chinese Communist Party
CIA	Central Intelligence Agency (U.S.)
CPA	Coalition Provisional Authority
DPRK	Democratic People's Republic of Korea
EU	European Union
GATT	General Agreement on Tariffs and Trade
GDP	gross domestic product
IAEA	International Atomic Energy Agency
ICC	International Criminal Court
ICISS	International Commission on Intervention and State Sovereignty
ICJ	International Court of Justice
NATO	North Atlantic Treaty Organization
NIE	National Intelligence Estimate (U.S.)
NPT	(nuclear) Nonproliferation Treaty
OAU	Organization of African Unity
P5+1	permanent members of the UN Security Council plus Germany
PLA	People's Liberation Army (China)
PRC	People's Republic of China
PSI	Proliferation Security Initiative
RDD	radiation dispersal device
ROK	Republic of Korea
UNSCOM	United Nations Special Commission
WMD	weapons of mass destruction
WTO	World Trade Organization

Preface

This book is the third in an unintended series. The first, *Rogue States and U.S. Foreign Policy: Containment after the Cold War*, traced the origins of the "rogue state" concept and its translation into policy. My research into rogue states grew out of my work on the National Security Council in the mid-1990s, when the term entered the official U.S. foreign policy lexicon. Rogue states—those pursuing weapons of mass destruction and sponsoring terrorism—were declared a distinct category in the post–Cold War international system by the U.S. government.

The central argument of the book was that the term, which had no standing in international law, obscured our understanding of, and distorted policy toward, the disparate group of states lumped together and demonized within this category. *Rogue States and U.S. Foreign Policy* advocated the development of a repertoire of differentiated strategies, each tailored to the particular circumstances of a specific country. Coinciding with the publication of the book in February 2000, I contributed an op-ed piece to the *Washington Post*, injecting the distilled argument into the public policy debate. Because the category had become a political straitjacket and a liability, the Clinton administration subsequently dropped the term "rogue state" in favor of "states of concern."

But the George W. Bush administration revived it before September 11, 2001, and after the 9/11 attacks, the concept was at the heart of its redefinition of threat and the radical shift in U.S. strategy. The administration linked the threats of the new era—the "nexus" of proliferation and terrorism—to the *character* of the regimes. The containment of rogue states would no longer suffice because the threatening conduct arose from the very nature of the ruling regimes. Changing their behavior required changing the regimes themselves. The emphasis on regime change was central to the argument for preventive war in Iraq in 2003. My second book, *Regime Change: U.S. Strategy through the Prism of 9/11*, published in 2007, analyzed these conceptual and policy developments. It contrasted Iraq with the other important precedent of 2003, Libya, where Muammar Qaddafi acceded to weapons of mass destruction disarmament in December 2003 without a change of regime. The book argued that in addressing the nuclear crises with North Korea and Iran, the Bush administration was sending a mixed message as to whether the U.S. objective was regime change or behavior change, and in the process, it was accomplishing neither. I recommended that the United States end the mixed message by making clear that the United States would "take yes for an answer" and offer North Korea and Iran a "structured choice" to test their nuclear intentions.

The Obama administration came to office with the avowed commitment to diplomatically engage North Korea and Iran, which the president referred to as "outliers." This third and final volume in the series, picking up the analysis where *Regime Change* ended, addresses the shift in strategy from the Bush to Obama administrations. To provide context, and as an aid to the reader, the core arguments of the previous two books are recapitulated. Extending the analysis from 2007 to the present, *Outlier States* seeks to inform the broader scholarly and policy debate about whether and, if so, how states that flout international norms can be brought into compliance and reintegrated into the "community of nations." The central policy dilemma explored in this study is that the "outliers," the rulers of states such as Iran and North Korea, view the very process of integration as a threat to regime survival.

Daniel Patrick Moynihan, the founding father of the Woodrow Wilson Center, believed that how we think about the world shapes how we act in the world. The issue is not just a matter of shifting nomenclature—"rogue" to "outlier." Rather, the words reflect and drive underlying concepts that have far-reaching practical consequences.

Acknowledgments

This book could not have been completed without the help and counsel of many colleagues and friends. First and foremost, I would like to thank Lee Hamilton, Jane Harman, and Michael Van Dusen for providing an ideal work environment at the Wilson Center to complete this project. I am deeply grateful to James Morris, Joseph Pilat, Mitchell Reiss, and Ronald Steel for reviewing and providing indispensable comments on the entire manuscript. I also thank those who critiqued draft chapters or with whom I discussed the book's argument: Michael Adler, Shaul Bakhash, Shahram Chubin, Martin Dmitrov, Haleh Esfandiari, Michael Glennon, James Goldgeier, Robert Hathaway, Bruce Hoffman, Bruce Jentleson, Melvyn Leffler, Christian Ostermann, Daniel Poneman, Walter Reich, Gary Samore, David Sanger, Joseph Sassoon, Thom Shanker, Sean Singer, Etel Solingen, Paul Stares, and Samuel Wells.

Essential research assistance was provided by a superb team of young scholars: Bronwen De Sena, Oliver Gilbert, Jasper Hicks, Chloe Lizotte, Gabriela Plump, and Rachel Tecott (who also edited the manuscript). I am indebted to the Wilson Center's resourceful librarian, Janet Spikes, and my assistant, Tonya Boyce. My sincere thanks also go to Peter Reid and Wilson Center Press director Joseph Brinley for expeditiously moving the book through production, as well as to editor Linda Stringer and designer Michelle Furman.

Finally, I could not have completed the book without the steadfast support of those to whom it is dedicated—my wife, Liz, and my father and late mother, Robert and Doris Litwak.

Washington, D.C.
March 2012

Outlier States

Introduction

In addition to ongoing wars in Iraq and Afghanistan, President Barack Obama inherited twin nuclear challenges with North Korea and Iran. President Obama described the two countries as "outliers"—states that flout international norms by defying their obligations under the nuclear Non-proliferation Treaty. Senior White House aides confirmed that use of the term, which appeared in an April 2010 interview with the *New York Times* about the administration's "Nuclear Posture Review," was a calculated departure from the George W. Bush–era moniker of "rogue state."[1] As with the Obama administration's effort to "reset" the strained U.S. relationship with Russia, so too was there an avowed interest in reorienting U.S. policy toward the disparate group of states that had been previously designated as "rogues." The shift in nomenclature from rogue to outlier was intended to convey that a pathway was open for these states to rejoin the "community of nations" if they came into compliance with international norms.

The rise of the rogue state concept coincided with the end of the Cold War and the end of the hot war in the Persian Gulf to reverse the Iraqi invasion of Kuwait. Saddam Hussein's Iraq was the archetype—a hostile state pursuing weapons of mass destruction (WMD) and employing terrorism as an instrument of state policy. The Clinton administration declared that rogue states (whose core group also included Iran, North Korea, and Libya) constituted a distinct category of states in the international system. Rogue status was linked to external behavioral criteria (i.e., activities with consequences beyond the state's borders) rather than internal behavioral cri-

1

teria (i.e., the conduct of the state's ruling regime toward its own people). The term, which had no standing in international law, was applied selectively. For example, Syria, which met the criteria, was excluded from the rogues' gallery because of its importance to the Middle East peace process, whereas Cuba, which met none of the criteria, was frequently included on U.S. domestic political grounds. In addition to clouding U.S. policymakers' understanding of this diverse set of countries, the rogue optic also distorted policy. Relegation of states to rogue status complicated the ability of the Clinton administration to conduct normal diplomacy with them. And why not, since the connotation of "rogue" was that their ruling regimes were essentially irredeemable? The rogue policy came up against hard realities when the Clinton administration wanted to pragmatically engage North Korea (to address its nuclear program) and Iran (when the election of a reformist president created a diplomatic opening). National Security Adviser Sandy Berger's acknowledgment that the term "rogue state" had become a "sloppy convenience that obscures more than it clarifies" presaged the Clinton administration's decision to drop the term.[2]

The George W. Bush administration revived the rogue rubric before 9/11; however, in the aftermath of the terrorist attacks, the concept was central to the administration's definition of threat and the consequent recasting of strategy. Threat was linked to the *character* of the adversaries of the United States. The 9/11 attacks focused attention on the "nexus" of proliferation and terrorism—specifically, the driving scenario that an "unpredictable" rogue state, such as Iraq, might transfer a nuclear weapon to an undeterrable terrorist group, such as Al Qaeda. That assessment of threat precipitated a change in strategy—from a pre-9/11 emphasis on *containment* (for example, keeping Saddam Hussein in his box) to a post-9/11 emphasis on *regime change*. Regime change was depicted as the only way to bring about durable change in rogue states because their threatening behavior derived from their very nature and they were deemed incapable of evolving.

The Bush administration launched a preventive war of choice against Iraq in March 2003, without the legitimizing imprimatur of the UN Security Council, because it viewed the threat posed by Saddam Hussein through the prism of 9/11. Nine months after the fall of Baghdad, in December 2003, came the surprise announcement that Muammar Qaddafi had acceded to verifiable WMD disarmament. Although Bush administration officials claimed Libya as "a dividend" of the Iraq war, the crux of the deal was a tacit but clear security assurance to the Qaddafi regime: if the Qaddafi regime gave up its unconventional arsenal, Washington would eschew the objective of regime change. Without that assurance of nonbelligerence, Qaddafi would not have had an incentive to accept WMD disarmament; indeed, if the Libyan dictator had believed that Washington was intent on regime change regardless of any change in Tripoli's behavior, he would have had an incentive to acquire a nuclear deterrent as quickly as possible. Thus, in 2003, two important precedents were set: in Iraq, nonproliferation through a change *of* regime in Iraq; in Libya, nonproliferation through a change *in* a regime.

In dealing with the nuclear challenges in Iran and North Korea, the Bush administration was caught between the precedents set in Iraq and Libya. The administration could not replicate the Iraq precedent of direct military intervention, and it was unwilling to offer Tehran and Pyongyang the security assurance that had sealed the Libya deal. With this mixed message as to the objective of U.S. policy, it was unclear whether the Bush administration was prepared to take *yes* for an answer. Obama campaigned for the presidency on a platform of negotiating with Iran, North Korea, and other adversarial states, which his Republican opponent criticized as appeasement.

The rogue reset was evident in President Obama's offer in his January 2009 inaugural address to "extend a hand [to adversaries] if you are willing to unclench your fist."[3] The Obama administration eschewed regime change rhetoric and reframed the challenges posed by North Korea and Iran in terms of their noncompliance with established international norms rather than with reference to a unilateral American political concept. In his December 2009 Nobel Peace Prize acceptance speech, Obama defended his engagement strategy, citing the historical precedent of an earlier president and a state that, at the time, was viewed as the functional equivalent of a contemporary rogue state: "In light of the Cultural Revolution's horrors, Nixon's meeting with Mao appeared inexcusable—and yet it surely helped set China on a path where millions of its citizens have been lifted from poverty and connected to open societies." Declaring that it is "incumbent upon all of us to insist that nations like Iran and North Korea do not game the system ...," Obama concluded, "engagement with repressive regimes lacks the satisfying purity of indignation.... [But] no repressive regime can move down a new path unless it has the choice of an open door."[4]

The Obama administration's approach, captured under the rubric "comprehensive engagement," was laid out more fully in its National Security Strategy of May 2010.[5] The document stated that the United States sought the further development of a "rules-based international system." It offered "adversarial governments" a structured "choice": abide by international norms (and thereby gain the tangible economic benefits of "greater integration with the international community") or remain in noncompliance (and thereby face international isolation and punitive consequences).[6] The Obama administration unpacked the Bush administration's mixed message, making clear its openness to a Libya-type agreement. But the adversarial states rebuffed the extended hand and refused to walk through the open door: North Korea conducted a second nuclear test in May 2009 and sank a South Korean naval vessel; Iran balked at a proposed agreement by the P5+1 (the permanent members of the UN Security Council plus Germany) to bring the country's nuclear program into Nonproliferation Treaty compliance. Opponents of the Obama administration's engagement strategy, turning the Bush-era criticism on its head, asked whether Obama would take *no* for answer.

The nuclear crises with North Korea and Iran are playing out against the backdrop of potentially significant societal developments in both countries. In North Korea, the death of Kim Jong Il, the "Dear Leader," in December 2011 fueled concerns of a succession crisis, and in Iran, the civil unrest that followed the contested presidential election of June 2009 exposed a major rift within the clerical leadership and undercut the regime's domestic political legitimacy.

The U.S. dilemma is that the nuclear crises are immediate, whereas the prospects for regime change or evolution in these countries are uncertain. The timelines for nuclear weapons acquisition and societal change are not in sync. And U.S. policy-makers cannot defer the nuclear issue while some indeterminate domestic political process unfolds in the two countries. The dilemma may be managed, but it cannot be resolved. In fashioning an appropriate policy response, the U.S. administration should look to the strategic playbook of an earlier era. Containment—the strategy adopted by the United States to meet the global challenge posed by the Soviet Union—should be retooled to address these lesser threats of the contemporary era. A new strategy of containment, whose key element would be deterrence, would decouple the nuclear issue from the question of regime change and rely on internal forces as the agent of societal change. At the outset of the Cold War, George Kennan wrote that the Soviet system "bears within it the seeds of its own decay" and argued for a strategy of "long-term, patient but firm and vigilant containment."[7]

By externally balancing Soviet power until internally generated agents of change could transform the Soviet reality, containment *was* a strategy of regime change. That essentially revisionist outcome points to what one might call the "regime change conundrum." The United States both defends and aspires to change the status quo. That the United States seeks to promote a rules-based international system is consistent with America's role as a status quo power. Yet Washington's parallel efforts to bring other states, particularly adversarial governments, into compliance with international norms governing internal behavior (with respect to human rights and democratic government) are viewed by the target states as those of a revisionist power.

The regime change conundrum is at the heart of the issue of providing security assurances to outlier states. The Libyan deal incorporated a U.S. assurance of nonattack if the Qaddafi regime relinquished its WMD arsenal, and the Obama administration was willing, as part of its nuclear diplomacy, to extend a similar assurance to North Korea and Iran. The U.S.-assisted regime change in Libya in 2011 greatly complicates the U.S. administration's future ability to deploy such a security assurance in negotiations. That the North Atlantic Treaty Organization (NATO) intervention was undertaken on humanitarian grounds is a distinction unrecognized by Pyongyang and Tehran. North Korea and Iran now claim that the 2011 Libyan precedent proves that Qaddafi never should have given up his nuclear program, though it should be noted that both countries had rejected the Obama administration's diplomatic overtures more than a year *before* the NATO military intervention in Libya.

Yet beyond the traditional concern of states about external attack, outlier states seek a second, even more fundamental form of security assurance—namely, an affirmative assurance from the United States that a regime will survive if it integrates more fully into the international system. The United States neither can nor should offer such assurance. The outlier regime will seek to gain the tangible economic benefits of integration while insulating itself from the political consequences.

Although the focus of this study is contemporary, the central issue it engages is one of the most traditional in world politics: the challenge to international order posed by states that defy its governing norms. The book's argument unfolds through its structure.

Chapter 1 provides historical and conceptual context. What is an "outlier state"—and what is the character of the international system within which it occupies an estranged status? The chapter examines the development of terms such as "pariah" and "outlaw state," which have also been used to describe such countries. It highlights the key conceptual shift that occurred around 1980, when the definition of "rogue," "outlaw," and "pariah states" shifted from its basis in internal behavioral criteria (i.e., how regimes treat their own people) to its grounding in external behavioral criteria (such as WMD acquisition and state sponsorship of terrorism). The chapter examines the rise and development of the "rogue state" concept and policy under the Clinton and Bush administrations, as well as the shift to the use of "outlier state" under the Obama administration. It also provides a brief assessment of significant power shifts reshaping the international system (i.e., the rise of the BRICs — Brazil, Russia, India, and China). The redistribution of power among states will affect how norms whose contravention defines outlier status are set and enforced. To what extent is there a consensus on the interests and values that allow one to refer to the international system as an "international society" or a "community of nations"? Finally, the chapter explores the operational meaning of "compliance" and how improved compliance can promote the reintegration of outlier states.

Chapter 2 explores four historical pathways by which states that defied international norms in the twentieth century have been reintegrated into the international system. The pathways and illustrative examples of each are (a) the assimilation of a defeated great power (Nazi Germany after World War II); (b) the evolution of revolutionary states into orthodox great powers (the Soviet Union under Mikhail Gorbachev and China under Deng Xiaoping); (c) regime change from without — that is, external intervention to oust ruling regimes, particularly by neighboring states (Tanzania's 1979 invasion of Uganda to overthrow Idi Amin and Vietnam's 1978 invasion of Cambodia to oust the Khmer Rouge regime); and, finally, (d) regime change from within (the 1989 overthrow of the Ceauşescu regime in Romania and the end of apartheid rule in South Africa in the early 1990s). Through a structured comparison, the chapter seeks to identify what political scientist Alexander George described as "conditional generalizations" — in this context, the identification of conditions favoring integration and conditions impeding that process. The cases make clear, though, that integration is not synonymous with compliance. For example, the former Soviet republic of Russia no longer poses a revolutionary threat to the international system, but as a country it has far to go in achieving democratic governance. (Vladimir Putin may not be democratic, but he is no Joseph Stalin.) From the foregoing cases, one can glean general historical patterns that can inform specific strategy development toward an outlier state.

Chapter 3 builds on the preceding conceptual and historical framework to address strategy development toward outliers. Kennan's pathbreaking article "The Sources of Soviet Conduct" highlighted how strategies are premised on concepts of societal change.[8] His containment strategy was based on what was essentially a prophecy of how the Cold War would end. Concepts of societal change constitute critical threshold assumptions for strategy development. Divergent concepts support alternative strategies. For example, in the case of Iran's nuclear challenge, the option of undertaking urgent military action is premised on the assumption that the Tehran regime is apocalyptic and undeterrable; alternatively, the option of imposing targeted sanctions on the regime's core interest groups (such as the Revolutionary Guards) assumes that the regime will respond to a cost-benefit calculation and change its behavior if meaningful pressure is brought to bear. Unfortunately, these concepts of societal change are often not subjected to the rigorous analysis necessary. Terms such as "containment" and "engagement" are general concepts that require specific content to be translated into strategies toward particular states. The chapter lays out an approach to target state analysis that incorporates a broad range of domestic and external (structural) determinants, while importantly distinguishing between factors that are specific to a particular regime and those that are generic and that would therefore pertain to a ruling regime of whatever character in the outlier state.

The discussion of target state analysis and the continuum of strategies (running from regime change to engagement) leads to case studies of Saddam Hussein's Iraq and Qaddafi's Libya, in which important regime change precedents were set. Yet over a period of decades, U.S. policies toward those regimes ran the gamut, from engagement to regime change, depending on different assessments of their circumstances. For example, after the Iran-Iraq War, the George H. W. Bush administration moved toward greater engagement with Iraq on the assumption that the Saddam Hussein regime would seek a quiescent regional environment within which it could focus on domestic reconstruction.

Chapter 4 focuses on the challenge posed by nuclear outliers. It addresses the covert efforts by North Korea and Iran to acquire nuclear weapons—and the parallel campaigns by the United States and others to thwart their ambitions. The analysis of these cases is framed within an initial discussion of proliferation dynamics (conditions of nuclear restraint and proliferation), as well as of terrorist acquisition of a weapon via the deliberate transfer from a state. Although the "leakage" of a nuclear weapon from Pakistan (or Russia) through theft or inadequate security is the more likely pathway of terrorist acquisition, the transfer scenario involving Iran or North Korea has dominated the U.S. strategic debate precisely because both countries are adversarial proliferators.

The Conclusion distills the study's policy-relevant findings with respect to strategy development and implementation. Like "rogue state," the term "outlier state" is used with reference to conduct that violates external behavioral norms. But states such as North Korea and Iran that engage in conduct with threatening implications beyond their borders also flout internal behavioral norms by mistreating their own populations. In contrast, not every human rights pariah (Burma and Zimbabwe) has a nuclear weapons program and is a state sponsor of terrorism. A major challenge for U.S. policy-makers is how to address conduct that violates external behavioral norms and poses a threat to U.S. interests while simultaneously calling out a regime on conduct that violates internal behavioral norms with respect to human rights.

Chapter 1

Outlier States and International Society

In its publicly released National Security Strategy of 2010, the Obama administration declared that "those nations that defy international norms … will be denied the incentives that come with greater integration and collaboration with the international community."[1] Integration or isolation —that is the stark choice presented to states whose regimes egregiously violate international norms. The administration's promotion of a "rules-based international system" raises the thorny issue of how and by whom those rules putting the outliers beyond the pale are set, interpreted, and enforced.[2] More fundamentally, what is the character of the international order from which outlier states stand apart?

States remain the principal units of international relations and constitute a "system," according to international relations theorist Hedley Bull, when "there is interaction between them sufficient to make the behavior of each a necessary element in the calculations of the other."[3] Moving beyond this minimalist definition of interstate relations, Bull argues that an international system becomes an international society when states "conscious of certain common interests and common values … conceive themselves to be bound by a common set of rules in their relations with one another, and share in the working of common institutions."[4] This definition of "international society" is essentially synonymous with the Obama administration's usage of "international community." Critics of diplomatic engagement with outliers such as Iran and North Korea dismiss the term as gaseous rhetoric. The substance of the alternative approach embodied in that criticism is addressed later in this chapter. But on the narrow point of rhetorical excess, in historical context, the "community" metaphor is restrained: American presidents, including Thomas Jefferson, Abraham Lincoln, Franklin D.

Roosevelt, Richard M. Nixon, and, most recently, George W. Bush, have referred to the international system with the even more utopian-evoking phrase "family of nations."[5]

Although Bull propounded the concept of international society, he famously characterized the contemporary international system as an "anarchical society"—*anarchical* because there is no supreme supranational authority governing relations among competing sovereign states, yet a *society* nonetheless because of the convergence of interests and values among states that has yielded international norms and institutions. This contradictory term reflects the enduring tension in American foreign policy between two contending approaches to international order—realism and liberalism (or idealism). Whereas realists, such as Henry Kissinger, emphasize the maintenance of a stable distribution of power *between* competing states, liberal practitioners, best exemplified by Woodrow Wilson, focus on democratic governance *within* states and authoritative international institutions regulating conduct among states as key to the preservation of international peace. Throughout American diplomatic history, the pendulum has swung back and forth under the influence of these competing schools. Thus, for example, Nixon and Kissinger could not sustain American popular support for a realpolitik foreign policy seemingly divorced from American values, whereas Jimmy Carter subsequently encountered the opposite, when liberal idealism confronted the power realities of an increasingly assertive Soviet Union.

Policy Shifts in Washington

The Bush Administration: From Containment to Regime Change

A central element of presidential candidate Barack Obama's sweeping critique of the George W. Bush administration's foreign policy was the administration's approach toward adversarial states—notably, the two remaining members of Bush's "axis of evil," Iran and North Korea. "The lesson of the Bush years," then-senator Obama stated, "is that *not* talking does not work ..., that talking to other countries is some kind of reward."[6] The contentious debate about whether and how to engage these states—for example, setting negotiating preconditions, such as Iran's cessation of uranium enrichment—was predicated on a more fundamental question: what is the character of the threat posed by so-called rogue states—and what is the appropriate strategy for addressing that threat?

The term "rogue state" entered the U.S. foreign policy lexicon as the Cold War ended and after the 1991 Gulf War to reverse the Iraqi invasion of Kuwait. Saddam Hussein's Iraq was the rogue archetype: a regime pursuing weapons of mass destruction (WMD) and using terrorism as an instrument of state policy. The Clinton administration designated the "rogues"—whose core group was Iraq, Iran, North Korea, and Libya—as a distinct category of states in the post–Cold War international system. With the demise of the Soviet threat, a downsized U.S. defense force posture was reconfigured to address a "major regional contingency" involving a rogue state in the Middle East or Northeast Asia.

"Rogue state" was a unilateral American political concept, without foundation in international law, that was analytically soft and selectively applied against a diverse set of states that were hostile to the United States. The concept proved problematic in practice. Once a state was relegated to this category "beyond the pale," the default strategy was comprehensive containment and isolation. Diplomatic engagement, as when the Clinton administration concluded a nuclear deal with North Korea in 1994, was castigated by hard-line critics as tantamount to appeasement. The administration recognized that the term had become a political straitjacket, frustrating its ability to apply differentiated strategies tailored to the circumstances in each country, so it was expunged from the U.S. diplomatic lexicon by the Clinton State Department in June 2000 and replaced with the awkward moniker "states of concern."

Although the George W. Bush administration revived the term before 9/11, "rogue" rhetoric came back with a vengeance after the terrorist attacks of September 11, 2001. Despite assertions that "everything has changed" and likening the date to a demarcation as stark as B.C. and A.D., 9/11 did not change the structure of international relations. But it did lead to a redefinition of threat. In its 2002 National Security Strategy, the Bush administration explicitly argued that the dangers of the post-9/11 world derived from the very character of America's adversaries—irredeemable rogue states and undeterrable terrorist groups such as Al Qaeda, whose only constraints were practical and technical, not moral or political. WMD proliferation and terrorism created a deadly nexus of capabilities and intentions. U.S. policy-makers were driven by the nightmare scenario of a rogue state transferring a nuclear, biological, or chemical capability to a terrorist group to carry out a mass-casualty attack on the American homeland.

The redefinition of threat precipitated a major shift in strategy. The Bush administration asserted that the Cold War concepts of containment and deterrence were "less likely to work against leaders of rogue states [who are] more willing to take risks" and more prone than an orthodox great power rival (such as the Soviet Union or contemporary China) to use WMD.[7] The 2002 National Security Strategy elevated the use of force, as "a matter of common sense and self-defense," not only preemptively, against imminent threats (a usage consistent with international law), but also preventively, against "emerging threats before they are formed."[8] This assessment propelled the shift from a pre-9/11 strategy of containment and deterrence to a post-9/11 emphasis on regime change. Changing the conduct of rogue states was deemed unlikely and inadequate because their threatening behavior was inextricably linked to the character of their ruling regimes: it derived from "their true nature," as President Bush put it.[9]

The Bush foreign policy after 9/11 exhibited key characteristics of neoconservatism—often called "Wilsonianism in boots."[10] Neoconservatism combined the twenty-eighth president's emphasis on democracy promotion with an assertive nationalism that (a) sought to perpetuate American dominance and (b) rejected the constraints that international institutions might impose on American power—hence, the administration's assertive defense of American sovereignty. Channeling American power through international institutions may have been crucial to American diplomatic success before 9/11, but the Bush administration saw that arrangement as an unacceptable check on American power in the transformed security environment after 9/11.

The radical new approach extended to transforming other societies—nation-building—since the definition of threat was now linked to regime type. Bush the former realist became, as one observer quipped, Wilson on steroids—espousing democratization as the antidote to terrorism and declaring that America's mission was to "end tyranny."[11] It was an ambitious, revisionist agenda. The United States was "behaving more like a revolutionary state than one committed to preserving the arrangements that seem to have suited it well," political scientist Robert Jervis stated. "President Woodrow Wilson wanted to make the world safe for democracy. Bush extends and reverses this, arguing that only in a world of democracies can the United States be safe."[12]

Iraq became the test case for the new strategy. Before 9/11, Saddam Hussein was likened by Secretary of State Colin Powell to a "toothache."[13] Afterward, the asserted nexus between proliferation and terrorism—Saddam's resistance to the WMD disarmament mandated by the UN Security Council and the Iraqi regime's purported links to Al Qaeda—provided the rationale for preventive military action to topple this rogue regime as a matter of urgency. Secretary of Defense Donald Rumsfeld later acknowledged that the decision to go to war was based not on new intelligence, but rather on viewing old intelligence "through the prism of 9/11."[14]

After the successful U.S. military march on Baghdad in April 2003 to oust Saddam, Bush administration officials described the intervention in Iraq as a "type"—a model of coercive nonproliferation through regime change.[15] In the heady weeks after the cessation of "major combat operations," before the onset of the deadly Iraqi insurgency against U.S. forces, President Bush stated that the Iraq precedent had implications for how the United States would approach the challenges posed by other rogue states, specifically North Korea and Iran. In Iraq, he claimed, America had "redefin[ed] war" by demonstrating the U.S. ability to decapitate a regime without inflicting unacceptable collateral damage on the civilian population.[16] A senior administration official said that the message of Iraq for Iran's theocratic regime was "Take a number."[17]

Just eight months after the fall of Baghdad, in December 2003, Libyan dictator Muammar Qaddafi announced that his country was voluntarily terminating its covert WMD programs and voluntarily submitting to intrusive international inspections to certify compliance. The surprise announcement, which came on the heels of a financial settlement for the 1988 terrorist bombing of Pan Am 103 over Lockerbie, Scotland, was hailed by President Bush as an important step that would permit Libya to rejoin the international community. If Iraq had set an important precedent—nonproliferation through change *of* regime—Libya offered the alternative: nonproliferation through change *in* regime.

Competing narratives were advanced to explain Qaddafi's strategic turnabout. Bush administration officials proclaimed it a dividend of the Iraq war. Qaddafi had been "scared straight" (as one analyst put it) by the demonstration effect of the regime-change precedent. Alternatively, former Clinton administration officials, who had been involved in negotiations with Libya since the late 1990s, argued that the decision culminated a decade-long effort by the Libyan dictator to shed his country's pariah status and reintegrate into the global system in response to escalating domestic economic pressures. The respective external and internal factors emphasized in these competing narratives were necessary but not sufficient conditions for change. The crux of the Libyan deal was the Bush administration's tacit but clear assurance of security for the regime: in short, if Qaddafi halted his objectionable external behavior with respect to terrorism and proliferation, Washington would not press for a change of regime in Tripoli. Without such a credible security assurance, what incentive would Qaddafi have had to relinquish his WMD arsenal? Logically, the belief that he would still be targeted by the U.S. administration for regime change regardless of any change in his behavior would have created a powerful incentive for him to accelerate his regime's efforts to acquire unconventional weapons as a strategic deterrent.

The contrasting nonproliferation precedents of 2003—a change *of* regime in Iraq; a change *in* a regime in Libya—provided the political backdrop for the escalating nuclear crises with North Korea and Iran. Bush administration officials viewed North Korea as essentially a xenophobic failed state with an advanced nuclear weapons program whose leadership's all-consuming priority was regime survival. The collapse of the U.S.–North Korean Agreed Framework, negotiated by the Clinton administration in 1994 to freeze North Korea's plutonium production capability, created the occasion for the Pyongyang regime's move toward nuclear weaponization. Iran had a less advanced nuclear program but was perceived to be the more dynamic threat because of its oil wealth, its unpredictable president's radicalism and incendiary rhetoric, and its sponsorship of terrorism and destabilizing regional policies.

The Bush administration was caught between the Iraq and Libya precedents. It could not replicate the Iraq model of coercive nonproliferation through regime change in North Korea and Iran, and regime collapse in either country was not an immediate prospect. At the same time, the administration's hard-line rhetoric (Vice President Dick Cheney's bald declaration, "We don't negotiate with evil, we defeat it") negated the possibility of offering assurances of regime security that were central to Libya's accession to comprehensive and verifiable WMD disarmament.[18] The Bush administration's mantra was "all options are on the table." But to what end? Senior officials from the president down sent out a consistently mixed message, never clarifying whether the U.S. policy goal was to change regimes or to change their conduct. The administration did participate in negotiations with these rogue regimes—with Iran, indirectly through the European Union–3 (Britain, France, and Germany), and with North Korea, directly through the six-party talks (whose other members were China, Russia, Japan, and South Korea). But the second term of the George W. Bush administration, when hard-liners were reportedly less influential, could not get past the legacy of the first term. As a consequence, the administration missed opportunities to test Iranian and North Korean intentions—to determine, in short, whether these regimes would be willing to give up their nuclear programs. And it paid the price as both countries crossed important red lines: North Korea tested a nuclear device in October 2006, and Iran mastered the process of uranium enrichment, an important technological threshold for the production of weapons-grade fissile material.

The Obama Administration:
From Regime Change to Engagement

Obama's 2008 presidential campaign pledge to meet unconditionally with the leaders of hostile states such as Iran and Cuba was derided as naïve and irresponsible by his electoral opponents. President Bush, rejecting negotiations with Iran's president Mahmoud Ahmadinejad because of his virulent anti-Israel stance, responded, "Some seem to believe that we should negotiate with the terrorists and radicals, as if some ingenious argument will persuade them they have been wrong all along. We have an obligation to call this what it is—the *false comfort of appeasement*, which has been repeatedly discredited by history."[19] But former secretary of state Henry Kissinger declared his support for the next administration to conduct high-level direct negotiations with Iran "without conditions."[20] Two-thirds of the American public held this latter view, according to a Gallup poll in June 2008.[21]

President Obama assumed office in January 2009 amid unpopular wars in Iraq and Afghanistan and the worst economic crisis since the Great Depression. As if this daunting foreign and domestic policy agenda were not enough, Obama also inherited twin nuclear challenges with North Korea and Iran. Obama signaled a shift from the Bush policy in his inaugural address, telling Iran, North Korea, and other adversarial states that they are "on the wrong side of history," but that America would "extend a hand if you are willing to unclench your fist."[22] News reports likened the gesture to President George H. W. Bush's 1989 inaugural message to Iran that "good will begets good will."[23] In the months after Obama's inauguration, the crises escalated further—North Korea conducted its second nuclear test in May 2009, and Iran continued to flout Security Council resolutions requiring the suspension of its uranium enrichment program (which the United States and its European allies believe is central to Tehran's clandestine effort to acquire nuclear weapons).

The foreign policy dispute between the Obama administration and its critics centers on the appropriateness and efficacy of engaging hostile states—

notably North Korea, Burma, Sudan, Syria and, most pressingly, Iran. But this debate over *means* has been a surrogate for a more fundamental debate over *ends*. The crucial issue remains the character of the regimes—the persisting policy tension between the objectives of behavior change and regime change, and whether the former can be achieved only through the latter. Hard-liners view engagement as tantamount to appeasement—rewarding bad behavior—and doomed to failure. This attitude betrays an essential misunderstanding of engagement. Engagement and its complement, containment, are general concepts that require specific content before the terms can be translated into targeted strategies that take the unique circumstances of each case into account (see Chapter 3).[24] The strategies derive from an assessment based on sound target-state analysis. Containment and engagement should be conceived not as a dichotomy, but rather as a continuum of choice for policy-makers. Nor, as regime-change proponents contend, does engagement preclude the threatened application of punitive instruments, including the demonstrative use of force, as a complement to inducements, to affect a particular regime's decision to alter its objectionable behavior.

The Obama strategy toward Iran has been described by Secretary of State Hillary Clinton as "a two-track approach of pressure and engagement."[25] That formulation would apply more broadly to the diverse set of states (in addition to Iran) that encompassed the Bush administration's "axis of evil" and "outposts of tyranny"—North Korea, Cuba, Zimbabwe, Belarus, and Burma. The Bush administration's all-stick approach (UN Ambassador John Bolton's memorable "I don't do carrots") has been supplanted by an alternative that integrates inducements and negative instruments.[26] The Obama strategy is a retooled version of "coercive diplomacy"—a traditional method of statecraft, whose underlying concepts and historical application were rigorously elucidated by political scientist Alexander George.[27]

The Obama administration's starting point was to clarify the objective of U.S. policy. It ended the mixed message that had been emanating from Washington, making clear that U.S. policy was focused on changing behavior rather than regimes and that the administration would take yes for an answer if the target state changed its conduct. This limitation of objective is a key condition for coercive diplomacy because the target state's leadership will perceive no self-interest in behavior change if the United States remains committed to the maximalist objective of regime change.

Because the objective of regime change runs contrary to the fundamental principle of state sovereignty, the Bush administration's mixed message had also hindered the U.S. ability to win international support for the imposition of tough multilateral measures against North Korea and Iran. Hence, fearing a repetition of the Iraq WMD precedent with Iran, Russia and China have rejected any language in Security Council resolutions that the United States could conceivably invoke as a pretext for military action. The Obama administration dropped the regime change rhetoric and has framed the issue not in terms of a unilateral political concept—"rogue state"—but rather with reference to violations of accepted international norms. The 2010 National Security Strategy laid out the strategy of comprehensive engagement: "To adversarial governments, we offer a clear choice: abide by international norms, and achieve the political and economic benefits that come with greater integration with the international community; or refuse to accept this pathway, and bear the consequences of that decision, including greater isolation."[28]

Primary among the administration's "multiple means ... to bring [recalcitrant states] into compliance with international nonproliferation norms" have been targeted sanctions on the regime's core interest groups—that is, imposing tangible costs on those responsible for the objectionable behavior (see Chapter 3).[29] With Iran, the focus has been on the Islamic Revolutionary Guard Corps, the hard-line military institution that controls the country's nuclear program and whose lucrative role in commercial and black-market activities has increased substantially under Ahmadinejad. With North Korea, U.S.-targeted sanctions have sought to curtail illicit and deceptive activities, such as narcotics trafficking and currency counterfeiting, by freezing bank accounts of commercial entities with links to North Korea that are an essential source of hard currency to maintain the Kim family regime. Those foreign financial institutions then face the stark choice of either severing their shady links to North Korea or having their access to the American banking system blocked.

Targeted sanctions "have had real bite," and thereby "sharpened the choice" facing the Iranians, according to Secretary Clinton. But changing a regime's incentive structure to bring about compliance with international norms faces several challenges.[30] To begin with, a strategy of pressure and negotiations takes time to unfold and should not be expected to yield immediate dramatic results. As Clinton said of the administration's targeted sanctions on Iran, "these things have to take some time to work through the [Iranian] system. Nobody ever thought that there would be an immediate change."[31]

A compounding problem is that targeted sanctions have been undercut through deception and circumvention. Dubai, whose trade with Iran accounts for an estimated 20 percent of its gross domestic product (GDP), has turned a blind eye to shell companies set up on behalf of Revolutionary Guard members that have been designated by the U.S. Treasury Department. Chinese firms have similarly acted on behalf of North Korea to skirt sanctions. Sanctions, particularly in the financial sector, have had some effect, but their main impact has been to increase these regimes' transaction costs.

The bottom-line questions about the Obama administration's new strategy toward the outliers are these: Will their leaderships make the choice to come into compliance with international norms? And will they take the pathway to reintegration into the community of nations? Each case is highly context dependent, hinging on the complex and subtle relationship between the target state's foreign and domestic policies. Within Iran, for example, the nuclear issue is a surrogate for a more fundamental foreign policy debate over relations with the United States and broader outside world, and ultimately, over the Islamic Republic's identity—whether Iran will be a revolutionary state or an ordinary country (see Chapter 4). Hence, President Obama has speculated, "It may be that [the Iranian regime's] ideological commitment to nuclear weapons is such that they're not making a simple cost-benefit analysis on this issue."[32] In the case of North Korea, the calculus of decision is also linked to regime survival: its nuclear program has utility for a besieged regime both as a deterrent and as a perennial bargaining chip with which to extract concessions from the United States, Japan, and South Korea. Human rights pariahs such as Burma and Zimbabwe are similarly driven by domestic imperatives: their leaderships perceive the very process of integration into the international community (which the United States holds out as a tangible benefit) as a threat to regime survival.

The Obama administration's reset of U.S. policy toward outlier states has created a necessary but not sufficient condition for success. It reflects a structured choice offered by Washington to adversarial states. With Iran and North Korea, that choice has been complicated by the 2011 intervention of the North Atlantic Treaty Organization (NATO) in Libya, which recast the 2003 precedent. Central to Qaddafi's acceptance of WMD disarmament was the Bush administration's tacit but clear security assurance that the United States, in return, would lift the threat of coercive nonproliferation through regime change (as in Iraq, the other important precedent set in 2003). After NATO launched its humanitarian intervention, both the Tehran and Pyongyang leaderships declared that Libya's disarmament of its nuclear program had left the country vulnerable to outside military attack. The Libyan intervention further lowered the already dim odds of achieving a nuclear rollback in either North Korea or Iran. The question remains as to what measures, if any, can be negotiated to bound or circumscribe these countries' programs—with Iran, to establish verified limits on its uranium enrichment program; with North Korea, to forestall the further growth of its small nuclear arsenal. (See Chapter 3 for a full discussion of the Libyan case and its implications.)

The Obama administration's structured choice not only offers tangible benefits for compliance but also requires that meaningful pressure be brought to bear on a target state in the face of intransigence. Just as the United States has made a choice, so too must other key states: Russia, for example, must decide whether its pique with Washington over past issues, such as U.S. relations with Georgia or ballistic-missile defense, trumps its core interest in preventing the advent in Iran of another nuclear weapon state on its periphery. Does Russia view Iran through the prism of its relationship with the United States? The attitudes of Russia, China, India, and others toward the outliers are significantly affected by America's evolving international role and the shifting distribution of power among states in the international system.

Power Shifts in the International System

Unipolarity versus Unilateralism

The foundation of the current international system was laid in the wake of World War II. The late 1940s were years of remarkably creative institution-building, led by the United States. Indeed, one might say the post–World War II international system had a "made in America" stamp on it. Through initiatives ranging from the International Monetary Fund to the Marshall Plan, the Truman administration fostered the creation of a community of democratic, free-market states in North America, Western Europe, and Japan. These new institutions, rooted in the liberal school of international relations, became the keystone of the contemporary international order. They were complemented by a system of security alliances, which started with the establishment of NATO. These institutions, grounded in the realist tradition, were the West's collective response to the paramount challenge of the postwar era: the need to contain an expansionist Soviet Union.

What was unique about the liberal order that took root in the Western half of the bipolar Cold War divide was its consensual nature. The recovering European states outside the Soviet sphere looked to the United States for protection and economic assistance and willingly joined the multilateral institutions forged through American leadership. This scenario led Norwegian historian Geir Lundestad to characterize the U.S.-led Western system as an "empire by invitation"—in sharp contrast with the Soviet bloc, which required the coercive presence of the Red Army to hold it together.[33]

With the end of the Cold War and the disintegration of the Soviet Union, the United States emerged as the sole remaining superpower—a so-called hyperpower because of the asymmetry between the United States and other major powers. But contrary to what the classic realist approach would predict, no overt countercoalition of major powers emerged to balance American hyperpower in the post–Cold War era. Political scientist John Ikenberry persuasively argues that this historic departure derived from the unprecedented character of the post–World War II international order. It encompassed a web of multilateral economic and security institutions in which American power was embedded and through which American power was channeled.[34] The unique quality of this "empire by invitation" made American power more legitimate and less threatening to other states in the international system. "Strategic restraint," to use Ikenberry's term, fostered the perception of the United States as a benign superpower and proved key to American international success in the latter half of the twentieth century, through the Clinton administration, which continued that winning game plan through its policy of engagement and enlargement. Premised on the Wilsonian principle that "democracies don't attack each other," this strategy aimed to expand the liberal international order through the integration of emerging democracies with market economies in Latin America, East Asia, the former Soviet bloc, and elsewhere.

Al Qaeda's attack on New York and Washington on September 11, 2001, highlighted the vulnerability of the American homeland and other Western societies to mass-casualty terrorism. Yet the assault, however horrific and psychologically searing, did not alter the structure of international relations. Indeed, Russia and China perceived the devastating strike on the iconic World Trade Center towers as an assault on the global economic system into which they were increasingly integrating themselves. China, in the midst of an unprecedented economic boom, connected the dots— the potential of international terrorism to damage the global economy on which China's economic growth depended—and reacted accordingly. Relations between the United States, Russia, and China moved to their closest state since World War II. Their shared perception of 9/11 led to what would have been unthinkable a decade earlier: America's former Cold War adversaries acquiesced to the establishment of U.S. military bases in Central Asia to conduct military operations in Afghanistan.

Although 9/11 did not change the structure of international relations, it did radically alter the perception of threat—a shift that precipitated the U.S. transition from a strategy emphasizing containment to one emphasizing regime change. In response to this newly perceived vulnerability—which was fostered by the nexus of proliferation and terrorism—the Bush administration controversially elevated military preemption to official U.S. doctrine. The administration explicitly argued that the exigencies of the new era could require unilateral U.S. action outside the structure of international institutions and norms created through American leadership—a sentiment captured in President Bush's bald declaration that that the United States would "never seek a permission slip" from the Security Council to defend America.[35]

The international solidarity manifested after 9/11 quickly dissipated when the Bush administration extended the war on terrorism to Iraq. The UN debate over Iraq in early 2003 began with discussion of Saddam's flouting of Security Council resolutions and ended with criticism of the exercise of American power. At the heart of these contentious deliberations was the prime issue of state sovereignty. In 1990–91, George H. W. Bush was readily able to secure Security Council support against Saddam Hussein because the Iraqi leader had violated the cardinal norm of international relations by his invasion of Kuwait; as one observer colorfully put it, Saddam had murdered another state. The 1991 Gulf War, undertaken with the legitimizing imprimatur of the Security Council, was waged to restore Kuwaiti sovereignty. By contrast, in 2003, George W. Bush argued that bringing Iraq into compliance with Security Council resolutions on WMD disarmament, which were passed in the wake of the 1991 Gulf War, could be achieved only through a change of regime—that is, through the negation of Iraqi sovereignty.

On sovereignty grounds, the United Nations withheld authorization for the 2003 war. The Security Council's judgment was, in essence, that the international community considered the precedent of a U.S.-imposed regime change in Baghdad worse than leaving the Iraqi dictator in power. "The rush to war in Iraq in the absence of a 'first shot' or 'smoking gun,'" historian John Lewis Gaddis observed, "left ... a growing sense throughout the world [that] there could be nothing worse than American hegemony if it was to be used in this way."[36] The benign hegemon had become a rogue superpower. During the rancorous Security Council debate, a de facto coalition of France, Russia, and Germany had arisen to block this unilateral application of U.S. military power. Whereas the advent of unipolarity at the end of the Cold War era had not triggered a balance-of-power response, the contentious manifestation of American unilateralism during the Iraq crisis did trigger concerted diplomatic opposition by other major powers.[37]

From Unipolarity to Multipolarity?

Seven and a half years after the March 2003 invasion of Iraq, President Obama announced the end of the American combat mission. Drawing a direct link between U.S. foreign policy overextension and the country's domestic economic problems, he stated, "[O]ver the last decade, we've not done what's necessary to shore up the foundations of our own prosperity.... We spent a trillion dollars at war, often financed by borrowing from overseas."[38] The withdrawal of U.S. forces from Iraq capped a decade that had begun with the turn of a new millennium and 9/11. Gone were popular references to the United States as a latter-day Roman Empire or to American hyperpower. Debate instead focused on whether the "unipolar moment" had passed and the United States was sliding into decline relative to other major powers in the international system.[39]

Domestic popular support for an activist U.S. foreign policy was continuing the sharp decline that had started little more than a year after the U.S. invasion of Iraq. A majority of Americans, according to a June 2004 Gallup poll, believed that the Bush administration's decision to go to war had been a mistake and that the intervention had not made the United States safer from terrorism.[40] This collapse of public support for the war, coming in the face of mounting casualties from the Iraqi insurgency, fueled concern about the rise of a possible "Iraq syndrome," which, like the "Vietnam syndrome," could have a long-term restraining influence on U.S. foreign policy.[41] In November 2005, a Pew poll found that the Iraq war had had a "profound impact" on public attitudes toward America's global role and that isolationism was on par with that in the aftermath of the Vietnam War.[42] By December 2009, Gallup reported an isolationist sentiment held by roughly half of the American public—a level unprecedented in the post–World War II era. Increased isolationism has been compounded by a broad erosion of public confidence in governmental institutions. This process began with the Iraq war—from the WMD intelligence debacle to the incompetent postwar planning—and accelerated further after Hurricane Katrina in 2005, when a failure of government occurred at all levels. Abroad, America's image and moral standing were tattered by prisoner abuse at Abu Ghraib and allegations over the use of torture in the war on terrorism.

The biggest constraint on U.S. foreign policy activism for the foreseeable future is likely to be fiscal. The Great Recession of 2008, the most severe economic crisis since the Great Depression, along with ballooning entitlement costs, has created unsustainably high U.S. budget deficits.[43] Whereas 9/11 did not alter the structure of international relations, the Great Recession, which brought the world economy to the verge of a catastrophic contraction, almost did. That near meltdown of the financial system was seen worldwide as a made-in-America crisis resulting from laissez-faire "rogue capitalism."[44] Just as the Obama administration recommitted the United States to a rules-based international order internationally, so too did it push through meaningful regulatory reform in an effort to restore a rules-based financial system domestically.

As the American model was losing its luster, power shifts among the major powers were poised to reshape international relations. The question is whether unipolarity (which succeeded Cold War bipolarity) was a transitional structure now being supplanted by emergent multipolarity, and, if so, whether the defining condition of the post–Cold War era—the low risk of conflict between great powers—would remain durable. The "rise of the rest," exemplified by the advent of the so-called BRICs (Brazil, Russia, India, and China), reflects a diffusion of power that is unfolding unevenly across different types of power.[45]

Economically, the world is increasingly multipolar: in 2010, according to the World Bank, the U.S. GDP was roughly $14.5 trillion (approximately 23 percent of world product), the European Union's GDP was $12.3 trillion, China's and Japan's GDPs were each roughly $5.5 trillion (with China surpassing Japan as the second-largest national economy in mid-2010), Brazil's was $2.1 trillion, and India's was $1.7 trillion.[46] The Central Intelligence Agency has projected that the BRICs' share of world GDP will overtake the original G-7 states (the United States, Japan, Canada, Britain, Germany, France, and Italy) by 2040–50.[47] Yet militarily, the world remains essentially unipolar: in 2009, U.S. military expenditures were $663 billion (approximately 43 percent of the world share), with China at $99 billion and Russia at $61 billion.[48] What is remarkable is that while dwarfing that of the rest of the world, U.S. defense spending amounts to only 5 to 6 percent of U.S. GDP (compared with 14 percent during the Korean War and 40 percent in World War II). The paradox is that although no conceivable coalition of major powers could surpass the United States militarily, the sole super-power has struggled against low-tech insurgencies in Iraq and Afghanistan.

Capturing the mixed character of the international system (that is, uni-polar militarily, multipolar politically and economically), social scientist Samuel Huntington coined the term "uni-multipolar."[49] The U.S. National Intelligence Council's influential *Global Trends 2025* forecasts that the in-ternational system will be "almost unrecognizable by 2025. Indeed, 'inter-national system' is a misnomer as it is likely to be more ramshackle than orderly." Although not predicting a breakdown of the system, the report states that "the most salient characteristics of the 'new order' will be the shift from a unipolar world dominated by the United States to a relatively unstructured hierarchy of old powers and rising nations, and the diffusion of power from state to nonstate actors."[50]

The future course of former great-power adversaries of the United States—Russia and China—poses one of the key uncertainties of an emergent uni-multipolar world. In both countries, foreign policy is being renationalized. The consequent possibility of revived competition could re-create the cataclysmic Cold War danger of war between great powers. Al-though China's meteoric rise and Russia's resurgent authoritarianism have prompted balance-of-power realists to question the long-term durability of this current condition, neither great power is mounting a frontal assault on the existing international order. Russia's military intervention in Georgia in August 2008 prompted some commentators to declare a return of the Cold War. Although a State Department official called Russia a "revision-ist" state after its move into Georgia, its revisionism is in the conventional tradition of a great power seeking to create a sphere of influence on its pe-riphery. This stance is closer to the Monroe Doctrine than to the Comintern. Russia's new assertiveness carries risks of regional strife and inadvertent military escalation, but in contrast to its behavior during the Cold War, the Kremlin is not advancing an alternative vision of international order.

Likewise, China, to the increasing concern of neighboring states, is vig-orously asserting its national interests in its region but is not more broadly challenging the current liberal international order from which it tangibly benefits. Although the National Intelligence Council's *Global Trends 2025* assessment casts the BRICs and other rising powers as "unlikely to chal-lenge the international system,... their growing geopolitical and economic clout [will provide them] a high degree of freedom to customize their po-litical and economic policies rather than fully adopting Western norms."[51] Hence, the process of setting, interpreting, and enforcing international norms—those whose contravention sets the outliers apart—will become increasingly contested. Under such conditions of shifting power and competing values, can an international society flourish?[52]

The Anarchical Society Revisited

Since the advent of the contemporary state system, threats to international order have arisen from dissatisfied states that reject its governing norms and the status quo. Such challenges have typically come from revisionist states whose aims are limited—a claim to disputed territory, for example—and are pursued within the existing international system. In contrast, revolutionary states have unbound ambition and are seeking the wholesale transformation of the international order itself. The emergence of expansionist great powers with unbound ambition—Nazi Germany or Joseph Stalin's Soviet Union— led to the periods of greatest upheaval and tumult in the twentieth century. Notwithstanding uncertainties about the future trajectories of Russia and China, no major power currently poses a revolutionary threat to the system. Instead, the challenge is posed by a set of relatively marginal states—Iran, North Korea, Sudan, Burma, and Zimbabwe, among others—that violate international norms and threaten the stability of their regions but lack the capacity (unlike a Nazi Germany) to bring down the system itself. In *A World Restored*, his early study of the Congress of Vienna system, Henry Kissinger observed that "stability … has commonly resulted not from a quest for peace but from a *generally accepted legitimacy*," which he defined as "an international agreement about the nature of workable arrangements and about the permissible aims and methods of foreign policy."[53] International order thus reflects a degree of consensus and cooperation among states while not eliminating competition between them over contending national interests or the setting and enforcement of norms. In Kissinger's conception, the essential importance of a legitimate international order lies in its creation of acceptable bounds within which continued competition is pursued.

Norms and Sovereignty

Outlier states are defined by behavior that contravenes accepted international norms. Modern norms setting the bounds of acceptable international conduct arose in tandem with the spread of the modern state system from its European origins in the seventeenth century onward. The Westphalian system established the principle of state sovereignty and its corollary of nonintervention by one state into the domestic affairs of another. With an international system now numbering some 195 countries, this model of "the state" was one of Europe's most successful exports. The system has proved durable, withstanding major traumas—the Cold War and anti-imperialist decolonization—in the latter half of the twentieth century.[54]

To the extent one can speak of the international system as a society, it relates to the extension and acceptance of norms. Central to that process has been international law, which, unlike its national counterparts, is entirely voluntaristic. Most prominent and readily identified with international law are formal treaties and agreements among states to regulate behavior. Such codified norms, not surprisingly, started with bedrock principles governing relations among sovereign states, such as diplomatic immunity. A second source of international law is custom. Customary international law is commonly defined as "the general and consistent practices of states that they follow from a sense of legal obligation."[55] Less concrete than treaty-based law, customary international law encompasses norms that reflect a consensus among states based on widely accepted practice. Over time, customary practice can harden into treaty law, as in the cases of the Hague and Geneva Conventions, which codified rules of war that had already gained widespread acceptance. Customary law has an important psychological dimension because compliance derives from a sense of obligation rather than an explicit legal requirement.[56] But a legal standing based on custom raises the question of how one establishes a causal relation between the two key criteria underlying customary law: the practice generally engaged in by states and their belief that such conduct is obligated. Moreover, does that sense of obligation extend beyond each state's narrow pursuit of its national interest to some sense of responsibility to a broader "international society"?

Frequent flouting of the Westphalian principle giving exclusive control to each state over its territory, resources, and people led political scientist Stephen Krasner to characterize sovereignty as "organized hypocrisy." The international environment, he observed, "has been characterized by competing and often logically contradictory norms, not some single coherent set of rules."[57] Those contradictions stem from two major sources: first, the tension between equality and hierarchy inherent to an international system in which, on the one hand, states are notionally sovereign equals, while, on the other, the uneven distribution of power and population among them creates an international pecking order; second, the controversial question of establishing limits on sovereignty such that, in extreme cases, it does not provide a shield of noninterference behind which regimes can commit gross violations of human rights against their own populations.

The duality of equality and hierarchy is reflected in the structure of the United Nations. The UN General Assembly epitomizes not only the principle of sovereign equality (the body operates on a one-state, one-vote basis) but also the hard realities of power politics (its resolutions are not binding). By contrast, the Security Council, whose membership includes five permanent members with veto power, has primary responsibility under the UN Charter for "the maintenance of international peace and security." That privileged position, however, has fueled criticism that the Security Council, through either its members' collective action or an individual member's use of the veto as an instrument of national policy, exercises "legalized hegemony" over less powerful states in the international system.[58] Since the end of the Cold War, the composition of the Security Council, its selective activism, and the scope of its powers have fueled calls for UN reform.[59] The right of the Security Council to impose punitive measures on a state in the absence of a judicial finding of guilt was unsuccessfully challenged by Libya in a suit arising from the UN sanctions imposed because of the Qaddafi regime's complicity in the 1988 terrorist bombing of Pan Am 103. More recently, in the ongoing nuclear dispute with Iran, the Tehran regime has mounted a similar defense, declaring UN sanctions illegal and the Security Council a tool of American foreign policy.

Although Iran charges the United States with gaming the system to its benefit, in point of fact America has a long-standing ambivalence toward international institutions. While the Obama administration declares an interest in promoting a rules-based international system, those very rules create what neoconservatives and some realists consider an unacceptable constraint on the country's freedom of action. The dual identity reflected in that ambivalence was captured by the French political philosopher Raymond Aron when he called the United States the "imperial republic."[60] By "imperial," Aron was referring to the country's unique role of providing what social scientists call "global public goods" (such as the U.S. Navy's protection of the sea lanes on which global commerce depends) to maintain international order. Yet Aron also acknowledged that the United States was a republic; like any other state, it acted to further its parochial national interests. The balance between these dual identities dramatically shifted after 9/11, which exposed the vulnerability of the American homeland to a mass-casualty attack. That redefinition of threat yielded an expansive redefinition of U.S. sovereignty. The Bush administration, declaring that the United States would not be constrained by international institutions in this new era of vulnerability, asserted a right of preemptive (and even preventive) unilateral military intervention. Critics argued that military action in the absence of a demonstrably imminent threat would erode the international norm governing the use of force and thereby create a precedent that others could seize on—for example, an Indian strike on Pakistan's nuclear facilities. Accompanying this assertive defense of U.S. sovereignty was a circumscribed interpretation of others' sovereignty. States lacking the capacity or the political will to exert effective control to prevent terrorist groups such as Al Qaeda from freely operating on their territory were warned that they were subject to preemptive U.S. military action. In short, the failure to exercise sovereignty would lead to the forfeiture of sovereignty.

The roots of the contentious debate over sovereignty and norms in the post-9/11 era can be traced to an important conceptual and policy shift that occurred in 1980. Before then, the term "rogue" was used to characterize states whose ruling regimes egregiously violated international norms with respect to the treatment of their civilian populations. Hence, in a then-characteristic usage of this "rogue state" concept, the *Washington Post* editorialized, "How does the international community deal with rogue regimes, those that under the color of national sovereignty commit unspeakable crimes against their own citizens? We have in mind not the mass deprivation of rights practiced by police states everywhere but the virtual genocide perpetrated by such regimes as Pol Pot's Cambodia and Idi Amin's Uganda."[61]

"Rogue" status before 1980 was thus linked to *internal* behavioral criteria (how a regime treated its own people) rather than to *external* criteria (how its conduct affected other states in the international system). This formulation pitted competing norms at stake: standards to protect citizens within states versus the cardinal principle of national sovereignty shielding states from outside interference in their internal affairs. However, in two extreme cases—Vietnam's 1978 intervention in Cambodia to overthrow Pol Pot, and Tanzania's 1979 incursion into Uganda to assist anti-Amin forces in ousting Amin—the international community turned a blind eye to violations of the norm of national sovereignty and the inviolability of state borders because of the two regimes' brutal conduct toward their own civil populations (see Chapter 2). Cambodia and Uganda were the archetypal rogue, outlaw, or pariah states of the pre-1980 period. The controversy over these externally induced regime changes presaged the post–Cold War debate over humanitarian interventions.

After 1980, rogue state status was linked to two defining criteria: state sponsorship of terrorism and the pursuit of WMD. Reflecting this shift from internal to external behavioral criteria was the State Department's inauguration of an annual listing of state sponsors of terrorism.[62] That development ushered in a heightened U.S. focus on the problem of state-sponsored terrorism that continued under the Reagan administration. President Ronald Reagan identified Iran, Libya, North Korea, Cuba, and Nicaragua as "outlaw governments who are sponsoring terrorism against our nation.... Most of the terrorists ... are being trained, financed, and indirectly controlled by a core group of radical and totalitarian governments—a new international version of Murder Incorporated."[63] In April 1986, the Reagan administration backed up its tough rhetoric with action: U.S. military aircraft struck targets in Libya in retaliation for the Qaddafi regime's role in the bombing of a Berlin discotheque in which American soldiers were killed.

In addition to state support for international terrorism, the second key criterion leading to "outlaw" or "rogue" designation was the acquisition of WMD capabilities. This factor rose in prominence in the late 1980s as the Cold War was reaching its denouement. Throughout the 1980s, a proliferation occurred of unconventional capabilities, particularly chemical weapons and ballistic missiles, in the developing world—mainly in states that were either American allies or countries with which the United States enjoyed close relations, such as Argentina, Brazil, South Korea, and Israel. Indeed, the state that received probably the greatest public attention because of its determined progress toward acquisition of nuclear weapons was Pakistan—America's key ally in Southwest Asia that was supporting the Afghan mujahideen's insurgency against Soviet occupation. Iraq, which the Reagan administration was courting through its famous "tilt" to counterbalance revolutionary Iran, was largely given a pass by Washington. The United States and the international community as a whole were largely silent when Iraq used chemical weapons against Iran in their lengthy attritional war in the 1980s. Though the United States did condemn the Saddam Hussein regime's gassing of the Iraqi Kurdish town of Halabja in March 1988, this heinous crime did not precipitate a U.S. policy reassessment toward the state that would go on to become the archetypal rogue after its invasion of Kuwait in August 1990.[64]

Characterizing the post–Cold War threat posed by rogue states in a widely discussed *Foreign Affairs* article in 1994, Anthony Lake, President Clinton's national security adviser, declared, "[O]ur policy must face the reality of recalcitrant and outlaw states that not only choose to remain outside the family [of nations] but also assault its basic values." He went on to argue that these outlaw states share common characteristics:

> Ruled by cliques that control power though coercion, they suppress human rights and promote radical ideologies. While their political systems vary, their leaders share a common antipathy toward popular participation that might undermine the existing regimes. These nations exhibit a chronic inability to engage constructively with the outside world ... [and] share a siege mentality. Accordingly, they are embarked on ambitious and costly military programs—especially in weapons of mass destruction (WMD) and missile delivery systems—in a misguided quest for a great equalizer to protect their regimes or advance their purposes abroad.

Lake concluded, "As the sole superpower, the United States has a special responsibility for developing a strategy to neutralize, contain, and through selective pressure, perhaps eventually transform these backlash states into constructive members of the international community."[65]

Rogue states were one of four distinct categories of states in the post–Cold War international system, according to the Clinton administration. The other three were advanced industrial states in North America, Western Europe, and Japan; emerging democracies with market economies in Eastern Europe, the former Soviet Union, East Asia, and Latin America; and failing and failed states, such as Somalia, which lacked state capacity and were unable to exert sovereign control over their territories. The Clinton administration's overarching grand strategy of engagement and enlargement aimed to integrate states outside the core of advanced industrial democracies, including the rogues, into the liberal international order by bringing them into compliance with the system's norms.

"Rogue state" rhetoric had some political utility for the Clinton administration in mobilizing domestic political support for tough measures toward these states. Yet the translation of the rogue concept into a coherent policy revealed significant liabilities, as previously noted, such that the Clinton administration elected eventually to jettison the term. The term "rogue state" had no standing in international law. As an American political construct, it was applied selectively and opportunistically—essentially to encompass hostile developing world states with which the United States had a history of estrangement. Thus, for example, Cuba (which had no WMD program and posed no credible security threat to the United States) met none of the criteria but was often included in the roster of rogue states because of the political clout of the Cuban émigré community. By contrast, Syria, which met the stated criteria for rogue status (with its WMD capabilities and designation on State Department's terrorist list), was pointedly not designated a rogue state because it was then being wooed by the Clinton administration as part of its Middle East peace process.

The definitional problem went further in that the rogue state policy's sole focus was on objectionable external behavior. It did not address odious actions within states that violated international norms, such as those by Rwanda and Serbia. The Clinton administration was philosophically inclined to engage in humanitarian interventions to forestall genocide, ethnic conflict, and other gross violations of human rights within states, but that impulse ran up against the more economical definition of U.S. interests in an international system no longer defined by the global East-West competition after the Cold War. Beyond the contested issue of interests, decisions relating to the use of force in cases ranging from Somalia and Haiti to Rwanda and Kosovo were highly contentious because no consensus existed—or exists yet—on the principle at stake in humanitarian intervention. Because external intervention in the domestic affairs of a state, even in defense of global norms, is at odds with the cardinal principle of state sovereignty, the international community has struggled unsuccessfully to formulate coherent rules governing the use of force.

In the cases of humanitarian intervention from Somalia to Kosovo during the decade between the end of the Cold War and 9/11, international law was a utilitarian instrument of U.S. foreign policy—a source of legitimacy when provided by Security Council approval, but not a significant constraint when the United States felt compelled to act in its absence. The authorization of the use of force by the Security Council in Haiti in 1994 was a reflection of the broad international consensus favoring intervention to end civil strife and restore democracy. For some legal scholars, however, that precedent-setting decision, no matter how well intentioned, was premised on a questionable interpretation of the UN Charter that circumvented the treaty's provisions on noninterference in the domestic affairs of a sovereign member state. Had the Security Council withheld its legitimizing approval, the Clinton administration would almost certainly have intervened in Haiti anyway. The 1999 Kosovo crisis was a telling case in which, despite the absence of a legitimizing Security Council imprimatur (because of Russian and Chinese opposition), the NATO alliance, led by the United States, intervened to stop the ethnic cleansing of Kosovar Albanians in Serbia. International legal expert Michael Glennon observed that "the Security Council chose to ride roughshod over Haitian sovereignty—setting the stage for NATO to override Yugoslavian sovereignty."[66]

The tortured formulation commonly used for the Kosovo intervention after the fact—"legitimate but not legal"—reflected the policy dilemmas created by the competing norms of sovereignty and human rights. The Canadian government–sponsored International Commission on Intervention and State Sovereignty (ICISS) grappled with the Kosovo precedent, strongly arguing that the Security Council should approve military intervention but acknowledging the reality that "a conscience-shocking situation" may prompt action by ad hoc coalitions in the absence of such authorization.[67] The ICISS report, titled *The Responsibility to Protect*, acknowledged the dilemma of clashing norms: "It is a real question in these circumstances where lies the most harm: in the damage to international order if the Security Council is bypassed or in the damage to that order if human beings are slaughtered while the Security Council stands by."[68]

The UN High-Level Panel, commissioned by Secretary-General Kofi Annan in 2004, addressed the radically altered security environment of the post-9/11 environment, including the U.S. assertion of a right not only to preemptive military action against imminent threats, but also to its preventive application against emerging threats. The panel—wanting to circumscribe the unilateral use of force yet allow for humanitarian interventions—grappled with the dilemmas of force arising from the Kosovo and Iraq precedents. Its report affirmed "the emerging norm of a collective international responsibility to protect," while also asserting, with reference to the U.S. invasion of Iraq, that "the risk to the global order and the norm of non-intervention on which it continues to be based is simply too great for the legality of unilateral preventive action, as distinct from collectively endorsed action, to be accepted. Allowing one to so act is to allow all."[69] Oxford University professor Adam Roberts concludes that attempts to develop doctrine governing the use of force with respect to humanitarian intervention and WMD proliferation "have failed, both politically and intellectually. Politically, because in neither case is there any sign of a really strong body of international support for them; intellectually, because in neither case is it at all clear how the proposed new norm relates to existing rules on non-intervention."[70]

Disputes arise not only from competing norms, but also from contending views over the setting and interpretation of norms. As the distribution of power shifts within the international system, rising states will inevitably seek to exert influence commensurate to their power and thus may increasingly question governing norms that they had no role in creating. Those contemporary norms emerged largely in tandem with the rise of the modern state system in Europe and reflect Western values. This clash of norms is exemplified in the dispute between the United States and China over human rights. The State Department's 2009 annual report found that the rights situation in that ascendant world power remained "poor and worsened in some areas."[71] The Chinese government rejected this criticism, not only claiming progress by Western standards, but also laying out an alternative conception of human rights. The Chinese definition focuses on *collective* rights, such as raising its people's economic standard of living and providing public education, in contrast with the West, whose political tradition focuses on *individual* rights, such as freedom of speech and the right of assembly.[72] This clash of perspectives highlights the limits to consensus on values within the international community. Even where differences in perspective are presumably narrower—for instance, norms codified in treaties to which states voluntarily acceded—the challenges of compliance and enforcement remain.

The relative salience of individual norms shifts over time. Consider one of the bedrock norms of international relations—the proscription of aggressive war by one state against another. Throughout most of the past century, the specter of interstate conflict, particularly among major powers, was the paramount concern. World War I, which resulted in some 37 million military and civilian deaths, led to the Kellogg-Briand Pact, whose aim was literally to outlaw war. But lacking any enforcement mechanism, the treaty failed to prevent three of its signatories—Germany, Italy, and Japan—from launching World War II, a global conflict that resulted in more than 60 million deaths. During the Cold War era of superpower rivalry, nuclear weapons made war unwinnable (if not unthinkable) and produced what historian John Gaddis referred to as "the long peace."[73] Even as the number of states greatly increased through decolonization after World War II, the incidence of interstate conflict declined in the latter half of the twentieth century. This trend stands in marked contrast during that same period to the increased incidence of intrastate violence, such as civil wars and ethnic strife—in part, a consequence of that very same proliferation of new states. The decline of interstate conflict is understandable. Nothing poses a more frontal challenge to the principle of state sovereignty than overt cross-boundary aggression; witness the relative ease with which the United States and Britain obtained the Security Council's authorization to reverse Iraq's invasion and occupation of Kuwait in 1990.

Although the danger of major interstate conflict is low, the durability of this condition is uncertain. Perhaps the most consequential open question about the evolution of the international order is whether an ascendant China will be successfully integrated. A broader concern was raised in the National Intelligence Council's *Global Trends 2025* report, which warned of "the growing prospect of ... possible interstate conflicts [in coming decades] over resources."[74] These alternative futures pointing to a revival of interstate conflict are possible but not inevitable. Moreover, not only does the relative salience of particular norms, like that proscribing interstate aggression, shift over time, but new norms may emerge. In the coming generation, to cite but one nascent norm, states responsible for massive environmental degradation may be treated as pariahs.[75]

Yet since the end of the Cold War, outlaw and outlier status continues to derive from objectionable state behavior that violates widely held international norms in three key areas—proliferation, terrorism, and human rights. The first two behavioral criteria are external, in that their contravention has direct negative consequences for other states in the system, whereas the third is primarily internal in its impact. In practice, however, the categories can overlap: states that violate norms with adverse implications beyond their borders also flout norms of conduct toward their civil populations within their borders. For example, North Korea, which commands the world's attention as a nuclear outlier (along with Iran), has been called one giant gulag because of the brutal and systematic mistreatment of its own people. Conversely, as in the case of Sudan, a regime's internal abuse of its own people can have adverse external consequences by triggering the flow of refugees or exporting violence to adjacent countries.

The Obama administration recast the policy debate by framing the threats posed by these states not with reference to a unilateral American political concept such as rogue states, but in terms of prevailing norms that enjoy broad acceptance in the international system through treaties or customary practice. The challenging goal is to induce or compel these diplomatically isolated states to come into compliance with those norms and thereby rejoin the community of nations.

Compliance and Integration

The policy dilemmas arising from the setting of norms extend to enforcing their compliance. The central issue remains sovereignty—the cardinal principle under which states voluntarily opt into international law, through treaty or custom, within an international system lacking a supreme supranational authority to enforce the observance of norms. Fortunately, most states obey international law without the need for enforcement, just as, in the domestic realm, most citizens comply with the law.[76] How, then, can states that flout international norms be brought into compliance? Is it a question of changing their regimes' calculus of decision—that is, the benefits of compliance versus the costs of noncompliance? Or is a change in behavior possible through the internalization of norms by their ruling elites?

One characteristic all these states of concern share is their nondemocratic nature. As political scientist Miroslav Nincic has observed, "Not all non-democracies are renegades, but all renegades are non-democracies."[77] Yet a nondemocratic domestic order has been no bar to a state's membership in the international community. During the negotiations leading up to the promulgation of the UN Charter in 1945, delegates had debated whether "rogue states" should be expelled from the new organization; in the end, they decided against that proposal on grounds that expulsion would create a lawless zone where "expelled members would be free of their obligations" and outside the United Nation's authority.[78] Consistent with that view, the charter accorded states "sovereign equality," however authoritarian or even criminal the character of their ruling regimes, and proscribed the United Nations from "interven[ing] in matters which are essentially within the domestic jurisdiction of any state."[79] This maximalist formulation of state sovereignty has provided a shield behind which the world's worst regimes have been able to abuse their own civilian populations with little fear of consequence. The UN Universal Declaration of Human Rights of 1948 created a diplomatic instrument to apply moral pressure on repressive regimes but did not constitute a meaningful limit on state sovereignty, let alone create a responsibility to protect. The nondemocratic nature of more than one-third of all states leaves the term "international community" open to derision. Particularly egregious is the UN Human Rights Council, whose members have shielded each other from criticism and refused to take up such flagrant cases as Zimbabwe, Burma, Sudan, and North Korea, while focusing almost exclusively on one country, Israel.

Although the United States played the lead role in creating the major institutions at the heart of the contemporary liberal international order, and although the embedding of American power in those institutions proved a highly effective strategy for furthering U.S. interests, Washington has been unwilling to cede its sovereignty to a supranational authority. U.S. attitudes contrast with those of the countries that constitute the international system's largest regional experiment in supranationalism, the European Union. Social scientist Francis Fukuyama observes that Americans tend to regard international law and institutions as legitimate to the extent that they reflect the consent of sovereign nation-states, whereas Europeans tend to view democratic legitimacy as flowing from the will of the international community and thereby superseding that of any individual nation-state. Given this persistent schism, Fukuyama concludes, "For better or worse, such international institutions as we possess will have to be partial solutions existing in the vacuum of international legitimacy above the level of the nation-state. Or to put it differently, whatever legitimacy they possess will have to be based on the underlying legitimacy of nation-states and the contractual relationships they negotiate."[80]

The writ of international organizations extends only so far as sovereign states permit in a consent-based system. Consider the institution that embodies the norm of nonproliferation—the nuclear Nonproliferation Treaty. Three nuclear-weapons states—India, Pakistan, and Israel—are not signatories of, and therefore not constrained by, the treaty. Conversely, the international furor over the Iranian and North Korean nuclear programs largely derives from the cheating both countries, though signatories, engaged in. Another prominent case in point is the effort to expand the authority of the International Criminal Court (ICC), which the United States has not signed, to prosecute the crime of "aggression." If adopted, the measure would permit the ICC to prosecute civilian and military leaders whose use of force the court deemed unlawful. State Department Legal Adviser Harold Koh argued that "if we accept a definition [of aggression], it has to take into account the many ways in which force can be lawfully exercised." The proposal has met concerted opposition from the United States and other permanent members of the Security Council that are concerned that the expansion of the ICC's purview to define "aggression" would undercut the council's authority.[81] The flipside of the UN founders' decision to allow universal membership and not to exclude rogue states on the basis of their objectionable conduct or nondemocratic governance is that all states are subject to the Security Council's authority, however selectively it is exercised.

Compliance has been defined as "a state of conformity" between a country's behavior and a specified norm.[82] But establishing a firm causal relationship between motivation and action is analytically difficult, to the point of being unknowable—the international relations version of nature versus nurture. Those policy-makers and analysts approaching the question from the perspective of realism or pragmatism view compliance as essentially a utility function: states calculate the benefits of acting in accord with a norm versus the penalties for noncompliance. The interests at stake need not be exclusively material, as a state's regime may attach value to intangible interests such as international reputation. Alternatively, those who explain compliance in terms of the development of social identities (so-called constructivists in social science terminology) emphasize the socializing role played by institutions: states internalize norms through their interactions within institutions, and this process, in turn, promotes their socialization within the international community. Thus, for example, in recent years, overt state sponsorship of terrorism has been a declining phenomenon. To what extent can that shift be attributed to a new calculus of decision after 9/11 (dramatically raising the costs of state sponsorship) or to the internalization of that norm by former state sponsors? Given the opaque nature of the regimes running these states of concern, one cannot say with confidence. "Demonstrating empirically the importance of socialization is ... difficult," political scientists John Ikenberry and Charles Kupchan conclude. "The core of the problem is that the outcomes we would expect to see if coercion were solely at work may not differ substantially from those associated with socialization."[83] The implication for policy analysis is to focus on a target state's observable behavior rather than on trying to surmise whether a norm has been internalized by its ruling elite as part of a socialization process. When a regime's conduct accords with the system's norms, perhaps one can more realistically speak of "assimilation," a condition under which the target state recognizes that "the gains of living within the system ... outweigh the potential advantages of seeking to destroy or dominate it."[84]

Compliance is context dependent and, therefore, inherently selective. As Michael Glennon observes, "No practical obligation obtains for all actors to honor all norms all the time, because some actors may, because of their situation, weigh the costs of violation differently in some circumstances than do other actors."[85] The situational nature of compliance suggests an approach toward international law that is instrumental. This attitude was exemplified in the case of the Iranian hostage crisis in 1979–81. As Stephen Krasner notes, for Iran, the contravention of a core international norm by the revolutionary regime in Tehran "served a domestic if not international political purpose." Although Washington broke diplomatic relations with Iran after the seizure of the U.S. embassy, other countries did not follow suit, and Iranian officials were not barred from international organizations: "Iran did not become a pariah state.... It was not in the interest of other states, which wanted to maintain communication, to isolate Iran."[86]

States draw important distinctions affecting compliance and enforcement on the basis of their perceptions of threat. For example, the United States may assert a *general* interest in the norm of nonproliferation, but, in practice, because of the perceived conjunction of capability with hostile intent that translates into *specific* threats, U.S. policy-makers focus on Iran and North Korea rather than on Israel and India. Hence, as President George W. Bush brushed aside nonproliferation concerns in 2005 to announce a nuclear cooperation agreement with India, a nuclear weapons state outside the Nonproliferation Treaty, he declared India to be a "responsible" member of the international community—in implicit contrast to irresponsible rogue states.

Compliance is easiest when important interests are not at stake and it conveys no risk. The Ottawa Treaty of 1999 banning land mines has been accepted by more than 150 states, yet the vast majority neither deploy land mines nor exist in a security environment vis-à-vis neighboring states that would create a powerful motivation for them to do so. Among the nearly forty states that did not accede to the treaty were South Korea, facing across its border the North's forward-deployed million-man army, and Finland, a state universally regarded as one of the international community's best actors, which was invaded by neighboring Russia, then under Soviet rule, in 1940.

Compliance is also obviously contingent on capacity. Failing and failed states, such as Chad and Somalia, lack the economic and military capabilities to assert effective sovereign control over their territories. This deficit in power makes them susceptible to terrorist groups, such as Al Qaeda, that are able to operate unfettered. In other cases, such as Pakistan with respect to Al Qaeda before 9/11, low capacity is compounded by a lack of political will that leads the regimes to turn a blind eye to threatening nonstate actors on their territory. Such passive sponsorship of terrorism has largely overtaken the traditional concern of overt state sponsorship.

The United States has regarded international institutions as a primary mechanism for promoting compliance with norms. The integration of states into the international order has long been America's preferred grand strategy. At the end of World War II, Roosevelt envisioned the integration of the Soviet Union into a postwar order as an alternative to the balance-of-power containment strategy that unfolded in the late 1940s in response to the challenge posed by Stalin. After the Cold War, this integration strategy was at the heart of the Clinton administration's strategy of engagement and enlargement. Former U.S. official Richard Haass has called integration "the natural successor to containment" and "the most coherent response to globalization and to the transnational threats"—such as terrorism, proliferation, and climate change—"that constitute the defining challenges of our time."[87]

Yet the dilemmas persist. An international system resting on the consent of its constituent states and lacking a supranational authority that can consistently enforce the compliance of norms will continue to be roiled by the enduring competition between anarchy and order. The attitude of states toward international law is situational and instrumental. It is a useful source of legitimacy for policy when it accords with a state's interests but not a meaningful impediment to independent action when it is at odds with a state's interests. Nonetheless, although interests and values are contested, a broad (albeit not universal) consensus on specific norms among states—especially those with democratic governance—permits the qualified use of the term "international society" without irony. That convergence of perspectives and interests creates a pragmatic opportunity for Washington to generate meaningful pressure on states that threaten U.S. interests.

Chapter 2

Pathways into the "Community of Nations"

"We want Iran to take its rightful place in the community of nations."
— President Barack Obama, April 5, 2009[1]

"Integration"—the acceptance by states of the dominant principles of international relations—has been called America's grand strategy.[2] Even when U.S. policy-makers have confronted the stark realities of power politics (as with Joseph Stalin's Soviet Union after World War II) or when the United States itself has acted outside institutions and norms in response to perceived exigencies (as in the 2003 invasion of Iraq), the Wilsonian vision of international order underlying integration has remained an aspiration. As such, it should be viewed less as an end state than as an ongoing political process that occurs along a continuum of change.

Integration is one of three approaches to international order. Countries rejecting integration may be dissatisfied—even revolutionary—states aspiring to a major or wholesale revision of international order or, alternatively, states seeking separation "from the orbit of prevailing norms and practices."[3] Among the states of contemporary concern, only Iran is an avowedly revolutionary state, whose theocratic leadership rejects an American-dominated international order. But unlike great powers of the past, such as Nazi Germany, Iran lacks the capabilities to overturn the established international order. In Iran, the core question underlying the leadership's policies—whether on the nuclear issue or the use of terrorism as a policy instrument—is whether it is a revolutionary state or an ordinary country. North Korea has pursued a brutal autarkic policy to separate that country from the international system and, in so doing, preserve regime stability by mitigating the threat of political contagion from outside. But for marginal actors in international relations, such as Iran and North Korea, neither posturing revisionism nor impoverishing separation offers viable long-term alternatives to integration into the liberal international order.

Pursuant to its strategy of comprehensive engagement, the Obama administration offered Iran, North Korea, and other states that defy international norms a structured choice with tangible benefits for behavior change and penalties for noncompliance. That choice lays out a "pathway [to] greater integration with the international community."[4] The contemporary challenge of inducing or compelling outlier states—those seeking either revision or separation—to comply with international norms should be informed by past experience.

A historical review reveals four distinct pathways of integration to be explained through a comparative analysis. Those distinct pathways and examples of each are as follows:

- Assimilation of a defeated great power (Nazi Germany after World War II)
- Evolution of revolutionary states into orthodox great powers (the Soviet Union under Gorbachev and China under Deng Xiaoping)
- Regime change from without—external intervention to oust ruling regimes by neighboring states (Tanzania's 1979 invasion of Uganda to overthrow Idi Amin and Vietnam's 1978 invasion of Cambodia to oust the Khmer Rouge regime)
- Regime change from within—changes of regime that were internally generated (the 1989 overthrow of the Ceauşescu regime in Romania and the end of apartheid rule in South Africa in the early 1990s)

An assessment of positive cases in which substantial or full integration has occurred would inform the consideration of negative cases, such as Iran and North Korea, which remain recalcitrant and, indeed, view the very process as a threat to regime survival. Although each case is context specific, a "structured, focused comparison" permits an assessment of cases across the four pathways to identify key determinants of change and, alternatively, factors that have impeded the process of integration.[5] Such a comparative analysis requires a common set of questions that fall within four categories.

First, what was the character of the normative challenge? Did the state seek the wholesale revision of the international order, or did its ruling regime violate established norms? Was the noncompliance with external behavioral norms—that is, with consequences beyond its borders relating to interstate aggression, proliferation of weapons of mass destruction (WMD), or state sponsorship of terrorism—or with internal behavioral norms related to the state's conduct toward its own population with respect to human and civil rights?

Second, what were the key determinants of change? What were the respective roles of—and interplay between—external and internal factors in determining the outcome? How did external pressures affect internal interest groups and shape intra-elite bargaining? Were the regime's own core interest groups the agent of change?

Third, what was the extent of the change? Was the magnitude of change total or partial—a change *of* regime or a change *within* a regime? What was the focus of change—leaders, institutions, policies, or across the board?

Fourth, and finally, did the state's increased integration or assimilation into the international order lead to improved compliance with international norms? Was compliance different for external and internal behavioral norms?

The Assimilation of a Defeated Great Power

Germany after World War II

As the principal power reestablishing international order in the aftermath of World War II, the United States faced twin challenges: the future of Germany (the paramount threat of the twentieth century's first half), and the future of the Soviet Union (the looming threat of the century's latter half). Washington's strategy to manage the defeat of the former was integral to its strategy to counter the rise of the latter. Central to this dual approach was the embedding of German power into the nascent structure of Western economic and security institutions, notably the European Economic Community (later the European Union) and the North Atlantic Treaty Organization (NATO).[6] That overarching policy toward Germany—assimilation through integration—provided the basis for economic revival as well as for large-scale rearmament (essential to containing Soviet military power in central Europe) that Germany's neighbors did not perceive as a threat. The Federal Republic of Germany (West Germany) became rooted in the U.S.-led community of industrial democracies. After the fall of the Berlin wall in 1989, this process of assimilation came to fruition with the integration of the Democratic Republic of Germany (East Germany), the former Soviet occupation zone, into the West German federal structure.

Nazi Germany was both a revolutionary state in the breadth of its challenge to international order and an outlaw state through its crimes of interstate aggression and genocide. Because the threat derived from the character of the Nazi regime, the Allied powers declared their objective nothing short of Germany's unconditional surrender. In the Allied debate about postwar Germany, France and the Soviet Union argued that the latent threat of revived German power in the heart of Europe necessitated that strict limits be set on its sovereignty. To ensure that Germany could never again be the instigator of war, Henry Morgenthau, the U.S. secretary of the treasury, advocated the deindustrialization (or what some called the "industrial disarmament") of Germany. By 1946, with the demise of the wartime alliance, the German question became subsumed within the broader deterioration in East-West relations. As Winston Churchill chillingly described an "iron curtain" descending on Europe, the VE (Victory in Europe) Day armistice line separating Anglo-American and Soviet forces hardened into the front line of the Cold War. The establishment in 1949 of independent West and East German states out of the former occupation zones codified this new status quo.

West Germany's domestic renewal and international assimilation were mutually reinforcing: economic reconstruction and democratization facilitated its integration into the U.S.-led community of states, which, in turn, supported West Germany's postwar recovery. The Federal Republic regained sovereignty but remained what historian Konrad Jarausch characterized as a "surrogate state" for a Germany that one day would be reunited.[7] The Basic Law of 1949—essentially the Federal Republic's constitution—established the legal framework for a democratic civil society and the election of Konrad Adenauer as West Germany's first postwar chancellor. The Basic Law was designed to avoid the fatal flaws of the Weimar constitution, whose unqualified democratic provisions had been exploited by the Nazis to subvert democracy. Hence, the Basic Law created an institutional structure that has been described as "value laden" through its explicit requirement to preserve the "free democratic basic order."[8]

Institutionalization took the lead role in altering Germany's political culture and allowing its population's attitudes to catch up through generational change. In marked contrast, East Germany became the western frontier of the Soviet empire under Stalin and developed a totalitarian system of civilian surveillance and control that dictators like Saddam Hussein and Kim Jong Il would later envy.[9]

Complementing the process of democratization in West Germany, economic policies adopted under U.S. military occupation—the breakup of industrial cartels through antitrust policy, free trade unions, trade liberalization rather than protectionism, and currency reform—created the foundation for sustained economic growth. External assistance through both the Marshall Plan and the newly established International Monetary Fund was important, but probably less for the relatively modest direct assistance than for providing subsidies to Germany and other European countries to import goods needed for recovery before those states had the necessary export revenues to pay for them.[10] More broadly, the U.S.-designed Bretton Woods and GATT (General Agreement on Tariffs and Trade) system created a flourishing global economy in which West Germany became the world's second-largest trading state by the late 1970s.

Concern about German reindustrialization in early postwar years, such as that reflected in the Morgenthau Plan, was trumped by the urgent need for German production. But the potentially adverse reaction of neighboring states to German industrial revival was mitigated through the embedding of two industries essential for war-making into a new supranational organization: the six-nation European Coal and Steel Community, a key institutional precursor of the European Economic Community. Even before full restoration of German sovereignty, the crucial issue of rearmament was settled by Cold War developments in 1948–49: the Berlin Blockade, the coup in Czechoslovakia (which brought a communist regime to power), and the Soviet acquisition of the atomic bomb. The wholesale demobilization of the Nazi regime's armed forces and the subsequent drawdown of U.S. occupation forces had created an imbalance (on the order of ten to one) between Soviet and Western conventional forces in Central Europe.[11] This military asymmetry was exacerbated by the redeployment of U.S. forces to East Asia after the onset of the Korean War in 1950. To counter the Soviet threat to Western Europe through a collective security arrangement, the United States spearheaded the establishment of NATO in 1949. The embedding of German military power within a supranational organization, whether through NATO (which the Federal Republic joined in 1955) or a proposed European Defense Community, went far to allay the concerns of France and other states adjacent to Germany.

The Soviet interest in preventing German rearmament and integration into the Western security community precipitated a diplomatic gambit—the so-called Stalin note of March 1952 to the United States, Britain, and France—in which the Kremlin called for negotiations leading to the establishment of a neutral, united Germany that would be permitted to have armed forces solely for self-defense. Although the failure to convene such four-party talks has generated historical speculation about a missed opportunity to unify Germany before 1989, Soviet archival evidence reveals that Stalin viewed East Germany as an integral part of the Soviet empire whose loss to the West through unification would have had unacceptable consequences.[12] That paramount Soviet interest, indicative of the Kremlin's view toward unification, was brutally evident in June 1953, when the occupying Red Army suppressed a workers' uprising in East Germany in support of its Soviet-installed regime.[13] In short, for both the United States and the Soviet Union, the only acceptable terms for the unification of the two Germanys were their own. "What each superpower most feared," Cold War historian John Gaddis observes, "was that [a unified Germany] might align itself with its Cold War adversary: if that were to happen, the resulting concentration of military, industrial, and economic power could be too great to overcome."[14]

Although the geopolitical realities of the Cold War precluded unification, the de facto partition of Germany into two states did not enjoy de jure status. West Germany declared that it was the sole legal representative of the German people and sought to delegitimize East Germany by preventing its international recognition as a sovereign state. In the post-Stalin era, after the unsuccessful effort to block West Germany's rearmament and integration into the West, Nikita Khrushchev pragmatically recognized the Federal Republic in 1955 as part of a "two-states policy."[15] The failure of that Soviet diplomatic move to win cross-recognition of East Germany was the prelude to the Berlin Crisis of 1958–61. In November 1958, Khrushchev issued an ultimatum threatening to turn over authority for access to West Berlin to the East German government and calling for the withdrawal of Western military forces and the establishment of Berlin as a "free city."

Although the conventional interpretation of Khrushchev's brinkmanship has been that he was attempting to pressure the United States into diplomatically recognizing East Germany, new archival evidence points to Khrushchev's overriding interest in bolstering the East German regime and, in particular, staunching the flow of East German refugees through the easiest access point in West Berlin. East German leader Walter Ulbricht was able to exploit that Soviet interest in his regime's survival to create effective leverage that won Khrushchev's eventual acquiescence to the construction of the Berlin wall in 1961. As Cold War historian Hope Harrison concludes, "Ulbricht finally put the Kremlin leaders in a position where their only realistic option to preserve a stable socialist regime [in East Germany] was to agree to his request to close off access to West Berlin."[16] Although the wall became a potent symbol of Cold War oppression, its erection stopped the flow of refugees and stabilized the East German economy.

By 1969, when Chancellor Willy Brandt came to power, the West German policy of delegitimizing East Germany was increasingly seen as counterproductive. Under Brandt's policy of détente, or *Ostpolitik*, West Germany concluded treaties in 1970 with the Soviet Union and Poland renouncing the use of force and reiterating the Federal Republic's recognition of postwar borders. Those agreements, as well as the 1971 accord among the four wartime allies ending the dispute over access to Berlin, paved the way for the establishment of formal relations between West and East Germany and for their subsequent admission to the United Nations. Whereas the East German regime seized on this shift from de facto to de jure status to emphasize its separateness, West Germany's Brandt, characterizing the new status quo as "two German states in one German nation," reaffirmed his government's commitment to eventual unification.[17]

In 1989, forty-three years after Churchill's "iron curtain" speech, the wall unexpectedly came down, and the diplomatic pathway for unification was cleared. The climactic events were set in motion that summer, when popular discontent in East Germany over fraudulent elections triggered the flight of East German refugees to the West through Hungary (which did not intercede to halt the flow) and mass demonstrations inside East Germany. At this critical juncture, a major discontinuity occurred: Soviet leader Mikhail Gorbachev decided not to respond militarily—in sharp contrast to the Soviet Union's interventions in East Germany (1953), Hungary (1956), and Czechoslovakia (1968). Indeed, speaking in Leipzig in early October at an event marking East Germany's fortieth anniversary, Gorbachev pushed a reform agenda, which was soon followed by the ouster of East Germany's hard-line leader, Erich Honecker. On November 9, the wall was opened to allow the free flow of people. An East German proposal for the unification of Germany as a neutral state was rejected by West German chancellor Helmut Kohl, who reiterated the Western position dating back to the Stalin note that a German government brought to power through open and fair elections should be free to join international organizations of its own choosing. Free elections in East Germany in March 1990, the first since World War II, led to the creation of a monetary union with the West in July. A formal political union between the two Germanys was established in October through the integration of the five territorial *Lander* constituting East Germany into the Federal Republic's structure.

The bilateral talks between the Germanys in 1989–90 were conducted in parallel with intensive negotiations among the Soviet Union, the United States, Britain, and France over whether unification would be allowed to occur and, if so, whether a unified Germany would be permitted to join NATO.[18] The George H. W. Bush administration played a pivotal diplomatic role in overcoming the resistance of those other major powers—initially by forging a common Western position in favor of Germany's unification and full sovereignty, and subsequently by crafting security guarantees (including Germany's renunciation of WMD and acceptance of a multilateral treaty to reduce conventional forces in Europe) to overcome Soviet opposition to a united Germany's membership in NATO. Gorbachev and Kohl jointly announced that membership on July 16, 1990.[19] U.S. officials informally called the date "VE Day II" to signify the final liberation of the European continent forty-five years after the defeat of Nazism.[20] The postwar process of German reassimilation through integration into European institutions had come to fruition: a united democratic Germany, by then the region's dominant economy and the world's third largest, was poised to assume its position within what President George H. W. Bush called "a Europe whole and free."[21]

The Evolution of Revolutionary States

Russia: Kennan's Prophecy Fulfilled

American diplomat George Kennan, under the pseudonym "X," in a path-breaking 1947 article in *Foreign Affairs*, elucidated the strategy of containment to counter the geostrategic threat posed by the Soviet Union after World War II. More than a strategy, Kennan's analysis in "The Sources of Soviet Conduct" was a prophecy of how the then-emergent Cold War would end. Kennan argued that the underlying cause of the Cold War was structural, arising from the very character of Stalin's regime. The Soviet system, he concluded, "bears within it the seeds of its own decay" that would lead to "either the breakup or the gradual mellowing of Soviet power."[22] Kennan viewed the balancing of Soviet power by the West through containment as basically a long-term holding operation until that internal process could come to fruition.

Forty-two years after the article's publication, Kennan declared the Soviet Union under Gorbachev to have evolved from a revolutionary state into an orthodox great power. "What we are witnessing today in Russia is the break-up of much, if not all, of the system of power by which that country has been held together and governed since 1917," he told the Senate Foreign Relations Committee in April 1989. "That country should now be regarded essentially as another great power, like other great powers—one, that is, whose aspirations and policies are conditioned outstandingly by its own geographic situation, history, and tradition."[23] Seven months later, the fall of the Berlin wall brought an iconic end to the Cold War. Yet as Kennan predicted, though it was nonetheless unexpected at the time, a "mellowing" of Soviet power came at the finish of a decade that was ushered in by the Soviet Union's invasion of Afghanistan on Christmas Day 1979—an event that drove superpower relations to their lowest point since the Cuban missile crisis. The transformation of the Soviet Union from a revolutionary state into "another great power" arose from a complex interplay of domestic and international factors: Gorbachev's paramount role in advancing transformational political reform internally in tandem with Ronald Reagan's revitalized containment strategy externally.

The structural nature of the Cold War was an inevitable consequence of the Russian Revolution. Vladimir Ilyich Lenin espoused a radical alternative vision of international order to that propounded by the other revolutionary figure of 1917, Woodrow Wilson, proselytizing for his doctrine of national self-determination. Churchill repeatedly expressed regret over the failure of the Western powers "to strangle Bolshevism at its birth."[24] A communist revolution that Karl Marx had foreseen in industrial Germany instead occurred by historical happenstance in agrarian Russia. True to its revolutionary bona fides, the Bolshevik regime initially eschewed conventional interstate diplomacy. When asked to assume the position of foreign secretary, Leon Trotsky famously declared: "What sort of diplomatic work will we be doing anyway? I shall publish a few revolutionary proclamations to the peoples and then close shop."[25] Trotsky called for a "permanent revolution" to promote the wholesale overturning of the international capitalist order in Europe and beyond.

By the mid-1920s, however, when it was clear that Russia was not destined to be the vanguard of a world revolution, Stalin, who was ruthlessly consolidating political power as Lenin's successor, pivoted toward an alternative strategy of "socialism in one country."[26] For a fragile post-revolutionary regime that was asserting control over the vast territory that was Imperial Russia, acceding to and, in turn, being accepted into the international community had a major benefit. State sovereignty—the bedrock principle of international relations that ensures the noninterference by states in the domestic affairs of others— provided the Soviet regime a tacit security assurance. But "socialism in one country" did not signify that the Soviet Union was a status quo power. "The world-revolutionary ideology, rhetoric, and political efforts of the early Soviet leadership," as Kennan stated, posed an inherent challenge to international order that engendered Washington's hostility and the withholding of its diplomatic recognition of the Soviet Union until 1933.[27]

In the 1930s, Stalin launched what historian Robert Tucker described as "a revolution from above," a "second revolution when massive terror transformed the single-party state inherited from Lenin into an absolute autocracy."[28] In lieu of international integration, Stalin pushed a draconian strategy of autarky, forced industrialization, and agricultural collectivization to establish a socialist economy. Agricultural exports were expected to finance imports of foreign goods and technology necessary for industrialization, but forced collectivization and the coercive extraction of farm produce from the Ukraine and other agricultural areas triggered a famine that led to the deaths of millions of peasants. Stalin ordered mass purges of the Communist Party, the military, the intelligentsia, and the professional classes to squelch any dissent. In 1937–38 alone, the number of people executed by the NKVD (People's Commissariat for Internal Affairs), Stalin's dread secret police, has been estimated at 1 million. Undergirding Stalin's autocratic system was a pervasive cult of personality that was propagated to shape mass opinion. Internal repression was combined with opportunistic external aggression when Stalin attacked Finland and annexed the Baltic countries in 1939–40.

The Cold War was presaged by tensions that emerged during the wartime alliance to defeat Nazi Germany. Ambassador Averell Harriman wanted to leverage U.S. military assistance to promote a postwar settlement that would prevent the rise of a Soviet sphere of influence in Eastern Europe. Arguing for a quid pro quo policy linking U.S. aid to Soviet conduct, Harriman sought "to strengthen the hand of those around Stalin who want to play the game along our lines and to show Stalin that the advice of the counselors of a tough policy is leading him into difficulties."[29] The key assumptions of this policy were that Stalin would settle for something short of outright postwar control of the territories the Red Army occupied on its march to Berlin and that the Soviet supreme leader could be influenced by his circle of close advisers. Loath to use aid for bargaining leverage during wartime, President Franklin D. Roosevelt believed that Stalin could nonetheless be co-opted into a postwar settlement. According to historian John Gaddis, "F.D.R. sought to ensure a stable postwar order by offering Moscow a prominent place in it; by making it, so to speak, a member of the club."[30] The premise underlying Roosevelt's strategy—what Gaddis described as "containment by integration"—was that Soviet hostility derived from a sense of insecurity whose source was external. After the Allied powers defeated the Axis powers and thereby eliminated the source of that external insecurity, so Roosevelt's thinking went, a political accommodation could be reached between the Soviet Union and the United States.[31]

Kennan held the diametrically opposite view of Soviet strategic culture, arguing that the perpetuation of external threat was an important source of internal legitimacy for the Kremlin leadership: "A hostile international environment is the breath of life for [the] prevailing internal system in this country."[32] Roosevelt's neo-Wilsonian proposal for integrating the Soviet Union into the international community came up against the hard reality of Stalin's "compulsion … to retain totalitarian control over the state and society once the war was over."[33] As the Soviet Union and the East European states under Red Army occupation rejected the U.S. offer of Marshall Plan aid, the VE Day armistice line hardened into the Cold War divide.

After Stalin's death in 1953, his successor, Khrushchev, ushered in a period of political liberalization that became known as the "Khrushchev thaw." Though he remained faithful to Marxist-Leninist ideology, Khrushchev addressed the worst excesses of the Soviet system that derived from Stalin's pathology. His landmark "secret speech" at the Twentieth Party Congress in 1956 was a sweeping indictment of Stalin's cult of personality and autocratic rule. But de-Stalinization called the legitimacy of the system into question: the line between the Stalinist excesses and the Leninist requirements for coercively maintaining the Communist Party's monopoly of power was unclear. The incendiary secret speech fueled subsequent political uprisings in Hungary and Poland (which the Kremlin harshly suppressed to maintain its sphere of influence) and was a major precipitant of the Sino-Soviet rift, because Mao Zedong (who was pursuing his own variant of neo-Stalinism in China) rejected Khrushchev's revisionist line. To be sure, Khrushchev's erratic behavior and miscalculations, perhaps stemming from a bedrock conviction that the global correlation of forces was shifting in Moscow's favor, led to Cold War crises in Berlin and Cuba that brought the United States and the Soviet Union to the brink. Nonetheless, biographer William Taubman concludes that history will credit Khrushchev, through his frontal assault on the central issue of Stalinism, with having "begun the process that destroyed the Soviet regime."[34]

Leonid Brezhnev, who became Communist Party leader through an intraparty coup ousting Khrushchev in 1964, backtracked on de-Stalinization through an internal crackdown on dissent and praise for Stalin's foreign policy legacy. The crackdown occurred when the United States was militarily mired in Vietnam and when the Soviet Union was emerging not just as a Eurasian land power but as a superpower with a truly global reach. Henry Kissinger, then Richard Nixon's national security adviser, described the rise of Soviet power as "the problem of our age."[35] Nixon and Kissinger's détente policy toward the Soviet Union was a realistic variation of Kennan's containment doctrine.

The Nixon-Kissinger strategy was premised on the concept of "linkage," under which Washington sought to create a system of incentives and penalties to moderate Soviet behavior. Tangible economic benefits, such as financial credits and technology transfers, were intended to induce responsive Soviet policies—for example, Moscow's assistance in resolving the Vietnam conflict. Alternatively, positive inducements would be withheld if the Kremlin persisted in destabilizing Cold War policies. Superpower summitry in 1972–73 produced nuclear arms control agreements and a statement of "Basic Principles" that committed both sides to "exercise restraint" and eschew "efforts to obtain unilateral advantage at the expense of the other." Nixon likened the agreement to a road map that was to serve as a code of conduct regulating superpower behavior. Yet the implementation of the 1972 "Basic Principles" agreement was undermined by contending Soviet and U.S. conceptions of détente. Whereas Nixon and Kissinger saw détente as a variation of containment, the Soviet leadership viewed it as an updated version of Khrushchev's "peaceful coexistence" doctrine. The Soviets circumvented the U.S. effort to establish policy linkages and were able to compartmentalize the relationship so that arms control, regional conflicts, and economic relations were addressed as discrete issues. The superpower experience in the 1970s revealed détente to be a *condition*, not a *structure*, of international relations. The "Basic Principles" marked not the end of U.S.-Soviet competition, but rather a framework for continued superpower competition that lowered the risk of inadvertent military escalation as both superpowers jockeyed for unilateral advantage.[36]

Like Khrushchev, Brezhnev believed that Washington's interest in détente stemmed from a recognition that the political and military correlation of forces was shifting in Moscow's favor. For Brezhnev, "unilateral Soviet gains and détente were not only compatible, but mutually reinforcing," argues political scientist Jack Snyder.[37] The Soviet leader pursued a strategy of "offensive détente" that catered to the regime's core interest groups by "offer[ing] an arms buildup to the military, Third World expansion to the orthodox ideologues, and détente and technology transfer to the cultural and technical intelligentsia."[38] Although "offensive détente" served an important internal function for Brezhnev in managing intra-elite politics and bargaining, the strategy generated a strong external reaction. A loose anti-Soviet coalition emerged that included the world's other major powers, from the United States and Western Europe to China and Japan. Ronald Reagan's revitalized containment strategy led to a major increase in U.S. defense spending and aimed to reverse Soviet gains in the Third World through what became known as the Reagan Doctrine. The administration's Strategic Defense Initiative threatened to shift superpower competition to a new military realm that was based on advanced information-age technologies in which the Soviet Union lagged considerably.

The status of the Soviet Union, once described as the "incomplete superpower," derived solely from its military strength.[39] In the early 1980s, the perception of Soviet strength based on military might belied economic weakness. Structural problems augured a long-term decline in the Soviet Union's power position. The rate of Soviet economic growth slowed in the 1960s and declined sharply in the 1970s. Russians referred to the final years of Brezhnev's rule as the era of stagnation. The slowdown that stemmed from the inefficiencies of a command economy was exacerbated by the financial drain of high military expenditures, which rose to an estimated 15 to 17 percent of Soviet gross domestic product (GDP); by Moscow's geostrategic overextension, which entailed significant subventions to Cuba and other Third World allies; and by a sharp downturn in the price of oil, the export of which was the Soviet Union's prime source of foreign currency.

Gorbachev became Soviet party chief in 1985 after the death of Brezhnev in 1982 and the brief interregna of Yuri Andropov, head of the KGB (Committee for State Security), and Konstantin Chernenko, a career apparatchik. In an effort to end stagnation and revive economic growth, Gorbachev, originally viewed as a conservative because his rapid advancement had occurred under Andropov, turned Brezhnev's strategy on its head. Gorbachev called for the wholesale reconstruction (*perestroika*) of the Soviet economy, thereby ending the worst rigidities and inefficiencies of the ossified command economy whose origins dated to Stalin's "revolution from above." As part of an anticorruption campaign, Gorbachev instituted a policy of openness (*glasnost*) to increase governmental transparency. The easing of media censorship, however, had unintended political consequences by breaking the Communist Party's taboo on public discussion of the country's social and economic ills and the repressive history of the Stalin era. In launching a program of domestic economic reform, Gorbachev's goal was not to end socialism but to make it work better. He acknowledged that a source of inspiration for perestroika and glasnost was Alexander Dubček, the reformist Czech leader toppled by the Soviet invasion of 1968, who had advocated an innovative, top-down, Communist Party–directed program of economic and political reform under the rubric "socialism with a human face."

Gorbachev's ambitious domestic program was contingent on a quiescent international environment. His new thinking in foreign affairs ended the policy inertia dating to Stalin under which the Kremlin sought to separate the Soviet bloc from the West with the expectation that the international capitalist order would eventually be overturned.[40] According to Gorbachev, "The new thinking wasn't just some policy shift, it required a major conceptual breakthrough" in which the Soviet leadership embraced "the fact that we live in an interdependent, contradictory, but ultimately integral world."[41] Gorbachev advanced a new "mutual security" paradigm to supplant the Brezhnev-era emphasis on class struggle, the correlation of forces, and peaceful coexistence. A Gorbachev aide warned an American audience of the new Soviet "threat": "We are going to take away your enemy."[42] Gorbachev's "new thinking" rhetoric was backed by action: negotiating the removal of intermediate-range nuclear missiles from Europe, withdrawing Soviet forces from Afghanistan, and above all, acquiescing to the fall of communist regimes in Eastern Europe in 1989.

In the arc of Soviet history, Gorbachev's rule was the great discontinuity. President George H. W. Bush and his national security adviser, Brent Scowcroft, recount their utter amazement at Gorbachev's decision to allow a unified Germany to join NATO—and the "firestorm" it created in the Soviet delegation.[43] Indeed, Gorbachev had earlier warned French president François Mitterrand that the day Germany unified "a Soviet [general] will be sitting in my chair."[44] Realist political theory, which focuses on the distribution of power among states as the key to explaining international politics, would not have predicted the Soviet Union's relinquishing control over its sphere of influence in Eastern Europe. In so doing, Gorbachev essentially accepted the vision of postwar order that Roosevelt had advanced in 1945 to integrate the Soviet Union into the international community. Any Soviet leader in the late 1980s would have had to confront the country's structural economic problems, which were exacerbated financially by geostrategic overextension and the Reagan administration's assertive containment strategy. Those material factors were a necessary condition for change but do not adequately explain the magnitude of change that Gorbachev championed. Kennan had prophesied an end to the Cold War when the Soviet Union "mellowed" or collapsed, but not that it would occur in 1989.

Gorbachev could have pursued an alternative course—for example, a strategy varyingly described as "status quo plus" or "détente plus" that would have combined economic reform with geostrategic retrenchment while maintaining the Communist Party's lead role.[45] Indeed, a former senior Soviet official claims that had Andropov lived, he would have pursued a Chinese-style reform along those lines. "Gorbachev's unwillingness to implement Chinese-style reforms," argue political scientists Deborah Larson and Alexei Shevchenko, "ultimately doomed the system he intended to refurbish, not to destroy.... Successful application of the Chinese-style reform program ... would have almost certainly produced dramatically different results." This assessment, based on Russia's post-Soviet economic performance, which benefited considerably from the higher price for its oil and gas exports, points to the possibility that a "getting-by" scenario was viable.[46] Incremental change within the context of the existing Soviet system is probably what Politburo hard-liners believed they were endorsing when they backed Gorbachev for the party leadership. Instead, he acted on the radical critique of Soviet foreign policy that had emerged in the late Brezhnev era. In embracing integration over isolation, Gorbachev initiated a dynamic process whose outcome was indeterminate, with consequences both intended and unintended. Certainly no consequence was more unintended for Gorbachev himself than the dissolution of the Soviet Union into fifteen successor states in December 1991.

Kennan's pseudonymous article argued that the structural nature of the Cold War derived from the ideology on which Soviet power was grounded.[47] Gorbachev eschewed Marxist-Leninist ideology in favor of new thinking that accorded with the political, social, and economic norms of the international community. That transformation—manifested in Gorbachev's remarkable address to the United Nations in 1988 renouncing the use of force and calling for "the supremacy of the universal human ideal"—prompted Kennan to declare that his prophecy had been fulfilled.

Since the dissolution of the Soviet Union in 1991, a revival of old think-ing has been evident in the antidemocratic policies adopted by Gorbachev's successors—Boris Yeltsin; Vladimir Putin; and Putin's hand-picked succes-sor, Dmitry Medvedev. Russian political power has been centralized in the presidency and the security services as parliamentary elections have been rigged, political dissidents assassinated, and freedom of the press and non-governmental organizations curtailed. This autocratic turn prompted Freedom House to downgrade Russia from "partly free" to "not free" in 2005.[48] The Russian economy, which has recovered from the debt default and devaluation of the ruble in 1998, remains overly reliant on oil and gas exports that account for one-quarter of the country's GDP.[49] Because of pervasive graft, Transpar-ency International ranked Russia 154th of 178 countries (behind Yemen and the Central African Republic) in its 2010 global survey of corruption.[50] The combined suppression of political rights and pervasive graft led the head of Russia's constitutional court to warn that the country was on the pathway to becoming a "criminal state."[51] Against that backdrop of domestic autocratic revival, post–Soviet Russian foreign policy is being boldly renationalized as Moscow tries to exert influence over its so-called near abroad: the four-teen other former Soviet republics—now independent states—ringing Rus-sia from the Baltic states to Belarus and Ukraine, then through Georgia and the south Caucasus to Central Asia. Russia's military intervention in northern Georgia in August 2008 and its subsequent unilateral recognition of Abkhazia and South Ossetia as independent states were emblematic of that assertive approach toward its geographic periphery.

Despite the revival of internal repression and foreign policy assertive-ness, contemporary Russia is nonetheless more integrated into the global system than its autarkic Soviet predecessor. As Kennan argued in 1989, Russia has evolved from a revolutionary state into "just another great power," with "aspirations" conditioned by geography and history.[52] Rus-sia's post-Soviet leaders will embrace greater integration with the inter-national community to the extent that they view it as advancing Russian national (as well as the ruling regime's own) interests.

China: The Rise of the Middle Kingdom

"The United States welcomes China's rise as a strong, prosperous, and suc-cessful member of the community of nations," declared President Obama to Chinese president Hu Jintao during his state visit to Washington in January

2011.[53] The Obama administration has pursued a strategy of engagement to "encourage China to make choices that contribute to peace, security, and prosperity as its influence rises."[54] Integrating China into the international order has been the consistent objective of U.S. policy since the Nixon administration initiated the process of normalizing relations to end two decades of estrangement. Writing in *Foreign Affairs* in 1967, eighteen months before assuming the presidency, Nixon telegraphed his intention: "We simply cannot afford to leave China outside the family of nations."[55] Four years later, Henry Kissinger's secret mission to Beijing paved the way for Nixon's presidential visit to China in 1972. China, traditionally known as the "Middle Kingdom," was then an isolated revolutionary state emerging from the domestic convulsions of Mao's Cultural Revolution.

Three decades after Nixon's pathbreaking journey, Hu came to Washington as the leader of a great power in ascendance. A Pew opinion poll indicated that a near-majority of Americans (44 percent) perceived China to be the world's leading economic power, even though China's GDP is roughly one-third that of the United States. Yet a still larger number of those polled (55 percent) considered "China's emergence as a world power [as] a major threat."[56] Americans increasingly perceive a threatening conjunction between China's growing economic and military capabilities and the Beijing regime's uncertain political intentions toward its neighbors and beyond. The crucial issue about China's rise is whether a state now driven more by nationalism than by revolutionary fervor can be successfully integrated into the international order as a "responsible stakeholder"[57] or whether modern China is an analogue to Imperial Germany before World War I that will evolve into what the Pentagon calls a "peer competitor."[58]

The contemporary debate about China's rise is being conducted within the context of the country's historical evolution from revolutionary state to orthodox great power. Three pivotal developments put China on that trajectory of change: first, Mao's strategic decision to normalize relations with the United States in 1969–72; second, the sweeping economic reforms launched by Deng Xiaoping in the post-Mao era; and third, the Beijing regime's response to the legitimacy crisis triggered by its brutal suppression of pro-democracy demonstrators in Tiananmen Square in June 1989.

"The Chinese people have stood up," declared Mao on the establishment of the People's Republic of China (PRC) in 1949 after the defeat of Chiang Kai-shek's Nationalist forces. As historian Chen Jian observes, this invocation was "a legitimacy statement" for Mao's revolutionary vision of domestic transformation and the revival of the Middle Kingdom's central position in international relations.[59] In 1958, Mao launched the so-called Great Leap Forward, which, like Stalin's "revolution from above," sought to create a strong socialist state through heavy industrialization and the collectivization of agriculture. But the Great Leap's terror tactics and mismanagement created a human and economic catastrophe: in the agricultural sector alone, it produced a disastrous drop in output, with famine leading to an estimated 30 million deaths.[60] In foreign policy, Mao broke the postrevolutionary alliance with the Soviet Union over Khrushchev's liberalizing de-Stalinization program at home and the Kremlin leader's doctrine of peaceful coexistence toward the United States.

In the early 1960s, U.S. policy-makers regarded Mao's revolutionary China as the functional equivalent of a contemporary rogue state. The perception of China as fundamentally more dangerous and irresponsible than the Soviet Union led the Kennedy administration to explore seriously the option of a preventive military strike on Chinese nuclear sites.[61] But as contingency plans were under consideration, State Department analysts questioned the underlying premise that China's acquisition of nuclear weapons would have an "intolerable" impact on U.S. security. Their classified assessment concluded that a nuclear-armed China would not fundamentally change the balance of power in Asia, that it could be deterred from aggression by U.S. conventional military and nuclear superiority, and that the Mao regime was unlikely to alter its risk-averse military policy. The bottom line was that the Chinese program was motivated primarily by a desire to deter an attack on China itself.[62] The military option receded when the Johnson administration, whether convinced by the less threatening assessment or fearful that a strike on China's nuclear infrastructure could trigger a Chinese escalatory response in Vietnam, rejected unprovoked military action against China, which conducted its first nuclear weapons test in October 1964.

Mao launched the Great Proletarian Cultural Revolution in 1966 with complementary domestic and foreign policy objectives: first, consolidating his autocratic control over the Chinese Communist Party (CCP) and society in the disastrous aftermath of the Great Leap Forward, and second, leveraging China's revolutionary transformation under his paramount leadership to enhance the country's international standing.[63] With respect to the former, Mao successfully suppressed the party faction of so-called capitalist roaders led by Liu Shaoqi and his protégé Deng Xiaoping, who had sharply criticized the Great Leap and proposed alternative economic reforms. The Cultural Revolution had a violently convulsive impact across

Chinese society as militant youth—the Red Guards—sought to root out alleged bourgeois influences threatening the revolution. But with respect to Mao's foreign policy goals, the pervasive instability unleashed by the Cultural Revolution only reinforced the country's international isolation.

In the late 1960s, as the Mao regime railed against "Soviet revisionism," Sino-Soviet relations sharply deteriorated, and the split became a full rupture. Military skirmishes along the Ussuri River border escalated into two major clashes in1969. The Chinese leadership received intelligence reports that the Kremlin had sounded out East European leaders about a possible Soviet preventive nuclear strike on China.[64] According to a Chinese historian using newly available documentary sources, the result was an "unprecedented war scare that, both in a strategic and a psychological sense, created the necessary conditions for the CCP leaders to reconsider the PRC's longstanding policy of confrontation with the United States."[65] An early indicator of the emerging rapprochement was U.S. support for the Beijing regime's assumption of the China seat at the United Nations. Although formal diplomatic relations between the United States and China were not established until 1979, seven years after Nixon's breakthrough visit, their common perception of the Soviet threat created the basis for a "tacit strategic partnership" during the Cold War's turbulent final phase.[66]

Mao's death in 1976 triggered a succession crisis, pitting the hard-line faction (the so-called Gang of Four, whose members included Mao's widow) that had risen to power during the Cultural Revolution against the CCP's pragmatic reformist faction (led by Deng Xiaoping) that harshly condemned the Cultural Revolution. Under Mao, the CCP had sharply deviated from ideological orthodoxy in foreign policy through its diplomatic opening to the United States. The core issue in the post-Mao power struggle was whether the CCP would similarly break with ideology in domestic policy by ending Mao's state of "continuous revolution," which had convulsed Chinese society. Two years after Mao's death, Deng had outmaneuvered his ideological opponents and emerged as the country's paramount leader. In December 1978, the CCP Central Committee plenum endorsed Deng's policies of reform and opening up.

Deng spearheaded what historian Chen Jian described as a process of "de-revolutionization," emphasizing the primacy of economics over politics.[67] His reform program sought to transform China's moribund Soviet-style economy (which was based on heavy industry and collectivized agriculture) into what was officially characterized as a "socialist market economy." The Deng reforms decollectivized agriculture by breaking up the Maoist system of communes and ended the country's autarkic isolation by opening the country to foreign investment through the creation of special economic zones. Deng's strategy launched the country on an economic trajectory that three decades later would allow a successor to visit Washington as the leader of the country with the world's second-largest economy. The domestic economic reforms Deng championed were essentially the antithesis of the Great Leap and the Cultural Revolution. But negotiating that departure from Mao's policies without calling the regime's legitimacy into question posed a challenge, much like that faced by Khrushchev when he embarked on de-Stalinization. Deng attempted to manage the tension between legitimacy and systemic change by emphasizing Mao's standing as a nationalist leader who had forged China into a strong, independent great power.

As Mao's legacy was recast, the lead role of the Communist Party within Chinese society, which Deng viewed as essential during a period of transformational change, was reaffirmed, thus ensuring that economic reforms would be kept within acceptable political bounds. China's move toward a market economy was marked by corruption and nepotism, as well as by high inflation in consumer prices. The resulting popular discontent triggered student demonstrations in 1986, a precursor to the Tiananmen Square demonstrations three years later. In spring 1989, China's pro-democracy movement emerged while systemic political change was unfolding in Eastern Europe. The immediate precipitant of renewed student demonstrations was the death in April of Hu Yaobang, a popular pro-reform figure who had risen within the CCP as a protégé to Deng. Hard-liners within the regime, led by Premier Li Peng, viewed the student movement as a frontal challenge to the CCP's authority. The irresolvable contradictions of Deng's position—breaking with Mao while retaining the CCP's lead role—were exposed in the Tiananmen tragedy. According to a Politburo member in a secret speech to party cadres, Deng faced the stark choice of either legitimizing the democracy movement (thus opening the door to opposition parties) or suppressing it. In the end, Deng and the CCP's senior leadership were unwilling to risk the repetition in China of Solidarity's success in Poland.[68]

The much-anticipated visit of Gorbachev to Beijing in May 1989, the capstone of Deng's efforts to normalize relations with the Soviet Union, became the occasion of another wave of mass demonstrations. Students thronged in Tiananmen Square and blocked People's Liberation Army (PLA) units from entering the city. The ensuing two-week stalemate, which captured the world's attention, was violently ended on June 4, 1989, after the CCP leadership had authorized the PLA to use "any means necessary" to end the student occupation and retake Tiananmen Square.[69] In the aftermath of the violence, the Chinese leadership instituted a sharp crackdown on dissidents and blamed foreign powers—principally the United States—for inciting the student uprising. Deng purged some close allies—notably Zhao Ziyang, general secretary of the CCP, who became the official scapegoat for the Tiananmen debacle—and ideological hard-liners retook the reins of economic policy. These domestic reversals occurred against the backdrop of events in late 1989 in Eastern Europe that reportedly shocked China's party elders: the collapse of Erich Honecker's East German regime (whose modern economy under tight party control Deng had looked to as a model) and the execution of Romanian dictator Nicolae Ceauşescu after a popular uprising in which key institutions and interest groups (notably the armed forces) that had long preserved the regime unexpectedly turned on it.

The Berlin wall came down, in November 1989, with cascading consequences for communist regimes in Eastern Europe, and the Soviet Union disintegrated two years later. Deng cautiously refrained from having China assume the mantle of leadership over what was left of the international communist movement. He opted instead to maintain the focus on domestic economic growth. After Tiananmen, the Chinese leadership's antireform faction reasserted the CCP's political primacy and threatened to retard the rapid economic growth that Deng considered absolutely essential to restoring the regime's legitimacy. Ironically, it was an external event—the failed Soviet coup against Yeltsin in August 1991—that provided renewed momentum for internal reform in China. In the Chinese leadership's internal deliberations over the Soviet coup, Deng stressed that China had avoided the instability that had overturned communist regimes in the Soviet Union and Eastern Europe; the CCP had taken decisive action to maintain party control while maintaining its commitment to economic reform.[70] The strategy put the country on its current economic trajectory. But as historian Chen Jian concluded, the legacy of 1989 remains "a knot that must be untied ... in China's continuous advance toward modernity. Without doing so, the legitimacy narrative of the 'Communist' state will always be burdened by the fundamental inability to justify itself."[71]

Deng's sharp break with Maoist economic dogma gave impetus to China's transition from a revolutionary state to an orthodox great power. His economic strategy of "reform and opening up" was predicated on China's integration into the global economy. The country's accession to multilateral financial and trade institutions—beginning with the International Monetary Fund and the World Bank in 1980 and culminating with the World Trade Organization (WTO) in 2001—was instrumental in promoting that objective. Integration became the engine of domestic development that the CCP hoped would bolster the regime's legitimacy by raising living standards. The post-Mao leadership sought the tangible economic benefits of integration (e.g., export earnings in foreign currency to fuel further industrialization and access to advanced technology) while mitigating the consequences of political contagion from the outside world. Conversely, Western countries—particularly the United States—benefited from cheap Chinese imports but also hoped that China's economic opening to the world would advance democratization and foster a more stable strategic partnership.[72] Notwithstanding trade disputes filed against China in the WTO over intellectual property rights and illegal subsidies to industry through a fixed exchange rate policy (which keeps the yuan at an artificially low level), Beijing has for the most part complied with WTO rulings and regulations. Yet Chinese compliance with international norms arising from the Western liberal economic order has "depended on the degree to which they resonated with existing Chinese values and met China's own economic and social needs."[73] Does compliance signify "socialization"? Because a utilitarian explanation would yield the same behavioral outcome, one cannot know whether Chinese leaders are "genuinely internalizing and embracing global norms and values."[74] (See Chapter 1.)

A similar pattern is evident in the realm of international security. By the mid-1990s, China had joined nearly 90 percent of all arms control agreements for which it was eligible, including the nuclear Nonproliferation Treaty and the Comprehensive Test Ban Treaty. That figure was up from the 10 to 20 percent of the early 1970s.[75] The increase signified a pragmatic recognition that participation in arms control institutions could serve China's national interests at low cost.[76] Michael Swaine and Alastair Johnston view this development as "a realpolitik adaptation to a changing security environment" through which China could bolster its image while working within institutions to keep important Chinese military capabilities off the negotiating table.[77] China, like the United States, has not acceded to agreements, such as the Mine Ban Treaty, that are deemed contrary to its interests.

In the aftermath of the Tiananmen crackdown, China was an international pariah. The United States and other Western states imposed a variety of political and economic sanctions, ranging from the suspension of export credits and high-level governmental contracts to the postponement of controls governing transfers of technology to the PRC. The CCP leadership went into "a defensive, crisis management mode."[78] To navigate this period of adversity, Deng Xiaoping enunciated epigrammatic foreign policy guidance: "Conceal capacities and bide our time; skillfully keep a low profile; avoid sticking [one's] head out."[79] His emphasis on rapidly restoring a tranquil international environment for China to permit the resumption of economic reform figured prominently in the new security concept that emerged in the mid-1990s under the slogan "peaceful rise" (later "peaceful development"). This declaratory policy was intended to signal to China's regional neighbors and the United States that the PRC's rapid economic growth posed no security threat. One manifestation of China's "keep a low profile" stance was the CCP leadership's decision, dating to the early 1980s, to maintain a minimum nuclear deterrent vis-à-vis the United States. Hence, as recently as 2004, a U.S. Department of Defense report on Chinese military capabilities said that China had only twenty nuclear-armed intercontinental ballistic missiles capable of targeting the U.S. homeland, and a 2010 report referred to a Chinese intention "to maintain a limited nuclear deterrence with regard to the United States."[80]

The new strategic concept for China's external relations complemented Deng's sweeping internal reforms and reflected the dominant view among elites that "only an intrasystem rise can be a peaceful one."[81] In short, China would seek to ascend within, rather than revolutionize and overturn, the established international order. That approach, according to Chinese foreign policy experts Zhang Yunling and Tang Shiping, entailed an acceptance of the United States as a "hegemonic power" within the system—that is, the lead power with special responsibility for maintaining international order—as long as the United States did not threaten core Chinese interests through "hegemonic behavior."[82]

The sharpest policy differences between the United States and China (aside from the unique issue of Taiwan) have arisen over the cardinal principle of state sovereignty. The CCP regime holds to a strict interpretation barring foreign interference in a state's domestic affairs. Thus, on sovereignty grounds, China opposed NATO's military intervention in Serbia in 1999 to liberate Kosovo (during which a U.S. aircraft accidentally bombed China's embassy in Belgrade), the U.S.-led invasion of Iraq to overthrow the Saddam Hussein regime in 2003, and the NATO air campaign in Libya in 2011. Likewise rebuffing Washington's efforts to raise human rights as a bilateral issue, China has asserted that U.S. criticism of China's record amounts to domestic interference and derives from Western norms emphasizing individual rights rather than a Chinese conception based on collective rights (see Chapter 1). Other U.S. policies are viewed as self-serving and hypocritical: for example, criticizing Chinese trade with Sudan while U.S. oil firms move into human rights pariah Equatorial Guinea, or concluding a nuclear agreement with India (which contravened three decades of U.S. nonproliferation efforts) while seeking to block China's nuclear commerce with Pakistan.

China's meteoric ascent carries uncertain implications for the United States and for international order. The ruling regime faces a fundamental challenge of legitimacy that derives from the unresolved contradiction between market-driven economic reforms to achieve modernity and the Communist Party's continued monopoly power. Political scientist Ashley Tellis has observed that contemporary Chinese domestic politics is "fundamentally about sustaining the high rates of economic growth in order to recover the great power status that Beijing had enjoyed historically and to avert the domestic instability that would arise if economic growth were to falter."[83]

The nub of China's unresolved legitimacy crisis is the legacy of Maoism. When Deng broke with Maoist dogma—policies that had produced the human calamities of the Great Leap and the Cultural Revolution—he effectively ended any claim of legitimacy that the CCP regime could make on the basis of ideology. Deng recast Mao's role in nationalist terms—the historic leader who had forged a strong, independent state that never again would be vulnerable to foreign imperialism. As China moves to develop military capabilities commensurate with its economic strength, the conjunction of China's great power status and the CCP regime's instrumental use of nationalism as a source of domestic legitimacy raises the historical comparison to Wilhelmine Germany. "The notion that [the United States and China] must be adversaries," President Obama has declared, "is not pre-destined."[84] Yet neither is the success of American policies aiming to manage China's peaceful rise by fostering its deeper integration into the liberal international order.

Regime Change from Without

Cambodia: Vietnam Overthrows the Khmer Rouge, 1978

On Christmas Day of 1978, the Vietnamese army invaded Cambodia and overthrew the Khmer Rouge regime, which had ruled the country since seizing power in April 1975.[85] Under Khmer Rouge rule, an estimated 1 million to 2 million Cambodians (roughly one-quarter of the country's total population) were executed in the "killing fields" or died of disease and starvation.[86] Declaring the human rights situation in Cambodia the worst "since Nazism," a UN commissioner coined a neologism—"auto-genocide"—to describe the Khmer Rouge's horrors.[87] In early January 1979, two weeks after the invasion's onset, Vietnamese troops, augmented by Cambodian exile forces based in southern Vietnam, occupied the Cambodian capital of Phnom Penh as the Khmer Rouge fled for refuge to the hinterland along the Thai border. Although the Vietnamese intervention had beneficial humanitarian consequences, it was justified at the time by the Hanoi government solely as an act of self-defense rather than as an act of humanitarianism. The international community, with the significant exception of the Soviet bloc, condemned the Vietnamese action as a violation of Cambodian sovereignty. Although the Soviet Union vetoed a proposed UN Security Council resolution demanding a Vietnamese withdrawal, the General Assembly voted to censure Vietnam for this cross-border intervention. The major powers—China, the Soviet Union, and the United States—viewed their stakes in Cambodia through the prism of their Cold War rivalry.

During the Vietnam War, Prince Norodom Sihanouk, the monarchical ruler from 1941 to 1970, declared Cambodia's neutrality but was unable to prevent his country from being drawn into that neighboring conflict. In April 1970, U.S. ground troops launched an "incursion" into Cambodia to root out North Vietnamese and Viet Cong forces that were using the border area as a sanctuary from which to mount attacks on South Vietnam. In its aftermath, Sihanouk was ousted in a coup headed by General Lon Nol, who abandoned neutrality in favor of an explicit alignment with the United States and South Vietnam. Cambodia descended into civil war as China and North Vietnam supported the Cambodian communist insurgent group, the Khmer Rouge, which was ostensibly fighting in support of a government-in-exile headed by Sihanouk in Beijing. In April 1975, as North Vietnamese tanks rolled into Saigon, in adjacent Cambodia the Khmer Rouge, headed by the hardened revolutionary Pol Pot, captured Phnom Penh. Because the Khmer Rouge had the link to Sihanouk, the international community accepted the new government, which assumed Cambodia's seat at the United Nations, as legitimate.

Declaring the Khmer Rouge takeover as the start of "Year Zero," Pol Pot avowed that his goal was nothing short of "restarting civilization." By September 1975, the *New York Times* described Cambodia as "a nation in a state of total revolutionary upheaval": emptied cities and towns, with the forced exodus of millions to the jungles and rural areas; mass executions of the country's educated class, as well as anyone else the Khmer Rouge deemed politically suspect; and the collapse of the economy, tangibly symbolized by the regime's abolition of money.[88] Sihanouk was soon ousted from his position as titular head of state, and the country was renamed Democratic Kampuchea.

Xenophobia, in general, and Vietnamophobia, in specific, were central to the Khmer Rogue's domestic political strategy. A senior Khmer Rouge official acknowledged that playing on the traditional ethnic animosity between the Khmer and Vietnamese peoples had political utility for the regime in deflecting popular discontent from the severe hardships created by its radically draconian program. In autumn 1977, a border clash between Cambodian and Vietnamese military forces moved China into a closer alliance with the Pol Pot regime to counter Hanoi's perceived regional ambitions. In turn, by 1978, Vietnam was publicly calling for a popular uprising against the Khmer Rouge and was organizing Cambodian exiles into guerrilla units to reinfiltrate the country. As for the United States, even though President Jimmy Carter decried the Pol Pot regime as the "worst violator of human rights in the world," his administration, which was then assiduously courting China, subordinated human rights, the professed centerpiece of its foreign policy, to geostrategic interests.[89]

Provoked by further deadly Khmer Rouge attacks on its southern border towns, Vietnam, which had bolstered its own geostrategic flank vis-à-vis China through the signing of a Treaty of Friendship with the Soviet Union, launched a full-scale invasion of Cambodia to oust Pol Pot and to install a new regime headed by Khmer Rouge defector Heng Samrin. The UN General Assembly, a number of whose delegates argued that the Pol Pot regime's atrocities could not justify Vietnam's use of force to oust the government of another sovereign UN member state, refused to seat the newly established People's Republic of Kampuchea. The *New York Times* similarly editorialized that "Vietnam's recourse to military force cannot be ignored, nor can it be justified by a recitation of the Cambodian regime's massive violations of human rights.... Vietnam's conduct reopens uncomfortable questions about Hanoi's intentions."[90]

At the heart of UN controversy over Cambodia was a fundamental difference about the nature of the conflict: Vietnam and the Soviet Union claimed that dissident Cambodians had overthrown a genocidal regime, whereas Vietnam's adversaries cast the invasion as an act of naked aggression in pursuit of regional hegemony.[91] With the Khmer Rouge leadership in hiding, Sihanouk reappeared as the face of Cambodian opposition to "Vietnamese imperialists and their Soviet masters." (Many years later, the prince would acknowledge, "If [the Vietnamese] had not ousted Pol Pot, everyone would have died—not only me, but everyone."[92]) China provided military assistance to the Khmer Rouge insurgency against the Vietnamese-imposed regime and, in February 1979, escalated the crisis with a retaliatory incursion of Chinese military forces into northern Vietnam. The United States did not provide material support to the Khmer Rouge, which enjoyed sanctuary in the borderlands of Thailand, but Washington tacitly supported Chinese actions, including the punitive border attack into Vietnam, and spearheaded diplomatic efforts to isolate Vietnam and Cambodia.[93] The Carter administration evidently did not consider the moral hazard of its policy had the policy proved successful: the return to power of the Khmer Rouge.[94]

A military and diplomatic stalemate persisted until the mid-1980s, when the sustainability of Soviet support for Vietnam was challenged by the advent of Gorbachev's new thinking, a central element of which was the resolution of regional conflicts that had roiled East-West relations. With the loss of its former superpower patron, as well as the continuing economic and diplomatic costs of occupation, Vietnam began to look for an exit from Cambodia. An initial Vietnamese proposal, linking a military withdrawal to international recognition of its client People's Republic of Kampuchea regime in Phnom Penh, was rebuffed. Negotiations convened by the French government at an international conference in Paris in 1989 were facilitated by improvements in Sino-Soviet and Sino-Vietnamese relations, which, along with the end of the Cold War, transformed the geostrategic context of the conflict.[95] In September 1989, Vietnam completed the withdrawal of its estimated 180,000 troops from Cambodia.

Two years after the end of Vietnamese occupation, in October 1991, a comprehensive settlement was signed in Paris that provided for the United Nations to organize free elections and for UN peacekeepers to enforce a cease-fire. Although the Khmer Rouge military had not been demobilized, some 4 million Cambodians participated in the May 1993 elections to a constituent assembly, which met to approve a new constitution establishing a constitutional monarchy under Sihanouk.[96] By 1997, the Cambodian civil war had ended as the last remnants of the Khmer Rouge accepted a government amnesty and were disarmed. In 1998, Pol Pot—the face of the Cambodian genocide—died under suspicious circumstances, reportedly the result of Khmer Rouge factional infighting. In 2004, the Cambodian government concluded an agreement with the United Nations to establish tribunals to bring Khmer Rouge leaders to justice. Although Cambodia faces continuing challenges of democratic governance as it strives to overcome the horrific legacy of "Year Zero," the country has emerged from isolation to rejoin the international community.

Uganda: Tanzania Overthrows Idi Amin, 1979

Idi Amin was remembered in a 2003 obituary as the "bloody tyrant [who] terrorized Uganda into penury in the 1970s."[97] His eight-year rule over the country that Churchill once described as "the pearl of Africa" came to an end in April 1979 when Tanzanian military forces seized the Ugandan capital of Kampala and Amin fled in exile to Libya and then on to Saudi Arabia. Although the Tanzanian invasion was undertaken without Security Council authorization and violated the Organization of African Unity (OAU) "twin pillars" of noninterference and nonintervention, the international community acquiesced to the overthrow of Amin. This external intervention to oust a despot has since been cited as evidence of an emerging international norm for humanitarian intervention. Yet the precedent set by Tanzanian President Julius Nyerere, the first invasion of one African state by another, was motivated more by hard strategic calculation than by humanitarianism.

Colonel Amin seized power through a military coup in January 1971 while Prime Minister Milton Obote, who had headed the Ugandan government since that country's independence from Britain in 1962, was out of the country. Obote had become increasingly autocratic in his determined concentration of state power at the expense of the ethnically based local kingdoms. Ironically, Obote had turned to Amin and the Ugandan army in 1966 to stave off political opposition to that centralization process. The Amin military coup was recognized by the United States and Britain, as well as by Israel (which then had a cooperative relationship with the Ugandan military), but was rejected as illegitimate by the OAU and President Nyerere, who offered Obote asylum.[98]

Amin brutally consolidated power by dissolving parliament, declaring himself president for life, and ordering the mass execution of Ugandan army troops from ethnic groups he considered loyal to Obote. Eighteen months after the coup, pro-Obote military forces based in Tanzania launched what proved to be an unsuccessful cross-border attack into Ugandan territory to reverse Amin's coup. A U.S. National Security Council assessment in November 1972 concluded, "The ill-fated invasion of Uganda by Tanzanian-backed Ugandan dissidents has greatly strengthened Amin and accelerated the elimination of any opposition to him."[99] Earlier that year, Amin, claiming God had spoken to him in a dream, had ordered the mass expulsion of Uganda's Asian population, whose skilled labor force was vital to the country's economy.

The Amin regime committed gross violations of human rights against the Ugandan people, with estimated deaths as high as 400,000.[100] The particular targets of Amin's repression were the pro-Obote Acholi and Langi ethnic groups. Amin's savage and bizarre behavior (the latter exemplified by his proposed memorial to Adolf Hitler in Kampala) was no bar to his serving as head of the OAU in 1975. In 1977, Amin's murder of Uganda's Anglican archbishop, whom he accused of complicity in an attempted coup, "disgusted the entire civilized world," in President Jimmy Carter's words.[101] The British government called on the United Nations to act, but African states, lining up behind Uganda on sovereignty grounds, were able to block even a toothless UN resolution condemning Amin for human rights violations. A *Time* magazine article on Uganda's descent called the dictator "an outrage to the world and a scourge to his own country."[102]

The events culminating in Amin's overthrow were set in motion in October 1978 by the mutiny of a Ugandan army unit. When the mutineers fled into Tanzania, Amin responded by ordering his troops to occupy a border area inside Tanzania, ostensibly as an act of self-defense. After intimating that Uganda would annex that territory, Amin offered to withdraw his forces if Tanzania would no longer provide safe haven to Ugandan dissidents seeking his regime's overthrow. Tanzanian president Nyerere demanded that the OAU exact compensation and punishment from the Amin regime for its territorial aggression and the atrocities committed against Tanzanian civilians by Ugandan forces. Nyerere further called for a revision of the OAU charter, arguing that the document's unqualified defense of state sovereignty, originally intended to protect weak newly independent states from external interference, had become a shield for dictators like Amin.[103] In November, in the face of OAU inaction, the Tanzanian army counterattacked to retake occupied territory; then, in January 1979, those troops, along with anti-Amin rebels, crossed the border into Uganda. Nyerere's political objective changed as the military opportunity presented: what started as a limited punitive action in retaliation for Uganda's cross-border attack shifted into a broader military operation to bring about a change of regime. With the Ugandan army in retreat, Libyan leader Muammar Qaddafi dispatched

3,000 troops to save the regime of his ally and fellow Muslim, but even Libyan intervention could not prevent Amin's downfall.

Was Tanzania's invasion a case of humanitarian intervention? Although the initial offensive to repel Ugandan forces from occupied Tanzania was a clear-cut act of self-defense consistent with international law, once Tanzanian troops crossed into Uganda and were marching on the capital, that justification was no longer valid. In that second phase of military operations, Nyerere switched rationales, declaring that Tanzania was fighting to promote "freedom, justice, and human dignity."[104] Although Nyerere's concern appeared genuine, this humanitarian interest fortuitously converged with Tanzania's paramount strategic interests in removing an adjacent state's unpredictable and hostile regime. The international community acquiesced to the Tanzanian intervention largely because the buffoonish Ugandan dictator had become a human rights pariah and his ousting did not conflict with the interests of any major power.

A cautionary postscript: Amin's downfall, far from restoring tranquillity to Uganda, ushered in a period of further domestic strife as Obote, who returned to power in 1980 through a sham election, brutally repressed opposing ethnic groups on a scale comparable to that of Amin. In 1985, Obote was again ousted by a military coup and, in 1986, Yoweri Museveni, leader of the insurgent National Resistance Army, came to power. Human rights conditions improved significantly under Museveni, winning praise from President Bill Clinton and other foreign leaders. In the 2000s, however, Museveni's increasingly antidemocratic tendencies—notably his refusal to relinquish the presidency to a successor—have drawn international criticism and resulted in a Freedom House rating of "partly free" for Uganda.[105]

Regime Change from Within

Romania: The Overthrow of Ceauşescu, 1989

Romanian dictator Nicolae Ceauşescu was deposed in late December 1989, capping a year of revolutions in which communist regimes were overturned across Eastern Europe. But unlike the other nonviolent transfers of power to postcommunist regimes, such as Czechoslovakia's aptly named Velvet Revolution, Romania's regime change had the appearance of a real revolution, complete with the Romanov-style execution of Ceauşescu and his wife, Elena, on Christmas Day by a military firing squad. But was it a change *of* regime or a change *within* a regime? A revolution or a coup d'état?[106] That Ceauşescu, who died an international pariah, was succeeded by a Communist Party insider fed the charge that a revolution instigated by a genuinely popular uprising had been stolen.

"One of Eastern Europe's most durable dictators," Ceauşescu, known simply as the *conducător*, or leader, was "a strangely contradictory figure, who showed one face to the outside world, another to his people," according to his *New York Times* obituary.[107] After gaining power in 1965, Ceauşescu won popularity at home through a relaxation in internal repression and in the West through an "independent" foreign policy. He condemned the Soviet invasion of Czechoslovakia in 1968, facilitated early U.S.-Chinese diplomatic contacts, hosted a state visit for President Richard Nixon, and forged diplomatic ties with Israel. Ceauşescu's foreign policy autonomy won him most-favored-nation trade status with the United States, as well as access to Western loans to finance domestic development. As political scientist Vladimir Tismăneanu observes, "Ceauşescu was not ... always unanimously hated or despised. Far from it: during the 1960s and early 1970s, many Romanians found themselves stirred and exhilarated by the Conducător's defiance of Moscow, the rapprochement ... with the West, and their country's imagined future grandeur."[108]

But Ceauşescu's flirtation with domestic political liberalization was short lived. His turn toward neo-Stalinism was reportedly cemented by a visit to North Korea in 1971, where he marveled at the total societal control exerted by his "beloved friend" Kim Il Sung. The key elements of Ceauşescu's "little cultural revolution" were economic autarky and heavy industrialization, mass mobilization for national development, and a cult of personality rivaling that of Stalin and Mao.[109] Ceauşescu's absolute power was maintained through his secret police force, the Securitate, whose pervasive reach prevented the rise of an indigenous dissident movement comparable to Poland's Solidarity movement or Czechoslovakia's Charter 77. With an estimated one in every five citizens a police informant, Ceauşescu kept Romania a closed society through travel restrictions on all but the country's privileged elite.[110] The country's media were devoted to propagating his personality cult, which was prominently symbolized by the erection of a gigantic triumphal arch in Bucharest bearing the legend "The Golden Epoch of Nicolae Ceauşescu."[111] Among Ceauşescu's multibillion-dollar vanity projects was a colossal presidential palace, an architectural monstrosity built on a razed historic neighborhood in Bucharest. According to Tismăneanu, the Romanian dictator "acquired the status of a communist pharaoh, an infallible demigod, whose vanity seemed boundless" and whose aim was the long-term institutionalization of his extended family's power through "dynastic socialism."[112]

By the early 1980s, the failure of Ceauşescu's grandiose economic plan, with the consequent sharp drop in living standards, had created a state of "institutionalized misery and despair."[113] Emblematic of Ceauşescu's economic mismanagement and indifference to its human costs were draconian austerity measures to pay off the country's foreign debt (e.g., large-scale exports of Romanian meats and produce to Europe even as foodstuffs were in critically short supply at home). In the West, Ceauşescu's political stock was in free fall as the importance of Romania's "independent" foreign policy faded with the general improvement in East-West relations and the Ceauşescu regime's gross human rights abuses were exposed. In the mid-1980s, the elderly and increasingly detached Romanian dictator—now castigated as "the sick man of communism"—presented a stark contrast to the energetic new Soviet leader, Mikhail Gorbachev, and the transformational reform agenda that Gorbachev was advancing.[114] Gorbachev gave his candid assessment of Ceauşescu's dynastic rule to West German chancellor Helmut Kohl in June 1989: "It is certainly strange that this kind of family clan would be established in the center of civilized Europe.... I could imagine something like that to emerge somewhere else, like it has in Korea; but here, right next to us—it is such a primitive phenomenon."[115]

The events culminating in Ceauşescu's ouster and execution began in mid-November 1989, a week after the fall of the Berlin wall, when students protested the Romanian Communist Party Congress's reelection of Ceauşescu. On December 17, the army brutally suppressed a protest in the western city of Timişoara, an act of violence that triggered further mass demonstrations and the regime's loss of control over that part of the country. Amid an escalating domestic crisis, Ceauşescu's supreme confidence led him to proceed on a state visit to Iran. On December 22, on his return from abroad, a mass demonstration Ceauşescu had ordered in the heart of Bucharest to denounce "counterrevolutionaries" instead turned on him. The sound of that crowd's anti-Ceauşescu chants and the conducător's shocked face on Romanian television marked the start of the revolution. Ceauşescu and his wife fled the capital by helicopter but were soon apprehended. Two days later, they were executed on order of the newly installed National Salvation Front (NSF).

Although questions remain about the Romanian "revolution," the most plausible explanation is that the popular uprising on December 22 precipitated a coup against Ceauşescu by his own inner circle. Indeed, the army general and deputy defense minister that Ceauşescu had entrusted with his own protection organized the perfunctory military trial that carried out his execution. As Tismăneanu concludes, "The end of the Ceauşescu regime was ensured by a plebian revolution, but Ceauşescu's personal end was carried out by his own Praetorian Guard."[116] That the demonstrators lacked strong leadership analogous to Solidarity in Poland created a political opening for second-tier apparatchiks of the communist regime, under the leadership of a former Ceauşescu lieutenant, Ion Iliescu, who had lost favor, to rebrand themselves as the NSF. As Romanian expert Dennis Deletant succinctly put it, "The NSF tried to blend into the present and bury the past."[117]

In the postcommunist era, Romania struggled to overcome the ruinous legacy of Ceauşescu's autocratic rule while avoiding a return to regressive nationalist-driven policies at odds with the "New Europe."[118] Notwithstanding the proliferation of vying political parties, a strong consensus quickly emerged in support of the country's integration into Europe's supranational economic and security institutions—the European Union (EU) and NATO. Political scientist Milada Anna Vachudova argues that Iliescu, elected to the presidency in 1990 and 1992, pursued "a strategy of formal compliance" with Western democratic norms to increase his domestic legitimacy and garner outside economic assistance. "The seven years of Iliescu's regime in Romania," she concludes, "provide a textbook case of the capture of a partially reformed economy by former communist cadres linked to the ruling political parties."[119]

Nonetheless, the tangible benefits of integration created powerful incentives and renewed impetus for domestic reform to bring Romania into compliance with the norms that were the prerequisites for EU and NATO membership in 2004 and 2007, respectively.[120] Since Romania's accession, the EU has been monitoring Romania's progress, or lack thereof, on such key issues as combating corruption and organized crime and developing an independent judiciary.[121] But compliance with international norms remains an ongoing process for this fragile democracy.

South Africa: A "Negotiated Revolution"

South Africa emerged from international pariah status to retake its seat in the United Nations after the April 1994 election of Nelson Mandela, the long-imprisoned black nationalist leader, to the presidency in the country's first multiracial election. His extraordinary ascension brought an end to the system of apartheid—the "institutionalization of racial discrimination"— imposed on South Africa's black and Asian population by its European white minority.[122] Mandela's election culminated years of negotiations between South Africa's ruling National Party and the banned African National Congress (ANC) for a peaceful transition to majority rule; the negotiations had begun in secret in the late 1980s and accelerated after Mandela's release from prison in 1990. Although the change of regime came from within, the National Party leadership's decision to cede power was affected by significant forces from without—most prominently, economic sanctions and the end of the Cold War. What was the relative influence of internal and external factors in ending apartheid rule and, with it, promoting South Africa's reintegration into the international community?

Racial segregation in the territories that made up the modern state of South Africa dated to the era of Dutch and British colonialism. In the pivotal 1948 parliamentary elections, the National Party, representing the Dutch-origin Afrikaner population, swept to power and instituted apartheid—Afrikaans for "separateness." The system's bedrock legislation divided the population into broad racial and ethnic categories—white, Indian, colored (of mixed race), and black—which were then further broken down into subgroups, with whites divided between the English and Afrikaans languages and blacks split into ten African ethnic groups, each with its own Bantustan, or territorial homeland. In thus fractionating the population, the National Party government sought not only to undercut black unity but also to create a political narrative in which the white population was simply one minority in a country of minorities.[123] The stark reality was that 5 million whites, controlling 87 percent of the country's land and the great preponderance of its economic wealth, dominated 29 million Africans, 3 million coloreds, and 1 million Indians, all of whom were disenfranchised and largely trapped in poverty.[124]

The apartheid system bureaucratized racial segregation and discrimination through regulations governing interactions between these groups (including a proscription against interracial marriage) and through "whites-only" jobs, schools, hospitals, and public services (from buses and beaches to restaurants and park benches). "Pass laws" restricted the movement of blacks from rural areas to the white urban centers, while a pervasive internal security state was established to maintain the system and suppress black resistance. South African apartheid arose in diametric opposition to the historic trend toward the universal extension of human rights and the wave of decolonization—the "winds of change," in British prime minister Harold Macmillan's phrase—that was sweeping the African continent. Under Mandela's leadership, the ANC organized a civil rights campaign against apartheid with an initial focus on the discriminatory pass laws. But civil disobedience was met with force when police fired on a crowd in a watershed event in March 1960, the Sharpeville Massacre. In the aftermath of that event, the Pretoria government declared a state of emergency, outlawing the ANC (which had shifted to armed resistance) and imprisoning Mandela and other ANC leaders on charges of treason.

The international outcry over the Sharpeville Massacre marked the beginning of South Africa's increasing diplomatic isolation. The violence triggered a first-time Security Council resolution condemning the Pretoria government and was soon followed by South Africa's withdrawal from the British Commonwealth. The United States supported the UN arms embargo on South Africa in 1963 but permitted business links under a policy that "neither encouraged nor discouraged" American investment until the 1980s.[125] In the 1970s, domestic political pressure mounted in Western Europe and North America to exert external economic pressure on the Pretoria government to end apartheid. A public divestment campaign sought to dissuade banks and corporations from investing in South Africa. The UN General Assembly had called for a general economic boycott of South Africa as early as the 1960s, but not until the mid-1980s were multilateral economic sanctions imposed by the governments of South Africa's major trading partners, including the United States. By the 1970s, the combined impact of the antiapartheid movement's economic divestment campaign and symbolic political sanctions—the UN General Assembly's refusal to seat the apartheid regime, as well as an international sports and cultural boycott—had essentially made South Africa a pariah state.

From Pretoria's perspective, the regional security environment was sharply deteriorating. Portugal's transition to democracy in 1974, for example, led to the devolution of Lisbon's colonial possessions in southern Africa. A white cordon sanitaire in Angola and Mozambique gave way to the rise of pro-Soviet, Marxist regimes. South Africa's abortive intervention in southern Angola from Namibia prompted the MPLA (People's Movement for the Liberation of Angola) regime in Luanda to seek Cuban military assistance, which led to the deployment of 50,000 troops. These adverse developments in South Africa's external environment coincided with a severe flare-up of internal violence and repression during the 1976 Soweto riots. Status as a pariah state reinforced the white minority regime's siege mentality and stimulated its interest in acquiring unconventional weapons. In 1979, with the South African Ministry of Defense warning of the specter of "total war," Prime Minister P. W. Botha authorized South Africa's nuclear establishment, which had mastered uranium enrichment in the early 1970s, to construct a small arsenal of nuclear weapons.[126]

The U.S. policy debate on South Africa from the 1960s to the 1980s was framed by the competing pulls of America's idealistic interest in promoting human rights and Washington's geostrategic interest in South Africa during the Cold War. Successive U.S. administrations oscillated between an emphasis on the former (Kennedy, Carter) and the latter (Nixon, Reagan). Eschewing the Carter administration's emphasis on majority rule, the Reagan administration (along with British prime minister Margaret Thatcher) expressed solidarity with the South African government and opposed economic sanctions.[127] That empathetic attitude was reflected in the administration's strategy of "constructive engagement," an incentive-based approach whose architect was Chester Crocker, the U.S assistant secretary of state for African affairs.

Reagan's constructive engagement policy linked South Africa's granting of Namibian independence to the withdrawal of Cuban forces from Angola and aimed for an overall improvement in bilateral relations between Washington and Pretoria. According to political scientist Pauline Baker, the administration's motivating assumption "was that the South African regime represented a reformist, pro-Western government that, with U.S. encouragement, would work toward regional settlements, check communism in Africa, and eventually give blacks political rights."[128] The experiment with constructive engagement was short lived, as renewed violence within South Africa reached an unprecedented level. A sham constitutional reform, which would have created a second-class parliament for Indians and coloreds while leaving blacks disenfranchised, precipitated mass demonstrations and harsh repression that left the country on the verge of a full-scale race war.[129]

With the Reagan administration widely perceived as an apologist for continued white rule, the U.S. Congress, overriding a presidential veto, seized the initiative to exert pressure on the Pretoria regime through passage of the Comprehensive Anti-Apartheid Act (CAAA) in October 1986. The CAAA imposed sanctions banning trade, investment, and air travel, which were linked not to a change of regime, but to a change in the regime's policies: Mandela was to be released from prison and a timetable set for the elimination of apartheid laws. The legislation also provided for direct U.S. financial support of black educational and civil society organizations in South Africa to promote the development of a democratic, postapartheid society. By the mid-1980s, the South African economy was stagnating: financial sanctions had staunched the inflow of capital, thereby impeding growth, and foreign corporations (including some 200 American companies) were pulling out of the country. The South African business community emerged as an important interest group advocating comprehensive political reforms (essentially meeting the conditions of the CAAA) that would lead to the lifting of international sanctions.

The economic crisis split the ruling National Party, with those members implacably opposed to systemic change moving to an ultraright party. Having shed its far-right wing of dead-enders, the National Party forged a coalition with the bloc of progressive English-speaking voters to create a pro-reform majority within the white community. An important source of reassurance as the white minority moved toward acceptance of systemic internal change was the transformation of the external security environment that came with the end of the Cold War. At their May 1988 meeting, which focused on resolving Third World conflicts, Reagan and Gorbachev achieved a breakthrough that paved the way for the withdrawal of Cuban military forces from Angola in tandem with the independence of Namibia. Yet the end of the Cold War, however salutary in its regional consequences, also denied the Afrikaner leadership the powerful anticommunist card that it had successfully played with successive U.S. administrations.

Years of secret contacts between representatives of the government and the ANC finally culminated in a direct meeting between President Botha and Mandela in early July 1989.[130] As important as the planning document Mandela presented to Botha on a democratic transition was his magnanimous manner. After Botha suffered a stroke, he was forced to step down in what one observer described as an intraparty "coup."[131] He was succeeded as National Party leader and president by F. W. de Klerk, a perceived hardliner who had not gone over to the ultrarightists, rather than by the candidate of the party's reformist *verligte* (enlightened) wing.

De Klerk proved a stunning surprise: like Nixon going to China, he did what no *verligte* politician could credibly have done. In February 1990, de Klerk ended the ban on the ANC and released Mandela from prison. In making these unilateral gestures, de Klerk declared that "there can no longer be any doubt about the Government's sincerity to create a just dispensation based on negotiations.... All of us now have an opportunity and the responsibility to prove that we are capable of a peaceful process in creating *a new South Africa.*"[132] When the extremist Conservative Party challenged de Klerk's right to negotiate an end to apartheid, he called a referendum of the white electorate to gauge public support for his policy. De Klerk astutely argued that negotiations would lead to power-sharing, not an outright ceding of power to the ANC, whereas the status quo would mean the continuation of strangling economic sanctions and spiraling racial violence. Nearly 70 percent of the white electorate voted in support of "the reform process ... which is aimed at a new constitution through negotiation."[133] Over the next three years, the National Party and the ANC were the primary interlocutors in multiparty talks that ultimately led to the 1994 elections in which Mandela was elected president, with de Klerk and Thabo Mbeki as deputies.

The end of apartheid and the peaceful transition to majority rule have been called a "negotiated revolution." The "new South Africa" of which de Klerk spoke arose from an amalgam of internal and external factors. Central to this process was the pressure for change coming from within the Afrikaner community itself. External pressure brought to bear by economic and political sanctions that raised the costs of apartheid was a necessary but not sufficient condition for change. It altered the Afrikaner community's calculus of decision. South African historian Hermann Giliomee observes that Hendrik Verwoerd, a founding father of apartheid who served as prime minister until he was assassinated in 1966, mistakenly believed that the Afrikaners, when "confronted with a choice between being rich and integrated and segregated and poor, would choose the latter."[134] A "regime change" (as Giliomee called it) came after Afrikaner leaders such as de Klerk and South African intelligence chief Niel Barnard concluded that the apartheid system was no longer viable and that a negotiated settlement with the ANC to end South Africa's international pariah status had become an imperative. Mandela's extraordinary personal qualities, as well as the safeguards for minority rights incorporated into the new constitution, provided the white community with the critical reassurance that undergirded de Klerk's decision to negotiate the revolution.

Assessment and Implications

Historical experience reintegrating revolutionary, outlaw, and outlier states into the international order should enlighten policy deliberations over how best to address the current roster of hard cases. For example, an understanding of the processes by which Russia and China evolved from revolutionary states into conventional great powers can inform the U.S. policy response to the contemporary challenge of revolutionary Iran. A structured analysis across the four pathways permits the delineation of what political scientist Alexander George characterized as "conditional generalizations"—in this context, the identification of conditions favoring integration and, conversely, the conditions impeding that process. Those conditional generalizations— "generic knowledge"—highlight broad causal patterns that provide a necessary but not sufficient basis for strategy formulation. Although general propositions can be developed through this approach, any specific decision by policy-makers will be contingent on an accurate assessment of the particular conditions within the target state (see Chapter 3). The conditional generalizations gleaned from this comparative case analysis can be categorized under three rubrics: sovereignty and intervention, leadership and intra-elite bargaining, and conditionality and compliance.

Sovereignty and Intervention

The pathways to integration divide between two alternative agents of change: external (imposed regime change from without) and internal (self-generated regime change from within). This bifurcation parallels the preceding chapter's discussion of normative challenges, which likewise distinguished between external behavioral criteria (how a regime's conduct affects other states) and internal behavioral criteria (how a regime treats its own people). With both of these alternative agents of change, the crucial issue in principle and practice is sovereignty—whether compelling a state's compliance with internal behavioral norms is permissible or amounts to domestic interference and whether externally induced changes of regime can ever be justified.

State sovereignty remains the cardinal principle of international relations, which arose as a historical protection to states against cross-border aggression and severely circumscribes the conditions under which external intervention can be legitimately undertaken.

The war against Nazi Germany was an ideal type—an externally imposed regime change of a totalitarian great power that sought to overturn the international order. The *casus belli* was Hitler's naked interstate aggression—a frontal assault on the principle of state sovereignty. A war of regime change (resulting in the negation of German sovereignty) was the legitimate response to the Hitler regime's violation of *external* behavioral norms. But such was the absolute authority then conferred on states over their populations that it is highly debatable (and ultimately unknowable) whether the international community would have intervened militarily solely in response to Hitler's violations of *internal* behavioral norms—for example, to consider the counterfactual, if Hitler had eschewed his territorial ambitions and confined his genocidal policy to Germany.

The most prominent contemporary instance of overt interstate aggression was Iraq's invasion of Kuwait in 1990. The Security Council resolution authorizing the use of force was confined to restoring Kuwaiti sovereignty through the expulsion of Iraqi military forces and not to extending the Gulf War into Iraq itself to topple the Saddam Hussein regime. By contrast, in the lead-up to the 2003 war, the George H. W. Bush administration controversially (and, ultimately, unsuccessfully) argued that only through a change of regime in Baghdad—in essence, the negation of Iraqi sovereignty—could Iraq be brought into compliance with the Security Council resolutions imposed on it in the wake of the 1991 Gulf War.

Humanitarian interventions, however well justified in preventing gross violations of human rights, are inherently contentious in international relations because they constitute to many states an unacceptable infringement on sovereignty. Humanitarian justifications will frequently mask strategic motivations.

Before 1980, outlaw or pariah state status was linked to the contravention of internal rather than external behavioral norms (see Chapter 1). Although the murderous regimes of Idi Amin and Pol Pot made them human rights pariahs, Tanzania's invasion of Uganda and Vietnam's invasion of Cambodia "were unilateral efforts geared to overthrow menacing and destabilizing regimes in contiguous countries, and all were explicitly justified as self-defense. [Neither] was approved by the Security Council—and Vietnam's was actually condemned. Yet they are now frequently cited as evidence of an emerging right to humanitarian intervention," according to former Canadian diplomat David Malone.[135] Both the extraregional powers and the neighboring states viewed the challenge posed by these outlaw regimes through the prism of their strategic interests. For example, in the case of Cambodia, the Carter administration subordinated human rights considerations to the nascent geostrategic relationship of the United States with China, which was the Pol Pot regime's great power ally against Vietnam. With Uganda, the United States and Britain acquiesced to the Tanzanian invasion to oust Amin because it accorded with their interests, whereas the OAU denounced the military action on sovereignty grounds.

In the post–Cold War era, the hostile attitude of developing states toward external interventions to address even gross violations of internal behavioral norms hardened. The so-called Group of Seventy-Seven (a loose bloc of developing countries) baldly declared in its April 2000 summit communiqué, "We reject the so-called 'right' of humanitarian intervention, which has no legal basis in the United Nations Charter or in the general principles of international law."[136] That categorical rejection came in the immediate aftermath of NATO's military intervention in Serbia in 1999 to halt the Milosevic regime's "ethnic cleansing" of ethnic Albanians in the province of Kosovo. Undertaken by a coalition of democracies rather than by the United Nations, the intervention was awkwardly rationalized by proponents as "legitimate but not legal." The opposition of China and Russia, countries facing their own ethnic separatist challenges and wary of creating a precedent for intervention, had precluded the possibility of UN authorization for the military action.

Kosovo's declaration of independence in February 2008 brought to a head the clash between competing principles: the Kosovar people's right to national self-determination versus Serbia's right of state sovereignty. The United States, along with most EU states, recognized the newly declared state, with Washington arguing that Kosovo constituted a special case and would not create a precedent for ethnic separatist minorities in other countries. (Citing the Kosovo precedent, Russia would recognize two breakaway regions of Georgia, Abkhazia and South Ossetia, as independent states after its August 2008 cross-border intervention.) At Serbia's request, the UN General Assembly referred the Kosovo case to the International Court of Justice (ICJ) in The Hague, where China, Russia, and Spain strongly advocated that the province remain under Serbian sovereignty. The ICJ's ruling of July 2010, sidestepping the fundamental question as to whether the state of Kosovo itself was legal, basically stated that "Kosovo's legitimacy will be conferred by the countries that recognize it rather than by the court," according to Balkans expert James Ker-Lindsay.[137]

The controversy over NATO's intervention in Libya, which began in March 2011, was also centered on the question of sovereignty (see Chapter 3). The United States and its European allies sent a mixed message as to whether the objective of the military operation was to prevent the mass killing of Libyan civilians by the Qaddafi regime (as narrowly authorized by the Security Council) or to bring about a change of regime in Tripoli.

The Libyan policy debate between the NATO allies and Russia and China echoed that surrounding the invasion of Iraq eight years earlier, when President George W. Bush and Prime Minister Tony Blair essentially argued that the fulfillment of the Security Council resolution could be achieved only through a regime change.

Although humanitarian intervention is intrinsically contentious on sovereignty grounds, the question remains: what can be done about human rights pariahs in countries where no prospect exists for change because their regimes have the coercive capacity to fend off serious internal challenges to autocratic rule? Under those circumstances, when the prospect of any internal agent of change appears remote, the political focus will invariably shift to a plausible external agent of change. Hence, in the case of Zimbabwe, many have called on South Africa, the neighboring regional power, to launch an intervention to topple the Mugabe regime or, at minimum, to exercise South Africa's unique influence to leverage a change in the regime's internal conduct. Similar hopes have been expressed with respect to a potential Chinese intervention to end North Korea's tyrannical Kim family dynasty. Yet the prospects of such intervention are unlikely, not only because of the high normative barrier to external intervention, but also because, on some level, the status quo in Zimbabwe and North Korea is acceptable to South Africa and China.

Leadership and Intra-elite Bargaining

Relative to external agents of change, internally generated changes *of* and *within* regimes are far more common and more legitimate in the eyes of other states. Those internal pathways depend on dynamics within a state's leadership and ruling elite. Each case is highly context specific, with the outcome hinging largely on how a regime's core interest groups (whether institutional, familial, class, ethnic, or sectarian) gauge their stakes for or against deeper integration into the international system.

Intra-elite bargaining among the regime's core interest groups is a key determinant of change, either promoting or blocking compliance with international norms. External pressure is a necessary, but not sufficient, condition affecting a regime's strategic calculus. When elite interests supportive of change reach a tipping point, a major discontinuity in policy can occur if advanced by the regime's top leadership. A regime's use of foreign policy as a source of domestic legitimation can be a major impediment to compliance with respect to external behavioral norms. Integration will likewise be eschewed if the leadership views that process as a threat to regime stability.

The evolution of the Soviet Union and the PRC from revolutionary states—outliers that shunned integration into the capitalist international order—into orthodox great powers occurred in response to both changes in the international environment and shifting alignments among key domestic interest groups.

In the Soviet Union, Khrushchev's pivotal de-Stalinization policy began the process of stripping the regime's claim to legitimacy based on ideology. Brezhnev's military buildup and developing world activism, which culminated in the invasion of Afghanistan, precipitated the formation of an anti-Soviet coalition of the world's other major powers and cut the Soviet Union off from access to advanced foreign technology. Those costs, coupled with the prospect of further decline if the Soviet Union failed to embrace the information-age technologies that were already transforming Western economies and societies, produced a shift among the Soviet Union's core interest groups that Gorbachev marshaled to further his reform agenda. At home, Gorbachev brought the process of de-Stalinization to fruition; abroad, eschewing the threatening Brezhnev activism, he fostered a quiescent international environment to provide cover for his ambitious strategy of domestic "restructuring" (*perestroika*). Perhaps the most consequential of the policy discontinuities under Gorbachev was the Soviet leader's historic decision not to intervene in Eastern Europe in autumn 1989 to prevent popular uprisings from toppling communist regimes.

In the case of China, a national security imperative—the threat of conflict with the Soviet Union in 1969—drove Mao's strategic decision to normalize relations with the United States. That discontinuity in Chinese foreign policy was the predicate for the similarly profound discontinuity in the country's domestic policies under Deng Xiaoping a decade later. The disastrous economic and social consequences of the Cultural Revolution, in tandem with the death of Mao, allowed Deng to overcome the opposition of ideological hard-liners in advancing his ambitious reforms, which have entailed deep integration into the global economy. This profound discontinuity in Chinese policy reflected a new elite consensus that only an intrasystem rise could be a peaceful rise.

Kennan's characterization of the transformation of Soviet Union under Gorbachev from a revolutionary state into "another great power" can also be applied to China under Deng. That evolution has created a challenge of political legitimacy as the two countries deal with the historical legacies of, respectively, Stalinism and Maoism. Now using nationalism as an alternate source of domestic legitimacy to communist ideology, both Russia and China seek to integrate into the international order (albeit on their own terms) rather than overturn it. But increased integration has not led to full compliance: both countries, which remain "not free" according to the Freedom House annual survey, flout internal behavioral norms.

Shifts in elite interests were integral to the changes *within* regimes in Romania and South Africa. Ceauşescu's overthrow occurred when the regime's own core support groups turned on the Romanian autocrat in what one analyst described as a "coup d'état." A radical change in the external environment (the cascading fall of communist regimes in Eastern Europe, with Soviet leader Gorbachev's acquiescence) combined with the disastrous consequences of Ceauşescu's internal economic policies, precipitated a nationwide popular uprising against the increasingly detached Romanian autocrat. The Romanian army's unexpected decision to oust and execute Ceauşescu reflected the shifting calculus of interests of Ceauşescu's own inner circle, who now viewed the "leader" as an anachronistic liability. In South Africa, the catalyst of change came from within the white minority community in response to international pressure from economic sanctions and rising domestic violence. Faced with the stark choice between being "rich and integrated [or] segregated and poor," the ruling Afrikaner party chose the former.[138] That discontinuity arose from hard-nosed recognition that the apartheid system was no longer viable. The shift in elite interests was a necessary condition for change. Leadership—de Klerk's pivotal role in ending apartheid and Mandela's reassurance to the white minority—was also essential in bringing about this "negotiated revolution."

Conditionality and Compliance

Integration into the international system does not automatically signify compliance with international norms. Just as defiant noncompliance by a state provides a basis for continued international isolation, the tangible benefits of integration can be leveraged to promote compliance. Here one must again distinguish between external and internal behavioral norms. The outlier states at the top of the American foreign policy agenda command attention because of threatening behavior that violates *external* behavioral norms (notably WMD proliferation and terrorism). In practice, states that contravene norms with external consequences also defy *internal* behavioral norms. The far larger group of countries (including human rights pariahs such as Belarus and Zimbabwe) that subjugate their own populations but do not pose a threat beyond their borders is beyond the scope of this study.

Perhaps the most successful case of reintegration in contemporary history was Germany after World War II. A rehabilitated Germany became an integral member of the Western community of industrial democracies, whose key institutions (NATO and the EU) were founded on the principle of democratic governance within their member states. Such *conditionality*, the linking of institutional membership to the meeting of political and economic criteria, was central to the process of NATO and EU expansion after the Cold War. In Romania, where an autocrat had been ousted by regime apparatchiks in a coup d'état, the conditionality of NATO and EU accession was instrumental in promoting democracy.

Since the end of the Cold War, the United States has pursued coercive diplomacy toward rogue states to counter the twin threats of proliferation and terrorism. One of the few successes of that policy was Libya's surprise decision in 2003 to undergo transparent WMD disarmament; the decision came shortly after the legal settlement over the Qaddafi regime's complicity in the terrorist bombing of Pan Am 103. The WMD negotiations used a method of coercive diplomacy that Alexander George characterized as "conditional reciprocity," which in this case linked demonstrable changes in Libyan behavior to the bestowing of inducements (such as the lifting of economic sanctions or establishment of diplomatic relations) by the United States.[139] This agreement, which offered Libya the prospect of rejoining the community of nations in exchange for compliance with external behavioral norms (with respect to WMD proliferation), did not address the Qaddafi regime's contravention of internal behavioral norms (with respect to human rights). As discussed in Chapter 3, the ending of Qaddafi's WMD programs and state sponsorship, which was the primary U.S. objective, allowed for Libya's international rehabilitation and the revival of its oil sector.

The Libyan case highlights a persistent problem in U.S. policy toward outliers such as Iran and North Korea—how to address external behavior of concern through negotiations without ignoring the countries' flouting of internal behavioral norms. The dilemma is twofold. First, Washington will accord greater priority to addressing objectionable conduct that has external consequences directly affecting U.S. interests than to halting behavior whose consequences are confined within states. And second, the cardinal principle of state sovereignty and noninterference makes holding regimes accountable for abhorrent conduct toward their own civil populations inherently difficult. The outliers have adopted a stance of wary pragmatism to compartmentalize their relationship with the international community. Tehran and Pyongyang aim to garner the tangible benefits of economic integration while insulating their regimes from political contagion (what the Iranian leadership calls a "soft revolution") that could threaten regime survival. Conditional generalizations about norm compliance gleaned from the comparative analysis of historical pathways to reintegration should inform the development of tailored strategies toward these outlier states.

Chapter 3

Strategies to Contain, Engage, or Change

An understanding of general pathways by which revolutionary or revision-ist states have historically been integrated into the international order is an essential but not sufficient first step toward developing specific strategies for dealing with contemporary outlier states. Conditional generalizations drawn from a rigorous comparative analysis of historical cases can reveal underlying dynamics, but an assessment of a particular case requires spe-cific knowledge about the target state (an "actor-specific model," to use political scientist Alexander George's term). For instance, conditional gen-eralizations identify circumstances under which deterrence has succeeded or failed throughout history, whereas a targeted strategy would focus on the specific requirements for deterring Saddam Hussein from launching an invasion of Kuwait.

Perhaps the most famous example of target state analysis informing strategy development was George Kennan's "X" article.[1] Tellingly titled "The Sources of Soviet Conduct," the article revealed how "the political personality of Soviet power" would shape "Russia's conduct as a member of international society." With a grasp of Soviet reality unparalleled among his contemporaries, Kennan had the genius at the time to divine that ideas and powerful forces shaping Russian political culture were seeds of change that would be as important as missiles and tanks in the Cold War struggle.[2] Kennan advocated containment as essentially a long-term holding process by the United States and its allies to balance Soviet power until the en-demic internal contradictions of the Soviet system became unsustainable and precipitated change. Kennan's strategy was predicated on a concept of societal change derived from his analysis of the Soviet state's strategic "personality."

Concepts of societal change similarly undergird the various strategies advanced to tackle the contemporary challenges of outlier states. But in contrast to Kennan's classic treatment in the "X" article, the sources of outlier state conduct are frequently not subjected to rigorous analysis. Key threshold assumptions about societal change are unarticulated or reflect an ideological predilection—or even a vain hope. The U.S. policy debate on Iran's nuclear challenge is emblematic. Three broad options have been advanced, each based on a different concept of societal change and the character of the Tehran regime:

• *A military strike on Iran's nuclear infrastructure.* The argument for urgent action rests on the assumption that the theocratic regime is undeterrable and that the acquisition of a nuclear capability is therefore unacceptable. One variant of this strategy is that a military strike might trigger a popular uprising against the regime.
• *Containment, relying primarily on economic sanctions.* The underlying assumption is that either targeted sanctions on the regime's core interest groups or general sanctions on the populace will create amplified pressure on the regime's leadership to alter its conduct.
• *Engagement, emphasizing incentives.* This option is based on the assumption that the basis of a nuclear agreement exists, but that the United States has not offered big enough "carrots" to induce the clerical regime's acceptance of an agreement.

Although current threats, such as that posed by Iran, differ from those of Kennan's era, the analytic challenge is analogous. Consider illustrative examples from recent history in which plausible but faulty assumptions have led to policy miscalculations of varying consequence:

• During the lead-up to the Iranian Revolution of 1979, the Carter administration operated on the assumption that Shah Reza Pahlavi would crack down militarily on street demonstrations if he believed they constituted a threat to monarchical rule. That the shah, who was perceived by U.S. officials as strong and decisive, did not do so was taken as an indicator of regime stability.[3]
• After the eight-year Iran-Iraq War, the George H. W. Bush administration concluded that the Saddam Hussein regime would seek a quiescent regional environment within which it could focus on domestic reconstruction. Two years later the Iraqi dictator invaded Kuwait.

- In the wake of the Gulf War of 1991, the George H. W. Bush administration assumed that the Iraqi military debacle in Kuwait would precipitate a coup overthrowing Saddam.

These cases highlight the need for policy-makers to have an accurate image of the target states before they attempt strategy development and implementation.

Sources of Outlier Conduct

In "The Sources of Soviet Conduct," Kennan invoked the term "political personality" metaphorically but never explained its meaning. Synonymous concepts, such as "strategic culture" and "strategic personality," have subsequently been used by foreign policy analysts. The terms share a common focus "on broad historical and cultural patterns that evolve over the whole course of a state's history (its historical plot) and identify the fundamental consistencies in its long-term strategic conduct in order to shed light on how they might shape its current and future strategic decisions. The methodology is not deterministic and, hence, not precisely predictive" because of the variance of regime types across time.[4]

Yet one must be cautious about the application of this approach in assessing the target state. As political scientist Alastair Ian Johnston warns, "Done well, the careful analysis of strategic culture could help policy-makers establish more accurate and empathetic understandings of how different actors perceive the game being played, reducing uncertainty and other information problems in strategic choice. Done badly, the analysis of strategic culture could reinforce stereotypes about the strategic predispositions of other states and close off policy alternatives deemed inappropriate for dealing with local strategic cultures."[5]

Developing an accurate image of the target state requires inputs from a variety of expert sources. Particularly relevant is the expertise of area specialists, whose knowledge of the target state's history and political culture can provide policy-makers with a much-needed context within which to frame their decisions. Yet different policy experts can review the same data and come to sharply divergent conclusions. In the official review of the failure of the Central Intelligence Agency (CIA) to predict India's nuclear test in May 1998, retired admiral David Jeremiah, the panel's chairman, stated: "We should have been [much] more aggressive in thinking through how the other guy thought."[6] Decision-makers must remain open to multiple viewpoints and foster a decision-making environment in which target state analyses can be openly vetted and their underlying assumptions challenged.[7] Flawed target state analysis can lead to misperception and miscalculation if decision-makers simply extrapolate future behavior from the past or impute some form of rationality on the basis of preconceived notions.[8]

Developing an Accurate Image

Target state analysis is a qualitative method that encompasses a broad range of domestic and international determinants.[9] The factors that should be considered in developing an accurate image of the target state include the geostrategic and historical context, the character of the regime and its leadership, the regime's declaratory policy and ideology, recent foreign policy behavior, the target state's economic and military capabilities, the impact of current U.S. policies on the target state, and the domestic context within the target state and the potential for alternative paths of political evolution.

- *Geostrategic and historical context.* An examination of the recent historical record can shed light on a state's intentions. Is its ruling regime revisionist? Does it seek a change in the territorial status quo with neighboring states? Is there a legacy of regional rivalry and enmity, as between Iran and Iraq? With respect to the target state's historical relationship to the United States, does that legacy continue to affect current perceptions and policies (e.g., with Iran, the 1953 coup and 1979 hostage crisis; with North Korea, the 1950–53 war that ended in an armistice, not a peace treaty)?
- *Character of the regime.* What is known or can be inferred from available evidence about the character of the target state's leadership and its decision-making process? Are decisions made by a paramount individual (such as Saddam Hussein) or by a collective leadership? What are the formal structures and, more significantly, the informal processes by which decisions are made? What are the key interest groups (such as the military and the security services) on which the regime depends for its survival?
- *Declaratory policy and ideology.* Public pronouncements by a target state's leadership can be an indicator of future intent. For example, prior to the May 1998 Indian nuclear test, CIA analysts discounted as

campaign rhetoric the Hindu nationalist Bharatiya Janata Party's public statements vowing to turn India into a nuclear power. Content analysis of leadership statements and of publications linked to interest groups can shed light on internal debates and a regime's belief system. The regime can use ideology as a source of domestic legitimation and a motivation for its foreign policy behavior.

- *Capabilities*. Intentions are inherently difficult to discern because they relate to the state of mind of the regime leadership. Intangible, often idiosyncratic factors affect decision-making—for example, Saddam Hussein's sense of regional grandeur. Capabilities, by contrast, are measurable indices, such as military spending or economic performance. They determine whether the regime possesses the wherewithal to act on its intentions. But the weapons of mass destruction (WMD) intelligence fiasco in Iraq in 2003 stands as an object lesson in the difficulty of estimating capabilities.
- *Foreign policy behavior*. Are discernible patterns or changes in the target state's pattern of behavior evident? Divergent or contradictory behavior may indicate divergent tendencies within the ruling regime. Are any perceived changes tactical (reflecting a short-term adjustment), or are they strategic (signaling a more fundamental foreign policy reorientation)?
- *The international environment*. A regime's perception of the distribution of power among states (and its perceived options within a potentially shifting alignment) will influence its foreign policy conduct. Because the United States is the sole remaining superpower with a global reach, U.S. policy-makers should take into account how their policies will be perceived by and affect the target state.
- *Domestic politics*. The maxim "all politics are local" can be extended to the realm of foreign policy. The goal of any strategy is to influence the target state, whether the objective is to moderate its foreign policy or to bring about a change in regime. Punitive strategies, such as comprehensive containment, aim not only to keep a "rogue" leader "in his box" (as the U.S. administration long said of Saddam Hussein) but also to up the ante internally by creating pressures that could precipitate change, such as a coup. Incentive strategies, by incorporating some degree of engagement, also seek to shape the domestic political milieu by giving interest groups within the target state a tangible stake in improved relations. A key determinant of success or failure is the extent to which the target state's leadership and decision-making process are insulated from or affected by political interest groups in the broader society.

Although target state analysis encompasses a broad range of factors, their relative salience is highly context dependent. Of particular importance is the need to distinguish between factors that are *regime generic* and those that are *regime specific*. Certain structural characteristics, such as geography and ethnic composition, are relatively durable and will influence the behavior of the state regardless of regime type. But other factors are idiosyncratic and transient because they derive from the particular regime in power. Thus, for example, the central question about Iraq's nuclear program was whether it was purely the manifestation of the megalomania of Saddam Hussein (i.e., regime specific) or arose from structural factors, such as the country's geostrategic position next to Iran, which would have stimulated Iraq's nuclear intentions under any regime in Baghdad (i.e., regime generic). The Iraq Survey Group's final report (known as the *Duelfer Report*) highlighted the paramount importance of regime-specific over regime-generic factors in its postwar assessment of that country's WMD capabilities: "*The former Regime was Saddam*, and he was the one person who made important decisions. It was his assessment of the utility of various policy options that was determinant."[10]

A rigorous assessment of the target state provides an analytic basis for strategy development. That process can identify key determinants of decision-making in the target state and explicitly articulate and vet the threshold assumptions about the target state on which U.S. policy will be premised. Ultimately, however, the issue for decision—whether to adopt a strategy to contain, engage, or change—comes down to public officials making a judgment about a target state. This decision is made under highly context-dependent circumstances in which various factors may be weighted differently and policy trade-offs (e.g., proliferation and human rights) must be taken into account.[11]

The Strategic Continuum

Policy-makers and analysts often use the terms "containment" and "engagement" without precision, almost as slogans to rally political support. Political scientist Alexander George observed that "containment" and "engagement" are general *concepts* that require specific content in order to become *strategies*.[12] The content comes from rigorous target state analysis that allows policy-makers to translate a general concept of containment or engagement into a targeted strategy. The goal is the reintegration (or "resocialization," to use George's term) of the outlier state into the international community. The degree of change necessary within the target state to realize that objective ranges from the narrow (behavior change) to the expansive (regime change). For this reason, regime change should be viewed as a dynamic process occurring along a continuum of change.

The range of possible relationships between states along the strategic continuum runs from all-out war to an alliance or regional economic partnership. The focus of analysis for the purposes of this study is on that segment of the continuum pertinent to the development of U.S. strategies toward "outlier states." Those strategies are (a) regime change, or rollback; (b) comprehensive containment (entailing politico-economic isolation and military deterrence); and (c) hybrid or mixed strategies that integrate a significant engagement component into a containment-dominant strategy.[13]

Regime Change or Rollback

Although the term "regime change" is closely associated with the Iraq war, its policy lineage can be traced back to the early Cold War era, when hardline opponents of containment, who viewed that strategy as too "passive" and "static," called for a "rollback" strategy to reverse the installation of pro-Soviet regimes in Eastern Europe. After the East German uprising of 1953 (which a National Security Council document, NSC-158, said created "the greatest opportunity for initiating effective policies to help roll back Soviet power that has yet come to light"), the Eisenhower administration flirted with a rollback strategy.[14] The strategy, which would have included "elimination of key puppet officials," was never implemented, out of concern over the escalatory risk of these proposed covert operations. The same restraining apprehension about rollback was evident during the 1956 Hungarian revolution. Notwithstanding Secretary of State John Foster Dulles's strong rhetoric in support of the rebels, President Dwight Eisenhower refused to take any action that would frontally challenge the Soviet sphere of influence in Eastern Europe and run the risk of conflict.

In the late Cold War, the issue of rollback returned under the Reagan administration, which had come to power in 1981 after a decade of Soviet activism in (what was then called) the Third World. The Reagan Doctrine aimed to assertively alter the status quo by overthrowing vulnerable, pro-Soviet regimes through the provision of military assistance to anticommunist insurgency movements, such as the Nicaraguan Contras and the Afghan mujahideen.[15]

Rollback strategies are more ambitious than containment strategies that seek to alter the behavior of the target state's ruling regime through punitive measures (notably, economic sanctions). Rather, the objective of a rollback strategy is to bring about a near-term change of regime in the target state through a variety of mechanisms, ranging from covert intelligence operations and support for domestic opposition groups to overt military action.

Iraq and Libya offer contrasting examples of the use of force to achieve regime change. In the case of Iraq, in 2003, the United States launched a large-scale air and ground offensive not only to oust the Saddam Hussein regime but also to occupy the country. The critique of the George W. Bush administration's policy was that it was applying to Iraq the post–World War II model for Germany without a commensurately scaled military force and carefully planned occupation strategy. By contrast, in Libya, in 2011, the use of force was limited to air power, which targeted Muammar Qaddafi's infrastructure of power to essentially decapitate the regime and create powerful incentives for core interest groups crucial for regime survival to flip to the rebels. As discussed later in this chapter, the U.S.-assisted regime change in Libya was undertaken under the rubric of a humanitarian intervention; however, such externally induced changes of regime are inherently controversial in international relations on sovereignty grounds.

Comprehensive Containment

Comprehensive containment uses the full panoply of instruments—economic, diplomatic, and military—to isolate the target state and deter its ruling regime from regional aggression. The strategy imposes tangible costs on the regime for behavior that contravenes accepted international norms. Comprehensive containment aims to moderate the target state's near-term behavior while generating domestic pressures that will eventually lead to either the toppling of the regime or its evolution into a norm-abiding state.

Kennan advanced containment as a strategy to promote either the "mellowing" (or moderation) of the Soviet regime or its "breakup." That strategy did not preclude pragmatic negotiations with a nuclear-armed superpower on issues central to American interests, such as strategic arms control. In the post–Cold War era, after the 1991 Gulf War, the Bush and Clinton administrations pursued comprehensive containment toward the

Saddam Hussein regime through sanctions and military exclusion zones in northern and southern Iraq not only to bring the Iraqi dictator into compliance with United Nations Security Council resolutions but also, with luck, to generate internal dissension that might lead to his overthrow.

Economic sanctions have been the primary instrument of U.S. containment strategy. Congress and the executive branch have had "the tendency to see economic sanctions as 'below' the use of military force on some imagined ladder of foreign policy escalation."[16] The United States used sanctions toward "rogue states"—Iraq, Libya, Iran, and North Korea—with mixed results. The correlates of success are the degree to which the sanctions are applied multilaterally and the extent to which they affect the core interests of the target state's ruling regime. Yet the challenge of forging multilateral support for economic sanctions rises in tandem with the ambition of the political objective (behavior change versus regime change). In addition, multilateral support is prone to political erosion ("sanctions fatigue") in the face of seemingly intractable opposition by the target state.

In the case of Iraq, sanctions failed both to coerce Saddam Hussein to withdraw from Kuwait before the Gulf War and to generate sufficient internal pressures to oust him from power in its aftermath. Imposed by the Security Council, those multilateral sanctions broadly targeted the Iraqi population on the assumption that the resulting popular discontent would create amplified pressure on the Iraqi regime to alter its conduct. Instead, Saddam was able to effectively insulate the regime's core constituencies from the consequences of general sanctions, to shift the focus of public ire to the external powers (the United States and United Nations) inflicting the pain, and to game the sanctions system to his financial advantage through his control of black-market activities. The unintended consequences of general sanctions have led to the increased usage of targeted or "smart" sanctions to bring pressure directly to bear on those regime elements (e.g., Iran's Revolutionary Guards) responsible for unacceptable behavior.

Mixed Strategies

A mixed strategy integrates diplomatic engagement and incentives into an otherwise containment-dominant approach. Under this hybrid strategy, the target state is offered a structured choice—with the enticement of "carrots" and the punitive threat of the "stick"—to induce or compel compliance with international norms. A prime example of this strategy—conditional containment—was Richard Nixon and Henry Kissinger's détente policy toward the Soviet Union in the 1970s. During a period of ascending Soviet power, the strategy aimed to constrain the Kremlin by establishing links between military, political, and economic issues. The underlying assumption was that positive inducements, such as favorable trade terms and access to Western technology, would give the Kremlin a tangible stake in what Nixon termed the "emerging structure of peace." The détente process would thereby promote more responsible Soviet foreign policy behavior, most notably in the developing world. The Nixon administration's efforts to establish policy links (particularly when a strong mutuality of interests existed, such as on strategic nuclear arms control) foundered on the Soviet leadership's ability to compartmentalize relations.

Although outlier regimes seek to insulate themselves from outside coercive pressures, they must be responsive to the core constituencies— the military, security services, key ethnic groups, and other elites—that make up the regime's power base. Analyzing this critical dynamic, political scientist Bruce Jentleson concluded: "To the extent that elite interests are threatened by compliance with the coercing state's [or international community's] demands, they will act as 'circuit breakers' by blocking the external pressures on the regime. To the extent that their interests are better served by the policy concessions being demanded, they will become 'transmission belts,' carrying forward the coercive pressure on the regime to comply."[17] A credible threat to the interest groups on which the regime's survival depends can be an effective source of leverage.[18]

"Engagement as a policy is not merely the antithesis of isolation," according to Richard Haass and Meghan O'Sullivan. "Rather, it involves the use of economic, political, or cultural incentives to influence problem countries to alter their behavior in one or more realms."[19] The scholarly literature on the role of incentives or inducements in strategy development toward problem countries distinguishes between two types of engagement—*unconditional* and *conditional*. These strategies vary significantly in terms of the actors involved, the incentives used, and the political objective desired.[20]

Unconditional engagement is typically conducted through nongovernmental actors operating at the societal level to promote the positive evolution of the target state's civil society. Economic, scientific, cultural, and other activities outside the regime's direct control can become seeds of long-term change by promoting the development of autonomous interest groups that can become the agents of that change. For example, China's increased links to the outside world at the societal level are eroding the Communist Party's monopoly of power by promoting democratization and the creation of a market economy.

Conditional engagement is conducted on the government-to-government level and requires reciprocity by the target state on essentially a contractual basis. It typically focuses on a discrete issue but can be broadened to encompass a range of issues in a "grand bargain" (as some have proposed in the case of Iran). "Conditional reciprocity" is a form of conditional engagement, elucidated by Alexander George, in which meaningful changes in behavior by the target state would be explicitly linked to each concession or benefit bestowed by the United States.[21] The "engagement" of an adversary under conditional reciprocity has three key features, which clearly distinguish it from "appeasement." First, the inducement must be tied to *specific* changes in the target state's behavior, not *general* expectations of improved behavior. Second, the reward should come only *after* the specific change in behavior. If the reward is provided in advance of behavior modification or is not linked to a specific behavioral change, it may be legitimately criticized as a bribe. And, third, such an approach depends on mutual adherence to the specific conditional reciprocal steps in the sequence. If the target state does not fulfill its obligations, the process can be halted and the benefit withdrawn.[22] An example of conditional reciprocity was the 2003 agreement with Libya under which the Qaddafi regime's verified WMD disarmament and foreign policy reorientation led to its removal from the U.S. list of state sponsors of terrorism and the restoration of diplomatic relations between Tripoli and Washington.

Central to the Libyan deal, which was concluded in the shadow of the Iraq war, was a tacit but clear security assurance under which the George W. Bush administration eschewed the objective of regime change in return for the Qaddafi regime's verified dismantling of its WMD arsenal. The proposition that the Obama administration came to office willing to test was whether the offer of a Libya-type security assurance to North Korea and Iran could constrain those countries' nuclear aspirations and bring them back into compliance with their nuclear Nonproliferation Treaty obligations.[23]

Yet beyond a narrow security assurance linked to the nuclear question, outlier states aspire to receive a broader form of security assurance that would guarantee their regimes' survival as they expand their interactions with the outside world. This motivation highlights the fundamental dilemma that engagement poses for the outliers. Their regimes' inability to survive in autarkic isolation creates a powerful incentive to expand foreign economic contacts and normalize relations with the United States. Yet the benefits of economic engagement are potentially "poison carrots" that could undermine the regime's control over the populace. Iran's clerical regime, for example, repeatedly charges that Western nongovernmental organizations are seeking to foment a "soft revolution" to topple the Islamic Republic. In the face of this perceived threat, outlier regimes may pursue a counterstrategy to compartmentalize their relations with the outside world so as to maximize tangible economic gains and minimize political risks of foreign contagion.

Two outlier states have experienced changes of regime in the decade since 9/11. In both cases, external agency in bringing about internal change was essential. The U.S.-led invasion of Iraq to overthrow Saddam Hussein and the U.S.-assisted toppling of Qaddafi set important precedents whose consequences affect the ongoing crises with North Korea and Iran. The cases exemplify the challenges of developing a sound understanding of the sources of outlier state conduct as a basis for strategy development and implementation.

Iraq: "Rogue" Rollback

Over three decades, U.S. policy toward Iraq spanned the continuum of strategies: initially, *engaging* Saddam Hussein through a "tilt" toward Iraq in its attritional war with postrevolutionary Iran in the 1980s; then *containing* the Iraqi dictator after the first Gulf War in the 1990s; and finally, *changing* the regime through military intervention to oust the Iraqi dictator in 2003. The various strategies were predicated on different assessments of Saddam Hussein's intentions and capabilities and of the threat that the Iraqi regime posed to the region and international order. The George W. Bush administration decisively shifted from a strategy of containment to one of regime change, not on the basis of new intelligence or in the face of an imminent threat, but rather, in the words of then–secretary of defense Donald Rumsfeld, because U.S. officials viewed old evidence about Iraq's WMD programs and sponsorship of terrorism "in a dramatic new light—through the prism of our experience on 9/11."[24]

The Bush administration's argument that Saddam's Iraq could be brought into compliance with Security Council resolutions only through a change of regime engendered wide opposition on sovereignty grounds among the council's members in the rancorous debate prior to the U.S.-led invasion in March 2003. The manner of the Iraqi dictator's ouster—imposed regime change from without—and the country's subsequent occupation by the United States (notwithstanding efforts to obtain ex post facto legitimation in the Security Council) have affected the perceptions and policies of states in the region and beyond. Early in his tenure, even as he laid out a plan to end U.S. military involvement, President Barack Obama acknowledged that "fundamental political questions about Iraq's future remain unresolved." With some of its neighbors "working at times to undermine its [security]," Iraq "is not yet a full partner, politically and economically, in the region or with the international community."[25] Post-Saddam Iraq continues to struggle, domestically, to build cohesion in a state divided along ethnic and sectarian lines and, internationally, to navigate the pathway to full reintegration.

From Reagan to Clinton

A conjunction of factors produced an improvement in relations in the 1980s between the United States and Iraq, whose ruling Baath Party had seized power through a 1968 coup. The two countries had severed diplomatic links in 1967 and had since been at odds over Iraq's staunch opposition to U.S. Middle East peacemaking efforts. In 1979, as Iran experienced a convulsive revolution bringing to power a radical theocratic regime under Ayatollah Ruhollah Khomeini, Saddam Hussein consolidated supreme leadership in Iraq after having suppressed challenges from within the Baath Party and from the country's Kurdish and Shiite populations.

Fearing political contagion from the Iranian revolution and perceiving a window of opportunity when the Khomeini regime deeply purged the armed forces' officer corps and the military balance tipped to Iraq's favor, Saddam launched an invasion across the two countries' long-disputed border in September 1980. According to a former Carter administration official, although the United States did not give a green light to the invasion (contrary to conspiracy theorists), Saddam may have perceived American acquiescence in the absence of an explicit red light. Such was Iran's diplomatic isolation that, even though Iraq had flagrantly breached the international norm proscribing interstate aggression, the Security Council passed a weak resolution neither citing Iraq as the belligerent nor designating the conflict as a threat to international peace and security under Chapter VII of the UN Charter.

The Reagan administration's 1982 decision to drop Iraq from the list of states supporting international terrorism was a tangible symbol of its engagement strategy. The strategic logic behind the administration's tilt was captured in the old axiom "the enemy of my enemy is my friend."[26] Iraq's exclusion from the terrorist list after 1982 ran contrary to evidence (such as providing sanctuary to Abu Nidal and other terrorist groups). The Reagan administration's flawed strategy toward Iraq was premised on the key assumptions that the Saddam Hussein regime's behavior could be moderated through engagement and that Iraq could serve as a regional counterbalance to Iran. Another manifestation of tilt was the Reagan administration's decision to reflag Kuwaiti oil tankers and provide them protection against Iranian naval and air attacks. When Iran accepted a cease-fire with Iraq under threat of mandatory UN sanctions, the widespread perception in the Gulf region was that U.S. support for Iraq had been a significant factor.

Ironically, the country later held up as the archetypal rogue state was being courted, not sanctioned, by Washington during a decade in which Iraq had by far the worst record of actual behavior with respect to WMD acquisition and use. The Reagan administration condemned specific Iraqi actions, such as the March 1988 gassing of the Kurdish town of Halabja, though not Iraq's earlier battlefield use of chemical weapons in the war with Iran (again, an indicator of Iran's pariah status with the United States). Yet the Saddam Hussein regime's horrific violations of the international norm proscribing the use of unconventional weapons did not trigger a reassessment of U.S. policy toward Iraq.[27] To the contrary, U.S. engagement of Saddam fostered a permissive multilateral export control regime that permitted Iraq, through open and covert procurement practices, to assemble a formidable arsenal of conventional and unconventional weapons.

In the aftermath of the Iran-Iraq War, the underlying assumption of U.S. policy toward Iraq was that Saddam Hussein would seek a quiescent regional environment within which he could focus on national reconstruction. Indeed, the George H. W. Bush administration's National Security Council Directive 26, adopted in October 1989, just nine months before the Iraqi invasion of Kuwait, concluded that Baghdad was "prepared to play a more constructive role."[28] The eight-year war with Iran had left the Baghdad regime not only financially strapped and exhausted, but also the dominant military power in the region. This conjunction of financial need and military dominance, as well as Saddam's demonstrated propensity for strategic miscalculation, led the Iraqi dictator to invade Kuwait in August 1990, less than two years after the end of the war with Iran. During that critical period, the Bush administration maintained its engagement policy toward Iraq, even as Saddam assumed an increasingly confrontational stance. The administration responded to Saddam's saber rattling with a weak deterrent policy whose signal of resolve was undercut by reassurances that the United States wanted improved relations. Political scientist Alexander George observed that the United States was unwilling to threaten *before* the invasion what it felt compelled to do *after* the invasion.[29]

After the liberation of Kuwait by the U.S.-led military coalition in February 1991, President George H. W. Bush was "disappointed that Saddam's defeat did not break his hold on power, as many of our Arab allies had predicted and we had come to expect."[30] Thus, though not the UN-authorized objective of the war—the restoration of Kuwaiti sovereignty—a key assumption of U.S. policy about the outcome of the Gulf War was that Saddam's military debacle would precipitate a coup ousting him. When the Iraqi dictator exhibited unexpected staying power, the Bush administration pivoted to a containment policy emphasizing economic sanctions. This postwar strategy exposed a sharp divide on the Security Council. On one side, the United States declared that the punitive measures imposed by the Security Council after the Gulf War would remain in place as long as the Iraqi dictator remained in power, thereby signaling to potential coup-makers the one pathway to easing outside pressure on Iraq. On the other hand, France and Russia focused on ending the Iraqi behavior that had led to the imposition of sanctions, thereby leaving open the possibility of the Saddam Hussein regime's political rehabilitation.

During the decade between the Gulf War and 9/11, the U.S. debate on Iraq revealed a persisting policy tension on whether the objective should be regime change or containment. Advocates of regime change or rollback argued that this maximalist end could be accomplished through minimalist means—that is, without direct U.S. military intervention—through a combination of punishing sanctions and covert support of anti-Saddam opposition groups in Europe and Turkey. The most visible manifestation of this policy impulse was Congress's Iraq Liberation Act of 1998, which provided $97 million in military aid to the Iraqi opposition. Less ambitious than rollback, comprehensive containment aimed to keep Saddam "in his box" through the deterrence of his regional ambitions and WMD disarmament. Whereas regime change was the clear U.S. aspiration, comprehensive containment emerged as the alternative default strategy when the prospects for Saddam's ouster receded after the Gulf War.

Saddam precipitated successive crises in the mid-1990s to pressure the international community into lifting economic sanctions before UN weapons inspectors had completed their work. Saddam's brinkmanship was met by the United States and Britain with the use or credible threat of force to end these episodes. Iraq's obstructionist resistance to UN inspections—what Clinton administration officials described as "denial, delay, and deceit"—culminated in Operation Desert Fox in December 1998.[31] Four nights of sustained air attacks by the United States and Britain (which aggravated the Security Council rift with France, Russia, and China) were aimed at "degrading" Iraq's WMD capabilities and attacking key elements of Saddam Hussein's domestic power base.

In January 2001, the incoming George W. Bush administration confronted the enormous policy gulf between the U.S. aspiration for regime change and the political reality that international support, even for the minimalist objective of Iraq's continued containment, was plummeting. The terrorist attacks on September 11, 2001, recast the debate on Iraq by redefining the nature of the threat and precipitating a radical shift in strategy.

Bush, 9/11, and the Iraq War

After 9/11, the Bush administration never seriously considered the continuation of a containment strategy toward Iraq. It argued that the new threats of this era derived from the very character of the adversaries of the United States. Bush's perception of Saddam Hussein as a madman meant that Iraq's mere possession of WMD capabilities constituted an unacceptable threat—one that could not be countered through a pre-9/11 strategy of containment and deterrence. Saddam Hussein personified the deadly new nexus of proliferation and terrorism. As the president declared to religious broadcasters in a speech making the case for preventive war, "Chemical agents, lethal viruses and shadowy terrorist networks are not easily contained. Secretly, without fingerprints, Saddam Hussein could provide one of his hidden weapons to terrorists or help them to develop their own."[32]

The Iraqi dictator profoundly misjudged how 9/11 would recast the national security debate in the Bush administration. Indeed, Saddam's reaction to 9/11 conformed to the strategic narrative that the administration was articulating in support of preventive war. Although his ministers urged him to condemn the Al Qaeda attacks on New York and Washington, Saddam refused to extend condolences and declared that the country responsible for the suffering of the Iraqi people had received what it deserved. As Iraq's state media praised the hijackers, Saddam's mishandled response to 9/11 diplomatically isolated the regime and confirmed the Bush administration's perceptions of him as an implacable adversary whose continued rule could not be tolerated.[33]

In the lead-up to the March 2003 invasion of Iraq, the administration offered two rationales, with contrasting policy optics, in support of its objective of regime change. One cast the crisis as the first test case of a so-called Bush Doctrine, under which the United States would strike not only preemptively against imminent threats, but also preventively against emerging threats. President Bush, candidly responding to press reports that some senior U.S. military officers preferred the continuation of containment in Iraq, declared, "The stated mission is regime change.... I believe there is casus belli and that the doctrine of preemption applies.... Success is the removal of Saddam."[34] Vice President Dick Cheney also made an unvarnished case for assertive unilateralism, including the preventive use of force in the case of Iraq.

The other policy optic framed the showdown in terms of the enforcement of Security Council resolutions, just as the Clinton administration had done to justify Operation Desert Fox. This alternative offered the possibility of developing a consensus for collective international action, with the political legitimacy and the material support from allies that such an approach could bring. The rub was the Bush administration's argument that bringing Iraq into compliance with Security Council resolutions could be accomplished only through a change of regime—that is, through the negation of Iraqi sovereignty. The Security Council withheld its legitimizing imprimatur for the military intervention on sovereignty grounds. (In sharp contrast, George H. W. Bush was easily able to obtain Security Council authorization for the use of force to reverse Iraq's occupation of Kuwait because the objective of the intervention was to restore Kuwaiti sovereignty.) After the UN rejection of a resolution authorizing the use of force and three days before U.S. forces crossed from Kuwait into Iraq, President George W. Bush told the nation that other Security Council members "share our assessment of the danger, but not our resolve to meet it.... The United Nations Security Council has not lived up to its responsibilities, so we will rise to ours."[35]

Before 9/11, Iraq was a low priority, likened by Secretary of State Colin Powell to a "toothache";[36] after 9/11, President Bush declared that Iraq posed an unacceptable threat to U.S. national security necessitating urgent action. The source of that urgency was the nexus between Saddam Hussein's alleged push to reconstitute Iraq's nuclear program and his regime's purported links to Al Qaeda. Nonetheless, the U.S. military invasion of Iraq in March 2003 was preventive rather than preemptive, given that the threat posed by Saddam Hussein was not imminent. Imminence is the prerequisite for the preemptive use of force in international law according to the customary interpretation of the UN Charter's Article 51 on the right of self-defense. The Bush administration's 2002 National Security Strategy had elevated the preventive use of force to address emerging threats *before* they became imminent. Without the critical elements conferring urgency on military action—the Al Qaeda link and Iraq's nuclear revival—the administration would have been hard pressed to justify the abandonment of the pre-9/11 strategy of containment.

The intelligence failure in 2003 regarding the overestimation of Iraq's WMD capabilities was the second in a dozen years. In 1991, after the first Gulf War, the WMD scandal was the U.S. intelligence community's glaring underestimation of Saddam's extensive WMD programs, which had included covert efforts to acquire nuclear and biological weapons. That historical legacy increased the propensity of intelligence analysts from the United States (as well those in Britain and other countries) to erroneously conclude in the lead-up to the 2003 war that Saddam had indeed secretly retained WMD stockpiles, in contravention of Security Council resolutions. What was particularly striking about the 1991 and 2003 intelligence failures was that they turned on assessments of Iraqi military capabilities, which by their tangible and potentially detectable nature are considered easier to ascertain than the political intentions of an outlier state, whose regime's decision-making process (often the will or whim of a paramount leader) is opaque.[37]

The baseline assessment of Iraq's WMD program before 9/11 derived from the final report of the United Nations Special Commission (UNSCOM), which was established by the Security Council after the 1991 Gulf War to oversee the dismantlement of Iraq's WMD programs. That January 1999 document detailed the chemical and biological agents that Saddam Hussein was known to have procured and whose destruction UNSCOM could not verify. The uncertainties in UNSCOM's final report left genuine ambiguity about the status of Iraq's WMD programs.

In October 2002, a secret National Intelligence Estimate (NIE) concluded with "high confidence" that Iraq "possesses proscribed chemical and biological weapons and missiles" and stated that the only major constraint on Iraq's ability to fabricate a nuclear weapon was access to fissile material. Bearing centrally on the administration's pressing case for regime change was the NIE's conclusion that Iraq's efforts to acquire specialized aluminum tubes "provide compelling evidence that Saddam is reconstituting a uranium enrichment effort for Baghdad's nuclear weapons program."[38] The NIE further warned of a scenario under which a "desperate" Saddam might either launch a WMD attack against the United States or transfer that capability to a terrorist organization, such as Al Qaeda, if he believed an attack threatening his regime's survival was imminent. When questioned as to whether the Bush administration's controversial remedy for Saddam Hussein's noncompliance with Security Council resolutions— regime change—carried the substantial risk of precipitating Iraqi WMD use or transfer, CIA director George Tenet downplayed that concern, maintaining that there was "no inconsistency" between administration policy and the NIE.[39]

The intelligence community's revised assessment in the NIE about Iraq's nuclear program was one source of urgency. The other, which came primarily from Vice President Cheney and the Department of Defense, was the Saddam Hussein regime's alleged links to Al Qaeda, the evidence of which Secretary of Defense Donald Rumsfeld described as "bulletproof."[40] Weaving these themes together to cast Iraq as the central front in the "war on terrorism," President Bush declared, "[We] cannot wait for the final proof—the smoking gun—that could come in the form of a mushroom cloud.... Understanding the threats of our time, knowing the designs and deceptions of the Iraqi regime, *we have every reason to assume the worst*, and we have an urgent duty to prevent the worst from occurring."[41] Although Bush referred to Iraq as "an ally of Al Qaeda," the 9/11 Commission later found "no evidence" that their contacts "developed into a collaborative operational relationship."[42]

The White House's depiction of Iraq's urgent threat was based on an unproven cooperative relationship with Al Qaeda and a highly speculative assertion of Iraqi interest in transferring WMD capabilities to Al Qaeda— not merely in response to a U.S. military action to topple the regime. Underlying this fear was the administration's assertion after 9/11 that the United States could no longer rely on deterrence and containment in dealing with the unbalanced dictators ruling rogue states. Was Saddam Hussein irrational and, therefore, undeterrable? The historical record indicates that Saddam was a miscalculator but not irrational. That Iraq did not use chemical weapons against coalition forces in the 1991 Gulf War is credited as a deterrence success. The occasions of Saddam's use of chemical weapons in the Iran-Iraq War and against the Kurds could be considered rational in the sense that neither foe had the ability to retaliate and, in both cases, the international community turned a blind eye.

On the possible revival of Iraq's nuclear program, the administration's new alarm arose from suspect sources (most egregiously, the known "fabricator," fittingly code-named "Curveball," who was linked to the Iraqi exile group lobbying Washington for a U.S. invasion) and flawed analysis. The presidential commission created in response to the failure to find WMD stockpiles after the toppling of the Saddam Hussein regime concluded that the intelligence community was *"dead wrong* in almost all of its pre-war judgments about Iraq's weapons of mass destruction."[43] Problems of intelligence collection were compounded by those of analysis. The presidential WMD commission stated that a hypothesis about Iraq's continued possession of WMD capabilities "hardened into a presumption." According to the Senate Intelligence Committee's parallel investigation, analysts operated within a culture of "group think" that reinforced their propensity to fit the thin available evidence on Iraq's WMD programs into their preconceived assumptions about Saddam's intentions.[44] Evidence at odds with that presumption was discounted, whereas information consistent with it was accepted without challenge.

The "not unreasonable" assumption, in the WMD commission's judgment, that Saddam retained chemical and biological weapons was based on logic and deduction. The truth—that he did not possess unconventional weapons—was simply implausible given the Iraqi dictator's history and the intelligence failure after the 1991 war. In his assessment of the most studied intelligence failure since Pearl Harbor, political scientist Robert Jervis concludes that "so much of the prevailing explanation for the failure is also wrong.... [W]hile there were not only errors, but correctable ones ... [an alternative process] would have been to make the intelligence assessments less certain rather than to reach a fundamentally different conclusion."[45]

The shocking failure to uncover WMD stocks posed a fundamental conundrum about Saddam's actions and strategic motivations. Given that Iraq had been successfully disarmed by UNSCOM in the 1990s, why did the Iraqi dictator cultivate ambiguity about the status of his WMD capabilities rather than simply come clean and thereby undermine the Bush administration's primary rationale for military action in Security Council deliberations?

The report of the U.S.-led Iraq Survey Group, which inspected suspect WMD sites and interviewed top Iraqi officials, provides broad insight into Saddam Hussein's worldview and calculus of decision. Saddam viewed WMD capabilities as a source of power and prestige. He credited Iraq's extensive use of missiles and chemical munitions as the decisive weapons that had averted defeat in the war with Iran. Saddam also believed that his regime's possession of and willingness to use chemical and biological weapons during the 1991 Gulf War had deterred the United States from marching on Baghdad after the liberation of Kuwait. But Saddam viewed the dismantling of Iraq's WMD stocks and infrastructure as an acceptable "tactical retreat" to free Iraq of UN sanctions. Rather than focus on existing munitions and equipment, his "guiding theme" was to sustain the "intellectual capacity"—the expertise of his scientists—to facilitate the rapid reconstitution of WMD capabilities once Iraq was free of UN sanctions.[46]

Saddam's intention to rebuild his WMD arsenal and the Security Council's disarmament mandate created a core contradiction that was never resolved. Saddam's urge to bluff about the status of Iraq's WMD programs derived from his perceptions of a hostile international environment (strikingly, he was fixated more on Iran than on the United States). For Saddam, who frequently told his inner circle, the "better part of war was deceiving," this ambiguity was instrumental. Uncertainty about whether Iraq retained WMD capabilities, he believed, could have an important deterrent effect on adversaries, both without (the United States) and within (the Shiites). This security preoccupation, compounded by megalomania, led him to resist making the reality of Iraqi WMD disarmament unequivocally clear.[47] In an interview after the regime's overthrow, General Raad Majid al-Hamdani, a Republican Guard commander, described Saddam's strategy of promoting uncertainty about his WMD capabilities as "deterrence by doubt."[48] Ironically, the ambiguity about unconventional weapons programs that Saddam cultivated to retain "a strategic deterrent" became the basis for the U.S. military intervention to overthrow his regime.

Post-Saddam Iraq

"[A]n invasion is never a very good basis for forming an alliance," observed diplomat Christopher Hill in the wake of President Obama's announced withdrawal of the remaining U.S. military forces from Iraq by the end of 2012.[49] As with post-Saddam Iraq's complicated relationship with the United States, the successor regime's relations with its Gulf neighbors and beyond have been affected by the legacy of the U.S. invasion and occupation. The political residue of the contentious prewar debate in the Security Council carried into the postwar period.

In the immediate aftermath of the fall of Baghdad, the White House and the Defense Department rebuffed advice to build ex post facto legitimacy for the military intervention through the involvement of the United Nations. The State Department had proposed a role in post-Saddam Iraq comparable to that played by the international organization in Afghanistan after the U.S.-led coalition had taken down the Taliban regime in late 2001. For the White House and the Defense Department, the rapid success of the hubristically dubbed "shock and awe" campaign in overthrowing the Saddam Hussein regime vindicated the decision to undertake unilateral military action with the aid of a "coalition of the willing" outside the UN institutional framework.

Former State Department official Richard Haass's memoir describes Iraq as a "war of choice," not only in the Bush administration's deciding to launch a preventive war against a nonimminent threat, but also in doing so with a bare minimum of 150,000 troops—a military force capable of swiftly toppling the Baghdad regime but woefully inadequate for securing the peace.[50] Prewar planning for the postwar period, Haass recounts, was "near useless" as preparations "were predicated on a short-duration, low-cost effort, as well as the notion that Iraqis would greet U.S. personnel 'with sweets,' as welcome liberators."[51] A profound mismatch was soon evident between the ambitious scope of the postwar mission that the United States assumed and the size of the U.S. occupying force. The inadequacies of the Bush administration's postwar planning—Phase IV operations, in the military's lexicon—were such that even those senior officials involved in the process cannot say with certainty when the decision for an extended occupation was made. Before the establishment of the Coalition Provisional Authority (CPA) in May 2003, American planning, according to a RAND Corporation study, "had proceeded along two ill-defined but divergent tracks, one moving toward the extended occupation, as finally eventuated, the other toward a swift handoff to a nonelected Iraqi successor regime, as had occurred in Afghanistan."[52] In the lead-up to war, Secretary Rumsfeld had publicly clashed with General Eric Shinseki, the Army chief of staff, after Shinseki's congressional testimony that the occupation of Iraq would require several hundred thousand troops—that is, three to four times the force eventually used in Operation Iraqi Freedom. The disastrous consequences of the decision on force size in that operation were evident in the first weeks after the fall of the regime with the outbreak of widespread looting, which American forces did not move to stop.

That the United States was embarking on an extended occupation was not clear until former ambassador L. Paul Bremer arrived in Baghdad to head the CPA.[53] In a memorandum to Pentagon officials, Bremer declared that he wanted his arrival to be "marked by clear, public, and decisive steps to reassure Iraqis that we are determined to eradicate Saddamism."[54] His early moves as American proconsul for Iraq are widely viewed as having put the country on its calamitous postwar trajectory. With clear echoes of de-Nazification, CPA Order No. 1, "De-Ba'athification of Iraqi Society," excluded individuals in the top tiers of Saddam's ruling Baath Party from government service. Opposing the depth of the proposed purge, senior U.S. military and intelligence officers in Baghdad warned that the envisaged de-Baathification would bring activity at Iraqi government ministries to a standstill and would exacerbate an already deteriorating security situation. With the CIA station chief warning, "You're going to drive fifty thousand Baathists underground," the CPA order moved forward nevertheless.[55] An Iraqi advisory committee established by Bremer to which former Baathist officials could appeal for an exemption was headed by the shady Iraqi exile leader Ahmed Chalabi, who issued no waivers. As former Baath Party members were barred from positions in government, the Bush administration, through the CPA, appointed Americans to key positions. Many had no experience in the Middle East region, and their selection was based on U.S. partisan political criteria rather than expertise. In his book *Imperial Life in the Emerald City*, a devastating chronicle of the CPA's fourteen-month rule, journalist Rajiv Chandrasekaran recounts numerous such missteps, including the appointment of a twenty-four-year-old college graduate with no finance background who was assigned to reopen the Baghdad Stock Exchange.[56]

In tandem with the de-Baathification decree, Bremer issued a second, even more consequential, CPA order disbanding the Iraqi army. That move is widely viewed by experts as having essentially jump-started the Iraqi insurgency by leaving nearly some 450,000 Iraqi soldiers armed and unemployed. Although President Bush famously declared an end to "major combat operations" in Iraq on the deck of the USS *Abraham Lincoln* in front of a "Mission Accomplished" banner in May 2003, by summer U.S. military forces were engaged in a "low-intensity conflict" against Sunni insurgents in central Iraq.

The U.S.-led invasion not only toppled a despotic regime, but also fundamentally altered the power relationship between the country's two rival sectarian groups—the Sunni minority (whose communal group ruled Iraq and enjoyed a privileged position) and the Shiite majority (whose population in the country's southern half had been brutally suppressed by the Saddam Hussein regime). That power shift has violently convulsed Iraqi society and frustrated efforts by its elected Shiite-dominated civilian leadership (to whom authority was transferred by the CPA on the CPA's dissolution in June 2004) to reintegrate into the Middle East regional order. Among the flawed assumptions that U.S. policy-makers brought to the invasion of Iraq was the vain hope that the change of regime in Baghdad would not aggravate the Sunni-Shia schism. Instead, in the so-called Sunni Triangle, a densely populated area northwest of Baghdad, a variety of armed Sunni groups (former Baathists and Iraqi military, Saddam loyalists, and foreign fighters) launched attacks against coalition forces, while in southern Iraq, rival Shiite militias vied for power.

In response to spiraling sectarian violence and growing congressional and public criticism of a U.S. military mission that had morphed from regime change to counterinsurgency, President Bush boldly announced a "surge" of 20,000 additional troops in January 2007. Whether that military escalation accounts for the subsequent decline in violence, as Bush administration officials claim, is still debated. Challenging the conventional wisdom about the surge, Middle East security expert Steven Simon credited the decrease to "the grim successes of ethnic cleansing" (which effectively separated sectarian populations), the tactical quiescence of the Shiite militias, a series of deals between U.S. forces and Sunni tribes that constituted a new bottom-up approach to pacifying Iraq, and "the violent nihilism" of the foreign fighters linked to or inspired by Al Qaeda that alienated Iraqis.[57]

With the withdrawal of American military forces, Iraq's future as a durable, unitary state will hinge on the success of transforming tentative domestic power-sharing arrangements into a lasting structure of state institutions that transcends sectarianism and personalities. The key determinants of Iraqi stability are, first, the intentions of the Sunni community—whether it will reconcile to its diminished status in post-Saddam Iraq or will harbor revanchist designs of a restoration—and, second, the attitude and actions of the now-ascendant Shiite majority in providing reassurance to the Sunni community that minority rights will be respected. The inability of Iraq's Shiite prime minister, Nuri al-Maliki, to rise above narrow sectarian interests prompted then-senator Hillary Clinton in 2007 to call on the Iraqi parliament to replace him with "a less divisive and more unifying figure."[58] A 2010 study by the RAND Corporation concluded that "Iraq's future over the next five to ten years will resemble a variation of the present: a Shi'a-dominated Iraq marked by endemic instability, lawlessness, and violence in key portions of territory."[59]

The Sunni-Shiite schism that roils the country's domestic politics also affects post-Saddam Iraq's attempted reintegration into the regional order. The toppling of the Saddam Hussein regime overturned the balance of power between the predominantly Sunni Arab world and Shiite Iran. Before 2003, Iraq played a pivotal role in balancing Iranian power. The advent of a Shiite-led government in Baghdad and the withdrawal of U.S. forces from Iraq and Afghanistan have created a strategic opportunity for a regionally ascendant Iran. The Saudi foreign minister declared that the American-initiated war had "handed Iraq to Iran."[60] The Saudi government balked at normalizing relations with Iraq until 2012, even though the government of Iraqi prime minister Malaki had moved against the Shiite militia, headed by Moktada al-Sadr, that is most closely linked to Iran. That post-Saddam Iraq has become an arena of competition between Saudi Arabia and Iran reflects the continued propensity of regional states to view Iraq, regardless of the political character of the ruling regime in Baghdad, through the prism of sectarianism.

Libya: U.S.-Assisted Regime Change

From the Cold War to 9/11

Colonel Muammar Qaddafi came to power in Libya in September 1969 through a "revolution" toppling the conservative monarchical regime that had been a close U.S. ally. Quietly accepting the coup d'état, the Nixon administration hoped that Qaddafi would emerge as a pragmatic Arab nationalist leader who would not shift Libya's strategic alignment in the Cold War from Washington to Moscow. The "benevolently neutral" stance of the United States toward the Qaddafi regime hardened after the Libyan dictator nationalized U.S. oil interests during the October 1973 Middle East war. Unable to purchase arms from the West because of his increasing foreign policy radicalization, Qaddafi turned to the Soviet Union, with which he concluded several large-scale arms deals to obtain bombers, tanks, and other military equipment during the 1970s. In December 1979,

U.S.-Libyan relations reached a new nadir with the sacking and burning of the American embassy in Tripoli—an action that purported to be a popular uprising in solidarity with Iran's revolutionary regime during the U.S. hostage crisis but that could not have been taken without Qaddafi's authorization. That same month, the Department of State placed Libya on its inaugural annual list of state sponsors of terrorism, thereby triggering the imposition of economic sanctions.

For the Reagan administration, Libya posed a challenge—but also an opportunity to demonstrate renewed American resolve in the wake of the Iranian revolution and the Soviet invasion of Afghanistan.[61] Though Iran and Syria were also active state sponsors of terrorism, the administration considered Libya (with its small population and advantageous geographic location on the Mediterranean) more vulnerable to U.S. military and economic instruments. The public elevation of Libya on the U.S. national security agenda was reflected in a July 1981 *Newsweek* magazine cover that featured a photograph of Qaddafi with the alarmist headline "The Most Dangerous Man in the World?"[62] A CIA assessment in June 1984 drew an explicit link between the regime's character and its objectionable foreign policy behavior: "No course of action short of stimulating Qaddafi's fall," the CIA report concluded, "will bring significant and enduring changes in Libyan policies." This intelligence assessment underpinned the administration's subsequent initiation of covert operations, including U.S. support of anti-Qaddafi exile groups, to weaken the regime's internal hold on power.[63] Publicly, however, President Ronald Reagan maintained that the United States would lift U.S. economic sanctions if Qaddafi would "reveal by action" that his regime was "no longer backing" terrorist groups.[64]

In April 1986, Libyan complicity in the bombing of a Berlin nightclub (killing several U.S. soldiers) led to a significant military escalation in the Reagan administration's coercive diplomacy toward the Qaddafi regime. In retaliation to that act of state-sponsored terrorism, the United States carried out a large-scale attack (involving some one hundred aircraft) on Libyan air bases and air defense complexes, naval installations, military barracks, and Qaddafi's personal command center.[65] The military action was publicly presented as a response to unacceptable behavior: to punish the Qaddafi regime for its prior bad acts (culminating in the Berlin bombing) and to compel its cessation of support for terrorism.[66] Although the action was couched in terms of behavior change, the choice of targets pointed to the continuing strong interest in promoting regime change. The bombing of Qaddafi's command center sought to achieve what policy analysts refer to as regime "decapitation" by targeting the leadership.[67] The air strike on that facility, which doubled as Qaddafi's personal residence, was essentially an assassination attempt. Failing decapitation, the large-scale U.S. air raid in April 1986 offered the possibility of destabilizing the regime and precipitating a military coup to oust Qaddafi.

Operation El Dorado, the code name of the April 1986 air raid, had two unintended consequences. First, rather than precipitating a coup, it actually solidified Qaddafi's internal hold on power by allowing him to play the nationalist card to rally popular support against foreign intervention. And second, contrary to the Reagan administration's public claim that U.S. air strikes would deter the Qaddafi regime from future adventurism, the Libyan leader instead retaliated in December 1988, when a Libyan terrorist bomb brought down Pan Am flight 103 over Lockerbie, Scotland. Three years later, after the forensic trail had been traced back to Tripoli, the United States and Britain indicted two Libyan security officials for their role in the terrorist attack. Rejecting the Qaddafi regime's cosmetic offer to turn over the suspects to an international tribunal, the Security Council imposed multilateral sanctions banning all arms sales and air links to Libya, as well as the transfer of production technology critical to the Libyan energy sector, and freezing Libya's foreign financial holdings. In winning broad diplomatic support for multilateral sanctions against Libya, the George H. W. Bush administration succeeded where the Reagan administration had been rebuffed. Timing was a critical factor: the Lockerbie crisis unfolded in the United Nations in the wake of the 1991 Gulf War—a paradigmatic application of the UN principle of collective security against interstate aggression that the United States had successfully led.

The George H. W. Bush administration's drive to enlist other countries for multilateral sanctions was facilitated by its deemphasizing regime change as a policy objective. The focus on Qaddafi's egregious behavior contravening international norms, rather than on the ambitious goal of removing a regime from power, avoided the inherently contentious issue of state sovereignty, which might otherwise have produced diplomatic gridlock.

The strengthening of UN sanctions in November 1993 marked the high watermark of international efforts to compel the Qaddafi regime's compliance with Security Council resolutions mandating the Libyan government to turn over the Lockerbie suspects for trial. Over the next six years, the Clinton administration struggled to maintain collective pressure on Libya in the face of dissipating international support for multilateral sanctions.

Yet, by the late 1990s, an amalgam of forces created mutual incentives for the United States and Libya to break the diplomatic impasse over the Pan Am 103 bombing. The key determinant of change was in Tripoli, where Qaddafi's mounting domestic political and economic pressures (a consequence of the multilateral sanctions) created a strong motivation to end Libya's pariah status.

Qaddafi's Strategic Turnabout

The pressure on the Qaddafi regime generated by the effectiveness of UN sanctions was compounded by a downturn in the international oil market. Not only were prices depressed, but also the Libyan oil sector, starved of Western capital and technology, sustained a production decline from a peak of 3.3 million barrels a day in the late 1970s to an estimated 1.4 million barrels per day when UN sanctions were finally lifted.[68] The sharp fall in oil revenues in the 1990s undermined the tacit national social contract, dating to the mid-1970s, under which Qaddafi was essentially given carte blanche to pursue his radical foreign policy as long as the welfare state generously provided for a rapidly expanding population.[69] In the mid-1990s, the collapse of Libya's economy reportedly triggered an "extraordinary dispute" within the regime that pitted pragmatic technocrats against hard-liners.[70] For the technocrats, Qaddafi's radical activist foreign policy, which the hard-liners viewed as a source of domestic legitimacy, had become an expensive liability that was hindering Libya's economic development. By the late 1990s, Qaddafi, bowing to the "new realities," swung his power behind the pragmatists and even embraced globalization.[71] During the economic crisis, Qaddafi faced, and successfully put down, significant domestic challenges to his rule from elements of the military (which staged a failed coup in 1993) and dissident Islamic groups (such as the Muslim Brotherhood). In 1999, secret trilateral talks began between Libya, Britain, and the United States.[72] Qaddafi signaled his interest in normalizing relations with the outside world by expelling the Abu Nidal organization from Libya and endorsing the Palestinian-Israeli peace negotiations that the Clinton administration was energetically pursuing. The 9/11 attacks, which Qaddafi publicly condemned as "horrifying, destructive," afforded him the perfect opportunity to accelerate the process of political rehabilitation. Yet the settlement of the Pan Am 103 case offered only the permanent lifting of UN sanctions, not the full normalization of relations with the United

States that Qaddafi sought. That latter objective hinged on resolution of the WMD issue. The secret negotiations that had begun prior to 9/11 accelerated in its aftermath—particularly after the U.S.-led invasion of Iraq. They culminated in the surprising announcement in December 2003 from Washington, London, and Tripoli that Libya had agreed to terminate its WMD programs.

Qaddafi's strategic turnabout came only days after Saddam Hussein was pulled out of his "spider hole" by U.S. forces. Bush administration officials cited the timing as evidence that the "demonstration effect" of the Iraq war had been a key determinant of Libyan decision-making. Qaddafi reportedly told Italian prime minister Silvio Berlusconi, "I will do whatever the Americans want, because I saw what happened in Iraq, and I was afraid."[73] Yet an alternative explanation came from Qaddafi's son Seif, who stated that his father had made the decision after receiving an assurance that the United States was not plotting to overthrow his regime.[74] Seif, who was educated at the London School of Economics, also claimed that in return for Libya's WMD disarmament, the United States and Britain had agreed to help his country economically—and even militarily—by encouraging foreign investment and providing "access to sensitive technology," including "necessary defensive weapons." Undergirding these expanded relations, according to Seif, was a security guarantee: "They said we, the West, and international society will be responsible for the protection of Libya."[75]

The external pressure on the Qaddafi regime from the Iraq precedent was a necessary but not sufficient condition for Libya's WMD disarmament. The crux of the Libyan deal was the Bush administration's willingness to eschew the objective of regime change in Libya and instead offer a tacit assurance of regime survival. If the Bush administration had not made that U.S. intention clear, Qaddafi would have had no incentive to give up his WMD option. Indeed, regime change rhetoric and policies toward Libya in the wake of Iraq would have created a strong counterincentive for Qaddafi to *accelerate* development of his unconventional weapons arsenal to deter the United States.

In January 2004, a month after Qaddafi's surprise announcement, more than twenty-five tons of nuclear and ballistic missile components were airlifted from Libya to the United States. Inspectors began the complicated process of destroying Libya's stockpile of chemical agents and munitions, and Russia removed highly enriched uranium from Libya's Soviet-designed nuclear research reactor.[76] The Bush administration reciprocated by lifting sanctions to permit American commercial activities in Libya, establishing diplomatic liaison offices in Tripoli and Washington, and ending U.S. opposition to Libya's entry into the World Trade Organization.[77] An important indicator of Libya's political rehabilitation was the March 2004 visit of British prime minister Tony Blair to Tripoli for a face-to-face meeting with Qaddafi. In May 2006, the State Department removed Libya from its state sponsors-of-terrorism list and fully normalized diplomatic relations.

The reopening of the U.S. embassy in Tripoli was a tangible symbol that Libya had shed its rogue state status. But even as Libya came into compliance with the external behavioral norms related to terrorism and proliferation, democracy advocates urged the United States to press the Qaddafi regime to come into compliance with internal behavioral norms related to human rights.[78] The Libyan leader sought to reap the economic benefits (i.e., oil revenues) of integration while insulating the regime from political contagion. The pattern was evident, for example, when Prime Minister Shukri Muhammad Ghanem, whose proposed reforms had put him at odds with Qaddafi's business cronies, was sacked and replaced by a hard-liner, Baghdadi al-Mahmoudi.[79]

Condoleezza Rice's historic visit to Libya in September 2008, the first by a U.S. secretary of state since 1953, reflected the state of the bilateral relationship—and the two states' contrasting priorities. Secretary Rice emphasized the Qaddafi regime's new compliance with external behavior norms regarding terrorism and proliferation: "It demonstrates that when countries are prepared to make strategic changes in direction, the United States is prepared to respond." By contrast, Qaddafi told Libyans in a televised speech that improved relations were a way for both countries to leave each other alone.[80] The Libyan dictator made clear through words and action that the country's normalization of relations with the outside world was a necessary concession to economic exigency and would not lead to political liberalization at home.

The Obama administration was the first since Nixon's to inherit a relatively quiescent relationship with Libya. In September 2009, Qaddafi journeyed to New York to reclaim his place on the international stage with his first-ever address to the UN General Assembly. Introduced to the body as "the king of kings of Africa," he delivered a bizarre, rambling speech that defended the Afghan Taliban's vision of an Islamic emirate, called for an investigation of the assassinations of John F. Kennedy and Martin Luther King Jr., and offered to relocate the United Nations to Libya.[81] Although Qaddafi was becoming increasingly erratic, his regime had a four-decade record of survival and appeared to retain the repressive capabilities to ward off an internal challenge. That conventional wisdom was unexpectedly overturned by the great discontinuity of 2011—the "Arab Awakening."

Libya and the Arab Awakening

In mid-February 2011, on the heels of the deposition of Tunisian president Zine El Abidine Ben Ali and Egyptian president Hosni Mubarak, civil protests erupted in Benghazi in response to the Qaddafi regime's arrest of a prominent human-rights activist. Benghazi, Libya's second-largest city, was the epicenter of the anti-Qaddafi movement, but the unrest quickly spread to other cities, including Tripoli and Tobruk. In contrast to the non-violent changes of regime in Tunisia and Egypt, Qaddafi unleashed the Libyan military and security services to suppress the protests before they gained momentum. Qaddafi vowed to track down and kill protesters house by house, and the resulting loss of life—reportedly in the hundreds—provoked international condemnation.[82] U.S. declaratory policy escalated as events moved rapidly on the ground and Qaddafi's forces (including mercenaries from African countries) deserted Benghazi and most of Libya's eastern province of Cyrenaica. The State Department's initial expression of "grave concern" about the regime's crackdown was soon followed by calls from President Obama and Secretary Clinton for the Libyan dictator to relinquish power. The White House press spokesman, announcing that the United States had frozen the Libyan regime's assets, declared that Qaddafi's "legitimacy has been reduced to zero."[83] The Libyan opposition established a Transitional National Council, which France recognized as the legitimate government.

Significantly, by late February 2011, the hold of the Libyan opposition in the east was bolstered by the defection of some regime loyalists.[84] The Obama administration viewed the continued defection of the regime's core support groups as the quickest pathway to resolving the Libyan crisis. Qaddafi's grip on power ultimately rested not on the regular army, but rather on what the BBC characterized as "a murky network of paramilitary brigades, 'revolutionary committees' of trusted followers, tribal leaders and imported foreign mercenaries [primarily from Niger and Chad]."[85]

Qaddafi's use of Libyan aircraft to attack the opposition led Western governments to propose the establishment of a no-fly zone in Libya. But Secretary of Defense Robert Gates, overseeing a U.S. military already engaged in two wars, injected a note of hesitancy and reality by baldly laying out to a congressional committee what the establishment of a no-fly zone would entail: "Let's just call a spade a spade. A no-fly zone begins with an attack on Libya to destroy the air defenses. That's the way you do a no-fly zone. And then you can fly planes around the country and not worry about our guys being shot down. But that's the way it starts."[86]

With the Obama administration already struggling to wind down two inherited wars, views within the U.S. policy community were sharply divided on the wisdom of undertaking yet a third military intervention in the Muslim world. Proponents of direct U.S. involvement focused on the impending slaughter of civilians in Benghazi at the hands of counterattacking Qaddafi-loyalist forces and cited the "responsibility to protect" norm as the basis for a humanitarian intervention. This moral case was buttressed by the cold calculation that the Qaddafi regime was a "low-hanging fruit" ripe for toppling. Opponents of intervention argued that Libya was not a country of vital interest to the United States, that the establishment of a no-fly zone would prove insufficient to oust the Qaddafi regime and would inevitably lead to a push to introduce ground troops, and that too little was known about the nature of the Libyan resistance or the type of government it might establish if successful.[87] Criticism was also voiced of the December 2003 agreement that had stripped Qaddafi of his WMD capabilities but had left him flush with petrodollars to perpetuate his autocratic rule at home—to be left alone, as the Libyan dictator had candidly put it.[88]

President Obama set a high bar for U.S. participation in a military intervention in Libya. His conditions included the willingness of America's allies in the North Atlantic Treaty Organization (NATO) to take the military lead, political support from Libya's Arab neighbors, and an authorizing resolution from the Security Council. This approach was infelicitously described by a White House official as "leading from behind." An Arab League request for the imposition of a no-fly zone over Libya set the stage for a complicated Security Council debate. Britain, France, and the United States were prepared to undertake military action but insisted that Arab League states participate in military action (lest it appear that NATO was unilaterally attacking another Muslim state) and help bear the financial costs of the intervention. On March 17, the Security Council passed Resolution 1973 approving the establishment of a no-fly zone and authorizing "all necessary means" to protect civilians within Libya. The resolution also imposed an arms embargo on Libya (which prevented NATO from providing weapons to the rebels) and ruled out any possible introduction of foreign ground troops. Two days later, the United States and its NATO allies launched the largest military operation in the Middle East since the Iraq war. U.S. naval vessels sent successive volleys of Tomahawk cruise missiles to take down Libya's air defense system, and NATO aircraft halted the march of pro-Qaddafi forces on Benghazi.

From the outset of the Libyan intervention, the U.S. objective was ambiguous. Even though the White House had previously called Qaddafi illegitimate, the Security Council resolution had authorized the use of force as a humanitarian intervention only and had been deliberately silent about dealing with the Qaddafi regime. An explicit mention of regime change in the proposed resolution, which passed unanimously, would likely have generated opposition on sovereignty grounds from Russia, China, and other states on the Security Council. As the imposition of a no-fly zone began, Admiral Mike Mullen, chairman of the Joint Chiefs of Staff, set the mission squarely within the parameters of the Security Council resolution: "Certainly the goals of this campaign right now, again, are limited, and it isn't about seeing [Qaddafi] go. It's about supporting the United Nations resolution, which talked to limiting or eliminating his ability to kill his own people as well as support the humanitarian effort." When asked if the military mission could be accomplished with Qaddafi remaining in power, Admiral Mullen replied: "That's certainly potentially one outcome."[89]

In a televised address to the nation on March 28, Obama declared that the United States had intervened in Libya to prevent "a massacre that would have reverberated across the region and stained the conscience of the world." The president reiterated that the role of the United States would be "limited," with no deployment of U.S. ground troops. He pledged "our unique capabilities on the front end of the operation," and then a rapid "transfer [of] responsibility to our allies and partners." Finally, he addressed the question of regime change: "Of course, there is no question that Libya—and the world—will be better off with Qaddafi out of power. I, along with many other world leaders, have embraced that goal, and will actively pursue it through non-military means. But broadening our military mission to include regime change would be a mistake."[90] On April 14, in a joint newspaper article, Obama, British prime minister David Cameron, and French president Nicolas Sarkozy argued: "Our duty and mandate under UN Security Council Resolution 1973 is to protect civilians, and we are doing that. It is not to remove Qaddafi by force. But it is impossible to imagine a future Libya with Qaddafi in power. It is unthinkable that someone who has tried to massacre his own people can play a part in their future government."[91]

The core tension between the humanitarian and regime change missions persisted but was successfully managed by the Obama administration. At an international conference of NATO and Arab states convened in London on March 30, UN Secretary-General Ban Ki-moon did not demur as successive world leaders called on Qaddafi to relinquish power, despite the limited scope of the UN Security Council resolution.[92] Among the factors favorable to the anti-Qaddafi coalition was that, in contrast to the case of Iraq in 2003, neither Russia nor China viewed the prospective fall of the Qaddafi regime as a major threat to its strategic interests. Indeed, China, after initially voicing its long-standing general opposition to internal interference by outside powers, established contact with rebel forces and declared an interest in playing a "positive role" in rebuilding postwar Libya.[93] Russian opposition was limited to pro forma complaints that NATO was overstepping Security Resolution 1973 by pursuing the objective of regime change. South African president Jacob Zuma, whose government had supported Security Council Resolution 1973, similarly voiced concern that NATO airstrikes violated the "letter and spirit of the resolution" and were part of a "regime-change doctrine."[94]

By late March 2011, the Libyan rebel advance from Benghazi into the country's western province stalled in the face of stiffer resistance by pro-Qaddafi forces. The rebel leadership complained that NATO was providing inadequate close air support to its irregular ground forces, and the military impasse fueled speculation of a prolonged civil war whose outcome might lead to the division of Libya into two states. As NATO sought to regain momentum in April, President Obama approved the use of the highly effective Predator drones for the Libyan mission. In a significant escalation, NATO aircraft began to strike Qaddafi's personal compound, communication centers, and other nonmilitary targets essential to the regime's ability to survival.

The International Institute for Strategic Studies characterized NATO's air campaign as "a gradual and coercive approach" that was not designed to remove Qaddafi from power quickly, even though removal was the ultimate objective. NATO's air mission was divided between tactical strikes to protect rebel enclaves from Qaddafi's regular forces and those to destroy the regime's infrastructure of power.[95] In June, NATO augmented its firepower with the introduction of attack helicopters for close air support of the rebels in urban areas and bunker-busting bombs for attacks on Qaddafi's compound (with the clear aim of killing the Libyan dictator). Further increasing the effectiveness of the NATO air campaign was the deployment of special forces from Britain, France, Qatar, and the United Arab Emirates, who reportedly provided targeting information for the coalition aircrafts' precision-guided bombs and missiles. The effective "coordination of foreign air power with the actions of rebel forces" broke the military stalemate on the ground.[96] NATO's higher tempo of strikes on the regime's power base (i.e., the secret police and regular army units) both eroded its coercive capabilities for control and caused a steady stream of defections over to the rebel side by Libyan government ministers, diplomats, and army commanders.

In late July and August, rebel ground forces made significant gains in their progress toward Tripoli. With its air force grounded or destroyed, the Qaddafi regime fired Scud missiles from a military installation near Sirte, Qaddafi's hometown, to blunt the rebel advance, but the missiles came down in the desert, inflicting no casualties. When Qaddafi resorted to ballistic missiles, U.S. officials were concerned about the status of the Libyan chemical weapons that had been declared when Libya joined the Chemical Weapons Convention in 2004 but that had not yet been destroyed. The fear was that a desperate Qaddafi might use these weapons against the rebels, or that, amid the chaos, they might fall into the hands of terrorists.[97] The Obama administration warned the Qaddafi regime that the United States still held it accountable for Libya's international obligations, including the Chemical Weapons Convention.[98]

In mid-August, after rebel forces, backed by NATO aircraft, had completed their sweep of the Libyan capital's surrounding towns, came the decisive battle for Tripoli. On August 22–23, rebels poured into the city with little resistance except around Qaddafi's compound, and Tripoli fell. But the Libyan dictator had already escaped to his hometown of Sirte, where he made his final stand. After a two-month siege, Qaddafi was killed by rebel fighters on October 20. A French aircraft and a U.S. drone had attacked his convoy of vehicles attempting to flee the city. Videos of the death (or, more accurately, summary execution) of the "king of kings" were widely circulated by the international media and on the Internet. On October 23, the Transitional National Council's leadership held a mass rally in "Martyr's Square" (the former "Green Square") in Tripoli, declaring the council's intent to hold elections and establish a new government based on Islamic tenets. Three days later, a unanimous vote by the Security Council ending its authorization of the use of force in Libya marked the conclusion of the country's eight-month civil war and the beginning of an uncertain postwar era. Qaddafi's forty-two-year rule left a ruinous legacy of squandered wealth and a hollowed state essentially devoid of functioning institutions.

Assessment and Implications

The preceding chapter focused on four broad pathways by which revolutionary powers threatening international order and outlaw states egregiously violating the system's norms can be integrated into the community of nations. A comparative analysis across cases (ranging from Nazi Germany and the Soviet Union to Idi Amin's Uganda and Ceauşescu's Romania) yielded conditional generalizations that inform this chapter's discussion of developing a repertoire of differentiated strategies, each geared to the particularities of the outlier state. The strategies—whether to contain, engage, or change—are premised on concepts of societal change that should flow from rigorous target state analysis (the qualitative method laid out in the initial section of this chapter). Policy-makers must distinguish between regime-specific and regime-generic factors and carefully weigh the relative salience of each factor. Failure to articulate and thoroughly examine the key threshold assumptions about the target state's character and plausible agents of societal change will yield a flawed assessment. The evolution of U.S. strategies toward Iraq and Libya was illustrative of this dynamic. The lessons and policy implications deriving from these cases vis-à-vis other outlier states fall under the following categories (which parallel those in the case analyses in Chapter 2): sovereignty and intervention, leadership and intra-elite bargaining, and conditionality and compliance.

Sovereignty and Intervention

State sovereignty, the cardinal principle of international relations, figured centrally as an issue in the UN debates preceding the U.S.-led and U.S.-assisted military interventions in Iraq and Libya, respectively.

In Iraq, in early 2003, the George W. Bush administration argued that only a change of regime—in essence, the negation of Iraqi sovereignty through the removal of Saddam—could bring that country into compliance with Security Council resolutions (passed in the wake of the 1991 Gulf War) mandating WMD disarmament. Administration officials viewed Iraq through the prism of 9/11, which produced a radical shift in both the definition of threat (the nexus of terrorism and proliferation, focused on unpredictable rogue states and undeterrable terrorist groups, such as Al Qaeda) and the recasting of U.S. strategy (from containment and deterrence to a new emphasis on military preemption and regime change). In short, a pre-9/11 containment strategy of keeping Saddam in his box would no longer suffice in a post-9/11 world. When the United States invaded Iraq without the Security Council's legitimizing approval, it acted outside the institutional structure within which American power had been embedded since World War II. As political scientist John Ikenberry has argued, that embedded quality (making U.S. power more legitimate and less threatening to other states) has been key to America's international success.[99] For many in the international community, leaving Saddam Hussein in power was seemingly preferable to the precedent that would be set by the United States in overthrowing the Iraqi regime. The opposition of Russia and China was also the product of strategic calculation to check the United States. The Bush administration characterized Iraq as a demonstration conflict: as one official put it, "Iraq is not just about Iraq.... It is of a type."[100] But the administration, particularly after the triumphalism following the fall of Baghdad gave way to an intractable insurgency, was unable to apply the Iraq precedent—coerced nonproliferation through regime change—in the nuclear crises with North Korea and Iran.

In Libya, in December 2003, an alternative nonproliferation model to that of Iraq emerged when Qaddafi acceded to verifiable WMD disarmament. The deal turned on the tacit but clear security assurance that the Bush administration provided the Libyan regime. Without such a pledge of nonintervention, Qaddafi would have had no incentive to relinquish his unconventional arsenal. The Bush administration, unable to replicate the Iraq precedent, was unwilling to offer North Korea and Iran the Libya deal by making clear that the U.S. objective was a change not of regime. Clarifying that mixed message, the Obama administration offered North Korea and Iran a structured choice to induce or compel these outlier states to come into compliance with nonproliferation norms. If the question for Bush was whether he would "take yes for an answer," the question for Obama, after North Korea and Iran rejected his overtures, was whether he would "take no for answer."

In Libya, in 2011, the U.S.-assisted overthrow of the Qaddafi regime set another important precedent. The Security Council authorized the intervention on humanitarian grounds and was calculatedly silent on the question of regime change so as not to create a divisive split on the council, as in 2003.

A UN-authorized intervention that began under a humanitarian rationale morphed within weeks into an overt regime change mission on NATO's part. The argument advanced by the Western powers spearheading the military action was essentially that only the removal of the Libyan dictator could ensure the achievement of the resolution's humanitarian objective. Russia and China issued pro forma objections to this mission creep but ultimately acquiesced. Neither power saw ousting Qaddafi as a major challenge to its strategic interests, but Moscow did make explicit that Libya did not set a precedent applicable to other cases, notably Syria. Russian foreign minister Sergei Lavrov bluntly declared, "We won't let Syria become a second Libya." Nor did Washington depict the U.S.-assisted regime change in Libya as a replicable precedent that was "of a type," as had been done with Iraq in 2003.

Leadership and Intra-elite Bargaining

Few regimes have exhibited the durability and longevity of Saddam Hussein in Iraq (with twenty-four years as paramount leader) and Qaddafi in Libya (with a record-breaking forty-two years). During these years marked by an extraordinary continuity of rule, U.S. strategy shifted in response to differing assessments of each target state and its societal trajectory.

Iraq was *engaged* by the Reagan administration in the 1980s to bolster it as a regional counterweight to Khomeini's Iran and then briefly by the George H. W. Bush administration after the Iran-Iraq War on the assumption that Saddam would focus on domestic reconstruction and would be prepared to play a more constructive role in the region. Iraq was *contained* in the 1990s after the Bush administration did not march on Baghdad during the Gulf War or tangibly support the Shiite and Kurdish uprisings against Saddam's rule in its aftermath. The George H. W. Bush administration viewed containment as part of a squeeze strategy that would press the regime to the breaking point.

Yet a Ceauşescu-style regime change in which Saddam's own inner circle would launch a coup never materialized. The key assumption (a surmise not evidently based on any hard intelligence about fissures within the regime) was that a humiliated Saddam, whose army had been forcibly expelled from Kuwait and whose capital had been bombed by coalition air forces, was vulnerable. From an Iraqi perspective, however, Saddam was able to depict himself as a strong Arab nationalist leader standing up to predatory outside powers; his internal security apparatus remained sufficiently intact to fend off a potential coup. As the immediate postwar prospect of a coup against Saddam faded, the concept of societal change shifted: punitive general sanctions imposed by the Security Council would put pressure on the Iraqi populace that would be transmitted to the leadership. In turn, that pressure would generate either the regime's compliance with the WMD disarmament requirements of Security Council Resolution 687 or a level of popular discontent that could undermine Saddam's grip on power. But Saddam was able to circumvent sanctions and thereby insulate his core constituencies from their consequences. Because sanctions did not threaten elite interests, they did not function (in Jentleson's metaphor) as "'transmission belts' carrying forward the coercive pressure on the regime."[101] After September 11, 2001, U.S. strategy shifted from containing regimes to *changing regimes* (on the assumption that these states' threatening behavior arose from the very character of their ruling regimes). The shift was driven by the redefinition of threat in response to the 9/11 terrorist attacks but was also, with respect to Iraq, a reflection of the prevailing view that no organic, internal agent of change was likely to dislodge the seemingly coup-proof Saddam Hussein regime.

In Libya, in 2011, the U.S.-assisted military intervention sought not only to avert a humanitarian calamity, but also to affect the calculus of decision of the Qaddafi regime's core constituencies (such as the security services, the regular army, business oligarchs, and key tribes). NATO airpower (operating with special forces on the ground to direct targeting in support of the anti-Qaddafi insurgents) created a military tipping point that produced a stream of political defections by former regime loyalists to the rebel side.

Iraq and Libya present contrasting precedents. In Iraq, regime change was accomplished through external agency (a military invasion by foreign forces) when the prospect for internal agency (a coup from within Saddam's inner circle or a successful Shiite and Kurdish uprising) to bring about societal change was remote. That it was accomplished through external agency was inherently controversial (witness the contentious Security Council debate in 2003) on sovereignty grounds. In Libya, regime change was accomplished through internal agency with external assistance. The precipitants of regime change (the rebel uprising that began in Benghazi) were indigenous and organic. But it was nonetheless an unexpected discontinuity that occurred under the catalyzing impact of the "Arab Awakening" in the broader Middle East region. NATO's military role in Libya—limited but decisive—was legitimized by the anti-Qaddafi insurgents and the Arab

League. But even as the United Nations gave its legitimizing imprimatur to military action, the Security Council omitted any reference to regime change in its authorizing resolution in deference to the principle of state sovereignty.

Conditionality and Compliance

Saddam Hussein's Iraq and Qaddafi's Libya were both part of the core group of countries designated as "rogue states." That status was rooted in conduct that violated important external behavioral norms with respect to proliferation and terrorism. Although these states also violated internal behavioral norms with respect to human rights, their conduct with external consequences (i.e., their WMD capabilities and sponsorship of terrorism) commanded Washington's attention.

In Iraq, the George W. Bush administration implemented not only a strategy of coercive nonproliferation through regime change, but also one of coercive democratization under the rubric of its "freedom agenda." The administration, whose officials often likened Saddam's regime to the Nazis, embarked on a Germany-style occupation, but without a Germany-sized force. The conditions (discussed in Chapter 2) that set the Federal Republic of Germany on a pathway into the community of nations (through democratization and reintegration) were present neither within Iraq nor among its neighboring states in the Middle East.[102]

Libya came into compliance with external behavioral norms through the resolution of the Lockerbie bombing case in the late 1990s and the WMD disarmament agreement of 2003. These agreements, however, did not address the Qaddafi regime's atrocious human rights record—that is, its violations of internal behavioral norms. In the aftermath of the December 2003 agreement, what concept of societal change underlay the Bush administration's strategy toward Libya? Although it was never explicitly articulated, official statements suggested that the underlying concept was evolutionary regime change through engagement. Under this optimistic scenario, Libya's increased integration into the global economy would create domestic constituencies for economic reform. In turn, the anticipated expansion of economic links with the outside world would have major implications for the political sphere by empowering technocrats and an entrepreneurial middle class.

Instead, contrary to that hopeful political scenario, Qaddafi was able to inoculate his ruling system from the political contagion that might occur through increased economic integration (primarily oil exports). Again, Qaddafi's characterization of the WMD agreement between the United States and Libya as "a way for both countries to leave each other alone" was emblematic of his approach to improved relations with the outside world. After the WMD agreement, Libya rejoined the community of nations, but the United States made no serious effort to link Libya's increased foreign economic ties to improvements in the Qaddafi regime's domestic conduct. In contrast to the experiences in Eastern Europe and Latin America, the United States and the European Union attached no political conditionality to their expanded economic relations with the Qaddafi regime. The Libyan case highlights the challenge that U.S. policy-makers face with other outlier states—Iran and North Korea—in addressing breaches of external behavioral norms (terrorism and proliferation) without ignoring egregious violations of internal behavioral norms (human rights).

Chapter 4

Nuclear Outliers

President Barack Obama has characterized Iran and North Korea as nuclear "outliers"—states that have violated or abrogated their commitment to the nuclear Nonproliferation Treaty (NPT).[1] Their noncompliance has raised the dark prospect of the international system's approaching a nuclear "tipping point" in which weapons acquisition by Iran and North Korea could trigger a cascade of proliferation by causing other states to reassess their non-nuclear status.[2] More ominous still is the specter raised by the nexus of proliferation and terrorism. Since 9/11, a driving concern of U.S. national security—indeed, the scenario central to the George W. Bush administration's case for preventive war against Iraq—has been the threat of an outlier state's either transferring or selling a nuclear device to a terrorist group that aspires to inflict a mass-casualty attack on the West. The United States may assert its commitment to the norm of nonproliferation, but in practice, Washington focuses (with reason) on adversarial proliferators—the outliers who combine nuclear capabilities with hostile intent.

But what of nuclear-armed Israel, India, and Pakistan? These states never accepted the NPT bargain and exercised their sovereign right not to join the treaty. From a U.S. national security perspective, none falls under the category of "adversarial proliferator." Of the three, however, the country of increasing proliferation concern is Pakistan, which the Bush administration designated as a "major non-NATO ally" in the "war on terrorism."[3] In contrast to Iran and North Korea, the perceived threat emanating from Pakistan is not that the Islamabad government would purposefully transfer a nuclear weapon to a terrorist group. Rather, a security breach within Pakistan's program (facilitated, in the most widely discussed scenario, by Islamic extremists who had infiltrated the country's nuclear establishment) could result in the inadvertent leakage of a weapon to a terrorist group. Although leakage from Pakistan (or Russia) is the more likely pathway of terrorist acquisition, the transfer scenario involving Iran or North Korea has dominated the U.S. strategic debate precisely because both countries are adversarial proliferators. This chapter addresses the efforts by North Korea and Iran to acquire nuclear weapons and the parallel efforts by the United States and others to thwart their ambitions. The analyses of these cases are framed within an initial discussion of proliferation dynamics (conditions of nuclear restraint and proliferation), as well as of terrorist acquisition of a weapon through the deliberate transfer from a state (because this is the scenario of concern with particular reference to North Korea and Iran in the post-9/11 era).

The ongoing nuclear disputes with Iran and North Korea are playing out against the backdrop of the important precedents set in 2003: coercive nonproliferation through a change *of* regime in Iraq and cooperative nonproliferation through a change *within* a regime in Libya. Central to the Libyan agreement was a tacit but clear assurance of regime security — that is, a pledge of nonintervention in return for the verified rollback of Libya's nuclear program. With Iran and North Korea, however, the Bush administration was caught between precedents; it was neither willing to offer the security assurance that sealed the Libyan deal nor able to replicate the Iraq model because of profound constraints on the military option.

The Obama administration's eschewal of the term "rogue state" in favor of "outlier" was calculated, a deliberate signal to Iran and North Korea that political rehabilitation was possible if their ruling regimes change course and come into compliance with international norms.[4] President Obama laid out the alternative if not: "We need real and immediate consequences for countries caught breaking the rules or trying to leave the treaty without cause."[5]

Even as Washington seeks to affect the strategic calculus of Iran and North Korea, the dilemma is that the outliers view the prospect of increased integration into the community of nations as a threat to regime stability, just as they view their nuclear programs—whether a weapon, hedge, or bargaining chip—as integral to regime survival. U.S. policy can realistically aim to mitigate, not eliminate, the threat posed by these adversarial proliferators.

Proliferation Dynamics and U.S. Policy

Regime Type versus Regime Intention

The nine states (the United States, Russia, Britain, France, China, India, Pakistan, Israel, and North Korea) that have "gone nuclear," as well as those seeking to acquire nuclear weapons, represent the full range of regime type—democratic, authoritarian, and military. Democratization can increase political transparency and accountability as well as facilitate open debate and scrutiny of motivation, but it will not, per se, restrain proliferation. Indeed, a majority of the states in the nuclear club are established democracies. The diversity of political systems among nuclear weapon states underscores that regime intention, not regime type, is the critical proliferation indicator.[6]

The extensive literature on nonproliferation highlights a range of domestic and international or systemic factors that have led states to abstain from or acquire nuclear weapons. President John F. Kennedy's famous nightmare vision of a world of thirty states with nuclear weapons by the 1970s, or other predictions of an impending proliferation cascade, did not come to pass.[7] For each state facing that choice, the strategic calculus has been highly context dependent. During the Cold War, the structure of bipolarity inhibited proliferation: the United States and the Soviet Union implemented strategies of extended deterrence within their competing alliance systems to assuage the security concerns of their smaller allies. For that reason, the North Atlantic Treaty Organization (NATO), which institutionalized the extended deterrent commitment of the United States, has been called one of the most effective nonproliferation instruments in history.

Nuclear abstinence and voluntary reversal have also been attributed to the combination of U.S. pressure in tandem with security guarantees (Taiwan, South Korea); transformations in civil-military relations (Brazil, Argentina); domestic political changes precipitated by a transformation of the international environment (Ukraine, South Africa); and the NPT's normative constraint on nuclear acquisition.[8] Of particular salience to this study of the outliers is political scientist Etel Solingen's research finding that "states [such as Japan, South Korea, and Taiwan] whose leaders or ruling coalitions advocate integration in the global economy ... have incentives to avoid the political, economic, reputational, and opportunity costs of acquiring nuclear weapons ... [whereas]

leaders and ruling coalitions rejecting internationalization incur fewer such costs and have greater incentives to exploit nuclear weapons as tools in nationalist platforms of political competition and for staying in power."[9] The nuclear issue is inextricably linked to the broader question of societal evolution. For the outliers, the perception of international integration as a threat to regime survival can strongly influence their nuclear intentions.

In developing effective nonproliferation strategies toward the outliers, distinguishing between regime-specific and regime-generic factors is essential. Was Iraq's nuclear program purely the manifestation of Saddam Hussein's megalomania? Or were these sources rooted deeper in the country's "strategic personality"—the long-term geographic, historical, and cultural forces that uniquely shape each state's worldview and calculus of decision-making—which would have motivated an Iraqi regime of whatever political character to pursue the nuclear option?[10] The 9/11 terrorist attacks recast the question of regime type. A state's proliferation motivations may be regime generic, but perceptions of that state as a threat by other states are regime specific. President George W. Bush's declaration that the threat posed by the states in the "axis of evil" derived from "their [ruling regime's] true nature" led to his administration's shift from a strategy of containment to one of regime change after 9/11.[11]

The Nexus of Proliferation and Terrorism

The mass-casualty terrorist attacks on September 11, 2001, overturned the old orthodoxy captured in terrorism expert Brian Jenkins's classic formulation from the mid-1970s: "Terrorists want a lot of people watching and a lot of people listening and not a lot of people dead."[12] Since 9/11, the consensus view across the American political spectrum is that the gravest potential threat to the U.S. homeland is a nuclear weapon falling into the hands of a terrorist group such as Al Qaeda. That the primary countries of proliferation concern (Iran, Iraq, Libya, Syria, and North Korea) were also designated state sponsors of terrorism by the U.S. Department of State reinforced the perception of a new nexus of proliferation and terrorism. Although a mass-casualty attack using conventional means (such as hijacked aircraft or truck bombs) is far more probable, the less likely but more consequential scenario of a nuclear 9/11 has dominated the U.S. strategic debate.

Pathways to Nuclear Acquisition

The two pathways by which a terrorist group could acquire a nuclear weapon are *transfer*, the deliberate handoff of a weapon from a state, and *leakage*, an unauthorized transfer or theft of a weapon from an inadequately secured site.[13] The transfer scenario undergirded the "nexus" concept and was central to the Bush administration's urgent case for preventive war to topple the Saddam Hussein regime, which was then accused—contrary to the assessment of the Central Intelligence Agency (CIA)—of having had direct links to Al Qaeda. The commonly attributed motivation for a "rogue regime" to hand off a nuclear weapon or technology to a terrorist group is a convergence of strategic interest between them. Yet even when a state-sponsorship link exists, as between Iran and Hizbollah, major constraints exert a powerful deterrent effect. For the transferring state, such an illicit transfer, if discovered, would run the extraordinary risk of a regime-terminating U.S. retaliatory response.

The only strategic interest that could plausibly justify the risk of a state-to-nonstate transfer would be regime survival itself. Of particular relevance to this issue is the controversial National Intelligence Estimate (NIE) of October 2002 on Iraq, which concluded that Saddam Hussein, "if sufficiently desperate ... might decide that the extreme step of assisting the Islamist terrorists in conducting a [weapons of mass destruction, or WMD] attack against the United States would be his last chance to exact vengeance by taking a large number of victims with him."[14] Ironically, the course on which the Bush administration was about to embark was the very scenario in which a "desperate" Saddam Hussein would most plausibly hand off unconventional capabilities to a terrorist group.

Another possible motivation for WMD transfer to a nonstate actor, cited with respect to impoverished North Korea, is economic. North Korea's status as an economic basket case with an advanced nuclear weapons program creates a chilling conjunction of dire need and dangerous capabilities. Past experience makes black-market sales a cause of concern, since the Kim Jong Il regime relied on illicit activities—from passing counterfeit money to selling drugs and ballistic missiles—to maintain power. North Korea has engaged in covert nuclear commerce on the state-to-state level: with Syria, by providing a prototype nuclear reactor that Israel bombed in September 2007, and with Burma, where suspicions of nuclear cooperation have prompted the Obama administration to express growing concern.[15] As a former U.S. official warned, a desperate, economically destitute North Korea "could be willing to sell anything [to anyone] if the price is right."

Although the deliberate transfer scenario focused on Iran and North Korea has dominated the post-9/11 security debate, the more likely route by which terrorists might gain access to nuclear or other WMD capabilities would be through unintended leakage of dangerous materials and technologies from inadequately secured sites. This acute concern centers primarily on Russia (which has an enormous legacy nuclear force and infrastructure from the Cold War) and Pakistan (which is rapidly expanding its nuclear arsenal and is poised to overtake Britain as the world's fifth-largest nuclear power, behind the United States, Russia, China, and France). Moreover, with China's announced plan to provide two civilian nuclear power reactors to Pakistan, the scope of the potential leakage problem will expand in tandem with Pakistan's increased production of fissile material.[16] In 2004, the existence of a long-suspected nuclear smuggling ring headed by Abdul Qadeer Khan, the so-called father of Pakistan's nuclear weapons program, was publicly confirmed. In a tearful confession on Pakistani television, Khan stated that his network had transferred nuclear components to Iran, Libya, and North Korea over a fifteen-year period but that the government had not authorized these illicit activities.[17]

In addition to the leakage of sensitive technologies from the Khan network to unpredictable states, another highly disturbing development was a reported meeting of Pakistani nuclear scientists with Osama bin Laden only weeks before 9/11. Supporters of the Taliban's ultraorthodox version of Islamic rule and jihadist causes, the scientists expressed the belief that Pakistan's nuclear capability is "the property of the whole Muslim community."[18] The episode underscored Al Qaeda's driving intention to carry out a mass-casualty attack using still more powerful unconventional weapons.

The Islamabad government responded to the embarrassing revelations about the Khan network by instituting additional measures to ensure the physical security of the country's nuclear stockpile against theft and unauthorized use. When questioned about the threat of Pakistani nuclear weapons falling into the hands of the Taliban or Al Qaeda, President Obama expressed confidence that "we can make sure that Pakistan's nuclear arsenal is secure, primarily ... because the Pakistani army ... recognizes the hazards of those weapons falling into the wrong hands. We've got strong military-to-military consultation and cooperation."[19] That assurance notwithstanding, Pakistan expert Stephen Cohen warned that the system of nuclear safeguards "could be circumvented in a determined conspiracy."[20]

Deterring Nuclear Terrorism

The principal routes to nuclear acquisition by a terrorist group—transfer and leakage—have been countered, respectively, by updated variants of traditional deterrence: deterrence by punishment and deterrence by denial.[21]

Although the transfer scenario drove the U.S. security debate after 9/11, the Bush administration did not issue a deterrent threat until the North Korean nuclear test in October 2006. As early as the collapse of the Agreed Framework in 2003, President Bush had warned North Korea that its efforts to acquire nuclear weapons would "not be tolerated."[22] Nonetheless, North Korea greatly augmented its stock of weapons-grade fissile material by separating plutonium from its Yongbyon reactor's spent fuel rods. Only after North Korea actually conducted a test in 2006 and became a self-proclaimed nuclear weapons state did President Bush enunciate a policy of deterrence by punishment: "The transfer of nuclear weapons or material by North Korea to states or non-state entities would be considered a grave threat to the United States, and we would hold North Korea *fully accountable* for the consequences of such action."[23] Although Bush's statement specifically referenced North Korea, the administration subsequently broadened that formulation into a general policy.[24] Yet the difficulty of enforcing red lines was evidenced in 2007, months after the North Korean nuclear test and the Bush administration's deterrent threat, when Pyongyang conducted a state-to-state transfer with Syria by providing a prototype nuclear reactor. And the Bush administration did nothing.

The Obama administration's Nuclear Posture Review of 2010 included a verbatim repetition of the Bush policy on transfer: "renewing the U.S. commitment to hold fully accountable any state, terrorist group, or other non-state actor that supports or enables terrorist efforts to obtain or use weapons of mass destruction, whether by facilitating, financing, or providing expertise or safe haven for such efforts."[25] But what precisely does "fully accountable" mean in practice? To the dismay of arms control proponents who hold that the sole purpose of nuclear weapons should be to deter other states' nuclear weapons, the Obama administration's calculated ambiguity left open "the option of using nuclear weapons against foes that might threaten the United States with biological or chemical weapons or transfer nuclear material to terrorists."[26] An alternative to calculated ambiguity would address the post-9/11 concerns about North Korea and Iran by establishing an explicit red line: the deliberate transfer of WMD capabilities by a state to a nonstate actor could trigger a non-nuclear, regime-changing response from the United States. Such a stance, which goes beyond current U.S. declaratory policy, could prove an effective form of deterrence by punishment. This policy would be pursued in tandem with, not as an alternative to, international efforts to prevent hostile proliferators from acquiring nuclear and other WMD capabilities in the first place.

The vast majority of work done in the nonproliferation area to counter nuclear terrorism falls under the rubric of deterrence by denial. This variant of deterrance covers a wide range of activities: export controls to limit access to technology; physical security at sensitive sites to lock down fissile material to prevent illicit diversion (an objective pioneered through the U.S. Cooperative Threat Reduction program, which the Obama administration has proposed expanding to regions beyond its original focus on the former Soviet Union); and the interdiction of contraband cargoes through the multinational Proliferation Security Initiative to prevent the trafficking of WMD technologies.

A highly contentious issue relating to nuclear leakage is whether, as with transfer, potentially negligent states such as Pakistan should be held fully accountable. Technical advances in the area of nuclear attribution will increasingly permit experts to determine the source of fissile material should an attack occur. Toward that goal, the Bush administration established the National Technical Nuclear Forensics Center within the Department of Homeland Security in 2006. According to this unit's mission statement, "Nuclear forensics may support attribution efforts that serve to bolster U.S. defenses against nuclear threats, across a wide spectrum, by *encouraging* nations to ensure the security of their nuclear and radiological materials or weapons to help prevent unwitting transfers to third parties through loss of control."[27]

But should states be encouraged or threatened to get them to safeguard nuclear materials? A highly controversial proposal would extend the deterrent threat to these countries by enunciating a policy of "expanded deterrence" under which the country of origin of the fissile material used in a nuclear terrorist strike on the U.S. homeland would be held responsible.[28] Yet despite improving attribution capabilities, the United States might be unable to determine the source of the material after an attack and would not want to retaliate against a negligent state such as Russia, which has a large nuclear weapons stockpile of its own. Opponents of "expanded deterrence" hold that "threatening retaliation against countries like Russia and Pakistan in response to terrorist attacks stemming from lax security practices is unwise. It undercuts efforts to work cooperatively with those states to improve their nuclear security, dissuades [them] from informing others if they discover that their nuclear weapons or materials [have been] stolen, [thereby] undermining any efforts to recover them, and makes it difficult to work with [them] in the aftermath of an attack to prevent further detonations."[29]

Yet a calculatedly ambiguous deterrent threat—such as the formulation, "in the event of a nuclear attack, the country of origin will be taken into account in determining the U.S. response"—would not commit the United States to a retaliatory response against the country of origin. The aim would be to compel countries that need to improve fissile material security to do more to deny terrorists access to nuclear and other WMD capabilities. The deterrent threat would complement the offer of political and economic inducements to these states to implement effective safeguard programs. In short, the fear of deterrence by punishment could lead countries that are the potential sources of nuclear leakage to implement more effective strategies of deterrence by denial.

To counter the threat of nuclear leakage from Pakistan, the United States has implemented a policy of deterrence by denial in the country through a $100 million program to secure Pakistan's nuclear laboratories and weapons (e.g., by separating warheads from triggers and missiles). Yet U.S. officials remain concerned about scientists who support radical Islamic causes infiltrating Pakistan's nuclear establishment and, more broadly, about the remote (but not unthinkable) possibility of an acute regime-threatening political crisis during which nuclear security is breached and a warhead falls into the hands of Islamic extremists.[30] Indeed, the Pakistanis—particularly in the aftermath of the unilateral U.S. military strike on Osama bin Laden's compound in Abbottabad that violated Pakistani sovereignty—perceive a similar U.S. commando threat to their nuclear arsenal. Hence, in a statement to parliament after the bin Laden raid, Pakistani prime minister Yusuf Raza Gilani warned, "Any attack against Pakistan's *strategic assets* [code for the country's nuclear arsenal] whether overt or covert will find a matching response. Pakistan reserves the right to retaliate with full force."[31] Gilani's use of that speech to also reaffirm Pakistan's strategic relationship with the United States is a reflection of the political tension inherent in the relationship. The prognosis is that U.S. administrations will pursue deterrence by denial through continued engagement with the Islamabad government, even as Washington and Islamabad view each other as both partners and threats.

Since 9/11, the Cold War concept of deterrence has been retooled to address the threats of a new era. Effective strategies on the state level to prevent nuclear transfer or leakage will go far in countering nonstate threats. The outliers—North Korea and Iran—will continue to command Washington's attention because of their status as adversarial proliferators and fear that their nuclear capabilities could become a pathway to terrorist acquisition.

North Korea: A Failed State with Nuclear Weapons

North Korea defies the neat typology of states that American officials have used since the end of the Cold War. The Democratic People's Republic of Korea (DPRK) is a "failed state," where endemic crop failures have precipitated famine and chronic fuel shortages have meant that the lights are literally out in the country. Yet North Korea, which is unpredictably aggressive and has active WMD programs, is a charter member of the countries that the United States has designated as rogue states.

The perverse incongruity of nuclear weapons and mass starvation is emblematic of the challenge posed by North Korea. The acquisition of "the bomb" by a totalitarian regime unable to feed its own people may give the lie to conventional wisdom that nuclear weapons confer prestige. But Pyongyang's possession of a nuclear arsenal (estimated at a dozen weapons by U.S. intelligence) ensures that the Kim family regime cannot be ignored. North Korea rises to the top of the U.S. foreign policy agenda not because it is a human rights pariah, but because it is a nuclear proliferator hostile to the United States and its East Asian allies. The nexus of nuclear weapons and impoverishment has raised the specter of the cash-starved Kim family regime's selling a nuclear weapon to another irresponsible state, or even a terrorist group.

Since the late 1980s, U.S. efforts to constrain North Korea's nuclear ambitions have focused primarily on blocking its access to the fissile material necessary for weapons fabrication. In Washington, the danger posed by North Korea's acquisition of weapons-grade fissile material under the guise of a civilian nuclear energy program created an imperative for diplomacy in the absence of a viable military option. The controversial Agreed Framework of October 1994, which the Clinton administration negotiated, froze activity at North Korea's nuclear complex.[32] However, the agreement collapsed eight years later, in October 2002, after the George W. Bush administration charged North Korea with pursuing a covert parallel uranium enrichment program to produce weapons-grade fissile material.

The Bush administration sent a mixed message as to whether the U.S. objective was to change North Korean conduct or to topple the Kim Jong Il regime. The Obama administration dropped its predecessor's regime change rhetoric and offered the Kim Jong Il regime a structured "choice" to come into compliance with international nonproliferation norms, but by then the administration faced a North Korea that had already withdrawn from the NPT and conducted threshold-crossing nuclear weapons tests in 2006 and 2009.

The North Korean nuclear crisis is embedded in the broader issue of regime survival. Although the privations of North Korean society have led to periodic predictions of regime collapse, the Kim family regime has proved remarkably resilient. The dilemma is that the regime change and proliferation timelines are not in sync. Although the threat posed by North Korea derives from the character of its regime, U.S. policy-makers cannot wait for an indeterminate process of regime change to play out.

North Korea's status as a failed state generates significant pressure on the regime to expand economic contact with the outside world to alleviate the country's plight. The nuclear weapons program is an impediment to normalization, but it is also the Kim Jong Un regime's only source of negotiating leverage. Since the 1980s, Pyongyang has repeatedly played its sole diplomatic bargaining chip in tandem with military brinkmanship (dangerously manifested in the North's unprovoked sinking of the South Korean naval vessel *Cheonan* in March 2010 and its shelling of the South Korean island of Yeonpyeong in November 2010). A foreign diplomat based in South Korea succinctly captured the consistent rationale underlying this erratic pattern of behavior: "Everything North Korea does, whether making peace or making threats, has a single goal: to sustain the regime."[33]

U.S. Policy toward North Korea

The Cold War Era

In the wake of World War II, the thirty-eighth parallel line separating Soviet and U.S. occupation forces became the official political demarcation between North and South Korea. With the rival north and south governments claiming sovereignty over the entire Korean Peninsula, the structure of this Cold War conflict was set.[34] North Korea's so-called Great Leader, Kim Il Sung, emboldened by a favorable balance of power after the 1949 withdrawal of U.S. forces, launched a surprise offensive in June 1950, after receiving approval from Joseph Stalin to "liberate" the south.[35] The Korean War was waged under the shadow of U.S. nuclear weapons: President Harry Truman gave "active consideration" to their use, and President Dwight Eisenhower's subsequent threatening ambiguity is credited by diplomatic historians as a major factor (along with the death of Stalin) influencing North Korea's acceptance of a cease-fire along the thirty-eighth parallel in mid-1953.[36] After the armistice, which remains in place today in the absence of a formal peace treaty, the United States retained troops in South Korea and deployed tactical nuclear weapons to deter the resumption of hostilities.

Despite the deterrent presence of U.S. nuclear and conventional capabilities on the Korean Peninsula, the Kim Il Sung regime engaged in covert operations and subversion against the Republic of Korea (ROK), including an audacious plot to assassinate the South Korean president in 1968. Kim also conducted risky brinkmanship with the United States directly: in January 1968, North Korean patrol boats attacked and seized the USS *Pueblo*, an intelligence-gathering ship, in international waters, and in April 1969, a North Korean MiG fighter shot down an unarmed U.S. reconnaissance aircraft flying in international airspace along the North Korean coast. The Johnson and Nixon administrations, already mired in Vietnam, refrained from strong military responses out of concern that retaliation commensurate with the provocations could inadvertently escalate to general war on the Korean Peninsula.[37]

North Korea's nuclear program was launched in 1964, when the Kim Il Sung regime established a nuclear facility at Yongbyon (sixty miles from Pyongyang) with a small research reactor provided by the Soviet Union.[38] In 1986, North Korea completed an indigenously engineered five-megawatt nuclear reactor at Yongbyon that was well suited to the DPRK: it depended only on locally obtainable natural uranium rather than imported heavy water and enriched uranium. U.S. concern about North Korea's nuclear intentions was triggered two years later with the construction of a new Yongbyon facility to chemically extract weapons-grade plutonium from the spent nuclear reactor fuel. Such a reprocessing facility served no purpose other than to support a nuclear weapons program. North Korea began construction of two larger graphite-moderated reactors (estimated at 50 and 200 megawatts), which, when operational, would have created a "nuclear factory" yielding plutonium sufficient for the fabrication of about thirty Nagasaki-sized nuclear weapons annually.[39]

The end of the Cold War created a diplomatic opening for negotiations between the United States and the DPRK, as well as between the two Koreas. The George H. W. Bush administration's announced withdrawal of tactical nuclear weapons from South Korea in 1991, as part of a global U.S.-Soviet agreement to eliminate most nonstrategic nuclear weapons, was followed by the Kim Il Sung regime's acceptance of an International Atomic Energy Agency (IAEA) safeguards agreement to ensure that North Korea was abiding by its NPT obligations and by the provisions of the ROK-DPRK Joint Declaration on the Denuclearization of the Korean Peninsula, which was concluded in 1991 and committed the two sides to forgo the production of nuclear weapons and the possession of nuclear reprocessing and uranium enrichment facilities.

The Clinton Administration

In the early 1990s, North Korea balked at IAEA inspections of its nuclear sites and sought to link international access to the cancelation of joint U.S.-ROK military exercises. The Clinton administration conducted direct negotiations with the North Koreans even as the Kim Il Sung regime made an escalatory threat to withdraw from the NPT. Of particular concern to U.S. officials was a CIA NIE that the North Koreans, during a 1989 shutdown of the Yongbyon reactor, could have separated enough plutonium from spent fuel rods for two nuclear bombs.[40]

The first nuclear crisis with North Korea was precipitated by Pyongyang's announcement in April 1994 that the Yongbyon reactor would be shut down so that spent fuel from its core could be removed. The alarming estimate was that these 8,000 fuel rods contained sufficient plutonium to produce four or five nuclear bombs. The Kim Il Sung regime refused to allow IAEA inspectors to conduct tests to clarify whether the spent nuclear fuel was part of the original load when the five-megawatt reactor became operational (as claimed by Pyongyang) or whether it had been replaced after the 1989 shutdown (as suspected by the Clinton administration) with the plutonium extracted and diverted into a weapons program.[41]

In June 1994, the crisis further escalated when the Clinton administration announced that the United States would seek the imposition of multilateral economic sanctions on North Korea through the UN Security Council. As the administration reinforced the U.S. military presence in South Korea as a deterrent, the Kim Il Sung regime remained defiant, proclaiming that economic sanctions would be an act of war. To meet the North Korean nuclear challenge, the Clinton administration adopted a strategy of coercive diplomacy based on economic sanctions after considering—and rejecting—the alternative of a preventive military strike on the Yongbyon nuclear installation. The overriding concern for U.S. officials, in effectively removing the military option from consideration, was that air strikes could have a catalytic effect, triggering a general war on the Korean Peninsula. General Gary Luck, then commander of U.S. forces in South Korea, warned that such a conflict would result in 1 million casualties and entail economic costs of $1 trillion.[42]

In mid-June 1994, as the Clinton administration was mounting a diplomatic campaign for economic sanctions, the escalating crisis was unexpectedly defused by former president Jimmy Carter's controversial mission to Pyongyang. After his meetings with Kim Il Sung, Carter announced on CNN that the North Korean leader had agreed to "freeze" the DPRK's nuclear program. He stunned the Clinton administration by declaring unilaterally that the United States was dropping its push for UN sanctions. The Clinton administration capitalized on the Carter mission by interpreting "freeze" to mean that North Korea would not refuel the Yongbyon reactor.[43] The administration's handling of the nuclear standoff was castigated by congressional hard-liners, who rejected the administration's acceptance of a freeze that did not roll back the North Korean program.

The Carter-Kim summit led to intensive negotiations over several months that culminated in the U.S.-DPRK Agreed Framework of October 1994. The accord embodied a series of carefully calibrated, reciprocal steps that would be implemented over a decade-long period and that could be halted or broken off in the event of Pyongyang's noncompliance. North Korea pledged to remain an NPT party and to cease reprocessing and traded its three graphite-moderated reactors and reprocessing facility for two 1,000-megawatt proliferation-resistant light-water reactors (which were to be constructed by an international consortium comprising the United States, Japan, and South Korea). In addition, the Agreed Framework obligated the Kim Jong Il regime to implement the 1991 ROK-DPRK denuclearization agreement, while the United States offered the DPRK a "negative security assurance," pledging that it would not use nuclear weapons against North Korea while it remained an NPT party. Washington and Pyongyang also committed to open diplomatic liaison offices as a first step toward full normalization of political and economic relations, though the Clinton administration linked that broader goal to further progress in North-South Korean relations.

Clinton administration officials defended the 1994 accord as the best of a bad set of options inherited from the George H. W. Bush administration. As U.S. chief negotiator Robert Gallucci acknowledged, "[E]veryone was reluctant about the Agreed Framework."[44] The agreement was structured as a series of reciprocal steps in which the North would discontinue activities of greatest concern to the United States before the transfer of sensitive light-water reactor components. Left deferred, however, was an accounting of the DPRK's nuclear history. That residual uncertainty about North Korea's capabilities left open the question of its nuclear intentions. In 1998, U.S. suspicions were fueled by the intelligence community's discovery of a large underground site (which raised the possibility of a covert program), as well as by the North's provocative test of a long-range Taepodong-1 missile over Japanese territory. Those developments threatened to undermine U.S. political support for the Agreed Framework, especially among congressional skeptics who were already hostile to engaging a "rogue state."

As a renewed crisis threatened, President Bill Clinton tapped former secretary of defense William Perry for a diplomatic mission to Pyongyang in July 1999 to address issues of concern with North Korean officials and to conduct a comprehensive review of U.S. policy. The resulting Perry report recommended a "comprehensive and integrated approach," linking the normalization of U.S.-DPRK relations (whose tangible benefits would include lifting of the U.S. trade embargo and economic sanctions) to Pyongyang's full compliance with the Agreed Framework and limits on the North's long-range ballistic missile production and exports. In the wake of the Perry mission, positive developments—notably, Pyongyang's announcement of a missile-test moratorium in September 1999 and South Korean president Kim Dae Jung's precedent-setting summit meeting with Kim Jong Il in Pyongyang in June 2000—created a perceived diplomatic opening. The North Koreans floated a plan linking restraints on the DPRK's long-range ballistic missile program to the establishment of diplomatic relations between the United States and North Korea. In October 2000, Secretary of State Madeleine Albright met with Kim Jong Il in Pyongyang to explore the North Korean proposal, as well as the possibility of a presidential visit.[45] Kim reportedly offered a moratorium on the production and deployment of long-range ballistic missiles in return for U.S. economic compensation. While follow-on negotiations grappled with the technical issue of verification, the incoming George W. Bush administration signaled opposition to a binding, eleventh-hour agreement concluded by its predecessor. President Clinton and other Clinton administration of-

ficials believed that a negotiated buyout of North Korea's long-range ballistic missile program was within reach and that they were handing off an
early foreign policy win to their successors.[46]

The Bush and Obama Administrations

An early signal of the hardening of U.S. policy toward North Korea was
the new administration's pointed revival of the "rogue state" category that
the Clinton administration had jettisoned in June 2000 (see Chapter 1). The
Bush administration reluctantly reaffirmed the U.S. commitment to the
Agreed Framework but opposed the broader effort through South Korean
president Kim Dae Jung's "sunshine policy" to normalize relations with
the DPRK. The administration was divided between pragmatists (such as
Secretary of State Colin Powell), who sought to build on the Clinton record,
and hard-liners (notably, Vice President Dick Cheney and Department of
Defense officials), who, in an early National Security Council memorandum, argued that a no-negotiations stance would maintain "moral clarity."[47]

Underlying the divergent policy options toward North Korea were contending assessments of the Pyongyang regime's durability and vulnerability.
As discussed in Chapter 3, strategies are predicated on concepts of societal
change in the target state. These critical threshold assumptions for strategy
formulation are frequently implicit and not subjected to rigorous analysis.
In the case of North Korea, which President Bush included in the "axis of
evil" after 9/11, the hard-line strategy was undergirded by an intelligence
assessment that the DPRK system was under extraordinary stress.[48] North
Korea "is teetering on the edge of economic collapse," Deputy Secretary of
Defense Paul Wolfowitz argued, and that "is a major source of leverage."[49]
The premise that North Korea was on the verge of collapse was marshaled
in support of a strategy of hard containment to squeeze the Pyongyang
regime and thereby hasten that collapse. Conversely, this assessment of
regime vulnerability suggested that the alternative engagement strategy,
which would incorporate economic carrots to induce a change in North
Korean behavior, could have the perverse effect of propping up the "teetering" regime. The Bush administration never reconciled the policy tension between these opposing approaches, with one official acknowledging,
"The problem is [that] people are operating from different assumptions."[50]

In October 2002, the United States, drawing on new intelligence from
Pakistan about the nuclear black-market activities of Abdul Qadeer Khan,

confronted North Korea about a covert uranium enrichment program, which would offer the DPRK an alternative route to nuclear weapons acquisition. In 2003, the diplomatic confrontation over North Korea's uranium enrichment activities turned into a much more urgent situation involving its renewed acquisition of plutonium. As Washington confronted Pyongyang through diplomatic channels, the Bush administration terminated the Agreed Framework, which had frozen the plutonium program. In 2003, North Korea withdrew from the NPT and prepared to reprocess 8,000 fuel rods that had been stored in cooling ponds pursuant to the Agreed Framework and to extract plutonium for approximately six nuclear weapons. While Mohamed ElBaradei, director general of the IAEA, recommended the North Korean case for referral to the United Nations in 2002–03, the Bush administration, then wanting to maintain the Security Council's focus solely on Iraq, conveyed no sense of urgency as Pyongyang threatened to cross the red line of plutonium reprocessing. The administration rebuffed suggestions from former national security adviser Brent Scowcroft and former defense secretary William Perry to intensively pursue bilateral negotiations with Pyongyang to reinstate the plutonium freeze.

In August 2003, with North Korea poised to acquire additional weapons-grade fissile material, the first of an eventual five rounds of six-party talks (involving the United States, North and South Korea, China, Japan, and Russia) was convened to pursue a diplomatic solution to the nuclear impasse. U.S. ambivalence about the six-party process was evident, with administration hard-liners concerned about "rewarding bad behavior," while pro-engagement pragmatists viewed the talks as a possible mechanism to constrain the North's nuclear intentions. In October 2006, North Korea conducted a nuclear test and became the world's ninth nuclear weapons state by a bold move that overturned the U.S. assumption that a Chinese red line would deter Pyongyang from crossing the nuclear threshold. In response, the Security Council, with Chinese and Russian support, imposed sanctions to block the Kim Jong Il regime's importation of luxury goods and authorized the United States and other states to interdict North Korean shipping to prevent "illicit trafficking in nuclear, chemical, or biological weapons, as well as their means of delivery and related materials."[51] In February 2007, during resumed six-party talks, North Korea agreed to dismantle the Yongbyon nuclear facility and to make a full disclosure of its past and present programs. In October 2008, after North Korea had halted activities at Yongbyon and released a document about its nuclear history (though omitting disclosure of its uranium enrichment program and its nuclear exports to other countries), the Bush administration removed the DPRK from the U.S. list of state sponsors of terrorism.[52]

President Obama campaigned on a platform of diplomatically engaging adversary states. His inaugural address metaphor of extending a hand to unclenched fists was a stark contrast to the Bush administration's regime change rhetoric. In practice, the emphasis on behavior change signaled a willingness to offer a Libya-type assurance of regime security to North Korea to seal a denuclearization deal. But the Obama administration's gesture of conciliation was met by renewed North Korean provocations to force concessions, including international recognition of the DPRK's status as a de facto nuclear weapons state. In 2009–10, the fist remained clenched. North Korea carried out long-range ballistic missile launches, a second nuclear weapons test, an attack on a South Korean naval vessel (killing forty-six sailors), and the shelling of a South Korean border island.

After the May 2009 nuclear test, President Obama, framing the issue in terms of Kim Jong Il's violation of international norms, declared, "By acting in blatant defiance of the United Nations Security Council, North Korea is directly and recklessly challenging the international community.... Such provocations will only serve to deepen North Korea's isolation."[53] The administration, adopting a stance that officials characterized as "strategic patience," maintained the emphasis on changing Pyongyang's behavior and ruled out any concessions merely to bring North Korea back to the negotiating table. U.S. intelligence analysts speculated that the spike in North Korean belligerence was linked to domestic politics; the ailing Kim Jong Il, who was reported to have suffered a stroke in August 2008, sought to bolster the position of his heir apparent, third son Kim Jong Un.[54]

The DPRK Domestic Context

The Kim Dynasty in Crisis

For a beleaguered regime whose paramount concern is survival, domestic politics are *the* key determinant of foreign policy. Assessing the domestic sources of external conduct is particularly challenging in this self-isolated country traditionally known as "the Hermit Kingdom." Yet despite the opacity of North Korea's Stalinist politics under the Kim family regime, U.S. policy formulation has been informed by observable indicators of the country's economic crisis and demographic stress. The conditions that led some Western analysts to categorize North Korea as a "failed state" manifested themselves in the 1990s, when an economy that had stagnated during the 1980s sharply declined, with national output contracting by roughly one-half. North Korean society was further beset by a mass famine that resulted in deaths estimated as high as 2 million. Average life expectancy dropped by more than six years during the 1990s, according to a senior North Korean official at a UN conference in 2001.[55]

North Korea's acute socioeconomic crisis in the 1990s coincided with a period of profound political change. With the end of the Cold War and the demise of the Soviet Union, Pyongyang lost a superpower patron and faced a precarious geostrategic situation. That transformation of the external environment was compounded by concomitant internal uncertainty with the death of Kim Il Sung in 1994. His son, Kim Jong Il, assumed power in the communist world's first dynastic succession. The so-called Great Leader, who ruled North Korea for nearly half a century, created a totalitarian system and pervasive cult of personality that was the envy of other despots, such as Romania's Nicolae Ceauşescu (see Chapter 2). To assert his autonomy within the international communist movement in the 1950s, Kim Il Sung enunciated his policy of self-reliance (*juche*), which tapped a deep vein of Korean nationalism. The continued political division of the peninsula after the Korean War had left the North with a preponderance of the country's industrial base and natural resources. Through the 1960s, these material advantages translated into a higher level of national output than in South Korea. But by the 1970s, South Korea, one of East Asia's economic tigers, had surged ahead of North Korea. By the early 1990s, the DPRK's gross domestic product was estimated to be a mere one-sixteenth that of the ROK. With national output plummeting, Pyongyang made the stunning public admission in 1993 that the North Korean economy was in a "grave" state.[56]

For Kim Il Sung, domestic exigencies created an imperative for external engagement. The "Great Leader" moved to ease relations with the outside world, which meant putting the nuclear program on the negotiating table with the United States as a means of alleviating the country's acute economic crisis. But the strategy carried the risk of political contagion that could weaken the regime's totalitarian grip over North Korean society. Chinese leaders, dating back to Deng Xiaoping in 1978, had counseled both Kim Il Sung and Kim Jong Il to end the DPRK's autarkic policies and to adopt market-based economic reforms. But whenever the North Korean leadership has faced the choice between integration and isolation, politics have trumped economics. The perceived threat of economic reforms to re-gime stability has ensured that their scope remains limited. Kim Jong Il's paramount interest has been in sustaining the estimated 1 million people who constitute the power base of his regime.

The ruling elite has been insulated from the adverse consequences of North Korea's failed *juche* policies through a "court economy" that distrib-utes food and foreign consumer goods to the regime's most loyal cadres.[57] But because North Korea, unlike oil-exporting Iran and Libya, does not have a ready source of hard currency, the regime has engaged in criminal activities (including counterfeiting and drug smuggling) to sustain its court economy. This illicit pattern prompted Alexander Vershbow, then the U.S. ambassador to South Korea, to brand North Korea a "criminal regime."[58] Bureau 39—a special government office described as Kim Jong Il's "per-sonal safes"—reportedly directs all illicit operations generating foreign currency. In addition to being responsible for procuring luxury goods for the ruling elite, Bureau 39 uses the hard currency generated through its illicit operations to acquire foreign technology for North Korea's nuclear and missile programs, thereby bolstering the regime's sole source of bar-gaining leverage with the international community.[59] While maintaining his power base, Kim Jong Il carefully guarded against the possibility of a palace coup through two major internal security agencies. With the impor-tant exception of the military, official government institutions (such as the Korean Workers' Party, which one would expect to play the lead role in a communist state) have atrophied because power is channeled informally through the Kim dynasty's core interest groups.

During the 1990s, North Korean society experienced famine and dein-dustrialization that fueled predictions the regime was on the brink of col-lapse. China's strategic decision not to allow that collapse led Beijing to extend an aid lifeline to minimally stabilize the situation. Conditions marginally improved a decade later, prompting *Foreign Policy*, in its 2011 "Failed States Index," to shift North Korea's status from "critical" to "in danger."[60] The North Korean system faces not only the traditional challenge of succession with the end of the Kim Jong Il era, but also novel challenges, such as the information age's encroaching threat to the regime's totalitarian control over society. North Korea's nuclear inten-tions must be viewed through the prism of regime security. The nuclear program is at the same time a driver of the country's international isola-tion and the primary source of its bargaining leverage with the outside world.

Nuclear Weapons and Regime Security

What are North Korea's nuclear intentions? Does it regard nuclear weapons as a deterrent capability vital to regime survival or as a bargaining chip to extract economic inducements from the United States, South Korea, and Japan? A 2004 study of North Korea's WMD programs conducted by the London-based International Institute for Strategic Studies (IISS) concluded, "The historical record suggests that the answer is both, and the emphasis that Pyongyang places on one or the other varies with domestic conditions and external circumstances."[61] That conventional wisdom may be changing as North Korea seeks recognition as a de facto nuclear weapons state.

Declassified documents from the archives of North Korea's former allies in the Soviet Union and Eastern Europe reveal the powerful motivation underlying Pyongyang's long-standing nuclear quest. These diplomatic cables clarify the North Korean leadership's thinking on nuclear weapons. The participants, including Kim Il Sung and his "best friend," East German leader Erich Honecker, believed the transcripts of their secret oral conversations would forever remain so. As early as August 1962, the Soviet ambassador to Pyongyang reported that the North Korean foreign minister had baldly asked of the DPRK's superpower patron, "The Americans have a large stockpile, and we are forbidden even to think about the manufacture of nuclear weapons?" In 1976, a senior North Korean official angrily emphasized his country's "front-line situation" after the Kremlin had rejected as "inopportune" yet another request by Pyongyang for nuclear technology.[62] The documents reveal the mind-set of a vulnerable regime that perceives the Korean War to have never ended. North Korea's nuclear intentions were fueled by perceptions both of vulnerability to superior U.S. and South Korean forces and, after the end of communist rule in Eastern Europe and the Soviet Union, of collapse.

A telling indicator of Pyongyang's determined pursuit of nuclear weapons is that its acquisition of uranium enrichment technology from Pakistani black marketer Khan (an alternative source of weapons-grade fissile material to the plutonium program at Yongbyon) occurred in the late 1990s, when the Clinton administration was engaging North Korea through the Agreed Framework and negotiations on ballistic missiles. The October 2002 crisis over the covert uranium enrichment program occurred amid U.S. preparations for a war of regime change in Iraq and President Bush's inclusion of North Korea in the "axis of evil." The chief North Korean nuclear negotiator told his U.S. counterpart, "If we disarm ourselves because of U.S. pressure, then we will become like Yugoslavia or Afghanistan's Taliban, to be beaten to death."[63] In June 2003, two months after U.S. tanks rolled into Baghdad to topple the Saddam Hussein regime, a North Korean Foreign Ministry official baldly declared that the DPRK would respond to any encroachment on its sovereignty "with an immediate, physical retaliatory measure. Neither sanctions nor pressure will work on us…. As far as the issue of nuclear deterrent force is concerned, the DPRK has the same status as the United States and other states possessing nuclear deterrent forces."[64] As Pyongyang claimed equivalence with the United States three years before conducting its first nuclear test, another senior DPRK official told visiting U.S. congressional staff members that Washington should "stop trying so hard to convince us to abandon our nuclear program and start thinking about how you are going to *live with a nuclear North Korea.*"[65]

Assessment and Implications

The North Korean nuclear challenge is intertwined in the broader question of the future of the Kim family system. As explored in Chapter 3, contending assessments of a regime's viability — and the critical threshold assumptions on which they are based — support alternative strategies. Consider the swings in U.S. assessments of North Korea from the Clinton to Obama administrations.

The Perry report of 1999 was premised on an assessment that economic weakness, though unlikely to lead to regime collapse, did create a motivation for the Pyongyang regime to negotiate. "[W]e must deal with the DPRK regime as it is," Perry argued, "not as we might wish it to be."[66] The Perry report advocated a strategy of comprehensive engagement that linked North Korean denuclearization (through compliance with the Agreed Framework) to the normalization of relations with the United States.

Three years later, in 2002, Deputy Secretary of Defense Paul Wolfowitz spoke of a "teetering" North Korea whose economic weakness was a "source of leverage."[67] This premise suggested that the nonproliferation and regime change timelines could be brought into sync. The United States could eliminate the North Korean nuclear threat through a comprehensive squeeze strategy to bring down the "rogue" regime. In short, a hard landing for the North Korean regime was inevitable, and the United States could hasten that outcome. The assessment also strongly argued against the alternative strategy of engagement, because any inducements offered to the Kim Jong Il regime to promote its compliance with international nonproliferation norms would merely serve to prop up a vulnerable regime. That perception of a regime living on borrowed time removed the urgency and utility of nuclear agreements with North Korea. Indeed, in October 2002, the revelation of the DPRK's covert uranium enrichment program led the Bush administration to declare the Agreed Framework "dead." As one former U.S. official put it, to confront the North Koreans about a uranium enrichment program of *unknown* scope, the Bush administration terminated the nuclear agreement that had frozen a plutonium program of *known* scope. An alternative would have been to address North Korean noncompliance within the Agreed Framework process, thereby maintaining the plutonium freeze and preventing North Korea from gaining access to fissile material sufficient for approximately six nuclear weapons.

In pivoting from a regime change strategy to engagement, the Obama administration was rejecting the target state assessment of the "collapsists" (to use economist Marcus Noland's term).[68] Though the approach was broadly similar to that in the 1999 Perry report, the circumstances were sharply different: North Korea had become an overt nuclear weapons state by this time. Underlying the Obama administration's offer to Pyongyang of normalization of relations for denuclearization was an assessment that the nuclear and societal-change timelines were not in sync and that the two issues therefore needed to be decoupled. The Obama administration sought to test North Korea's intentions by offering a structured choice to obtain a nuclear agreement curtailing the DPRK's capabilities in the near term; it relegated the internal process of societal change to play out on an indeterminate timetable.

North Korea's second nuclear test in May 2009 was a direct rebuff to the new U.S. administration's overture. Pyongyang's hardened position indicated an emphasis less on using its nuclear program as a bargaining chip to extract concessions than on obtaining international recognition as a de facto nuclear weapons state. As Asian security expert Jonathan Pollack concluded, "The DPRK was unprepared to conceptualize a strategic future without continued possession of nuclear weapons."[69] Secretary of State Hillary Clinton reiterated the U.S. objective of denuclearization and bluntly rejected Pyongyang's nuclear assertiveness: "Its leaders should be under no illusion that the United States will ever have normal, sanctions-free relations with a nuclear-armed North Korea."[70]

The Pyongyang regime has been able to defy its adversaries because it has also been able to defy its chief ally, China. The North Korean nuclear test in 2006 crossed what Western analysts widely viewed as a Chinese red line, given Beijing's logical apprehension that Pyongyang's provocative action could drive Tokyo and Seoul to reconsider their non-nuclear status. The Kims have likewise rebuffed Chinese calls for economic reforms and have maintained the North Korean economy's "military first" orientation. In North Korea expert Andrei Lankov's blunt judgment, "Reforms mean death."[71]

North Korea's alternative futures are often assessed with reference to an airplane metaphor—a "hard landing" versus a "soft landing." But what if neither is an imminent prospect? In short, what if the plane is not crashing? China plainly views an uneasy status quo as preferable to either. A hard landing—regime collapse—would, at minimum, create a refugee crisis and risk triggering a conflict on the Korean Peninsula. Alternatively, a soft landing—peaceful reunification between North and South Korea—would end North Korea's status as a buffer state and leave China with a formidable pro-Western regional power on its border. Facing unacceptable alternatives, Beijing has evidently made a strategic decision to prop up the vulnerable Kim family regime through economic assistance (food and fuel) and investments in politically connected North Korean trading companies. China turns a blind eye to UN sanctions adopted after the 2006 and 2009 nuclear tests by allowing the transshipment of North Korean military goods and technology to Iran and by serving as the primary conduit for luxury goods to maintain the lavish lifestyle of the regime's elite. An IISS study suggested that North Korea may increasingly become "a de facto satellite of China."[72]

China's sustaining assistance allows the North Korean regime to avoid the hard choice between impoverished autarky and destabilizing integration into the international system. In so doing, Beijing effectively undercuts the ability of the international community to bring meaningful pressure to bear on Pyongyang to alter its conduct. While asserting its status as a nuclear weapons state, North Korea remains ostensibly open to the goal of denuclearization, but Pyongyang's maximalist conception would require Washington to withdraw U.S. troops and essentially end its security relationship with South Korea.

What makes North Korea so dangerous is the regime's propensity for risk-taking and miscalculation. Border provocations and attacks, such as the sinking of the South Korean naval vessel *Cheonan* in March 2010, could easily escalate into a direct conflict. For the United States, North Korea's nuclear and long-range ballistic missile programs create a dangerous nexus. During his January 2011 visit to China, Secretary of State Robert Gates told Chinese president Hu Jintao that North Korea is no longer solely a regional problem and "is becoming a direct threat to the United States."[73] Just as the United States has made clear that Washington will never accept a nuclear North Korea, so too has the Kim regime remained adamant in not relinquishing its nuclear arsenal. U.S. policy can realistically aim to mitigate but not eliminate the threat through a combination of containment, deterrence, and engagement.

Iran: A Nation or a Cause?

The Iranian nuclear challenge must be viewed within the context of the country's societal evolution and attitude toward the outside world.[74] "Iran has to make a decision whether it wants to be a nation or a cause," in Henry Kissinger's apt formulation.[75] Yet since the 1979 revolution that swept the shah from power and led to the creation of the Islamic Republic of Iran, the country's ruling regime refuses to make that choice. On issues affecting Iran's national interests, Tehran fastidiously asserts its rights as a "republic" in an international order of sovereign states. At the same time, the theocratic regime pursues an ideologically driven foreign policy (such as its support of Hizbollah) to maintain revolutionary élan at home. Tehran's rejection of what it views as a U.S.-dominated international order is at the heart of the Islamic Republic's identity and worldview. Without these "revolutionary thoughts," as then-president Hashemi Rafsanjani once candidly acknowledged, Iran would become an "ordinary country."[76]

Iran's competing dual identities—revolutionary state/ordinary country—continuously roil the country's politics. This political schism underlies the violent clash between the country's hard-line theocratic regime and the reformist Green Movement in the aftermath of the 2009 presidential elections. While calling for democratic governance within Iran, the Green Movement leader, Mir Hossein Mousavi, also called for an end to foreign policy "adventurism," which, among other negative consequences, had led to Iran's international isolation and the imposition of UN sanctions over the regime's intransigent stand on the nuclear question. Iran's competing identities frustrate the ability of the United States to formulate a coherent strategy to meet the multiple challenges that Iran poses to the Gulf region and beyond. Impoverished, insular North Korea actually possesses a small nuclear arsenal, but U.S. policy-makers nonetheless regard Iran as the more dynamic threat because of its oil wealth and radical activism in an oil-rich region. The U.S. military withdrawal from a weakened and politically fractured Iraq has only reinforced the perception of Iran as an ascendant regional power.

Successive Security Council resolutions imposing targeted sanctions on the Tehran regime have varyingly expressed "deep concern about Iran's lack of compliance ... on ensuring the peaceful nature of its nuclear program," as required of an NPT signatory state.[77] Although the 2011 NIE concluded that Iran was making progress on the essential components of a nuclear weapon, it did not opine on whether the regime had made a strategic decision to acquire the bomb. The NIE described "serious debate within the Iranian regime ... on how to proceed."[78] The nuclear issue is "a surrogate for a broader debate about the country's future—about ... how it should interact with the wider world," observes Gulf security specialist Shahram Chubin.[79] In Washington, the nuclear challenge posed by Iran is shorthand for a more fundamental debate about how to deal with a state that is unable to decide whether it is a nation or a cause.

U.S. Policy toward Iran

From the Cold War to 9/11

U.S. estrangement from Iran, a bitter state of relations ushered in by the 1979 revolution, is exceeded in duration only by that of Washington with North Korea and Cuba. During the Cold War, the shah, who had ascended to power through a 1953 coup facilitated by Britain and the United States, became Washington's staunch anti-Soviet ally in the oil-rich region of vital interest to the West. In the 1970s, a conjunction of factors—the influx of petrodollars that filled Iranian coffers and the Nixon Doctrine, under which, in the post-Vietnam era, a retrenching United States looked to friendly local powers to play a more activist regional role—fueled the shah's ambitions. But as American arms transfers became the dominant currency of the bilateral relationship, the shah was increasingly viewed in Iranian domestic politics as a client of the United States.

Although the Iranian revolution should be viewed as a broader societal rejection of Western secularism and the shah's authoritarian rule, the political identification of the shah with the United States became a major driver of the revolution's virulent anti-Americanism. The seizure of the American embassy by radical "students" in October 1979 was essentially an extension of the revolution. In January 1981, Iran's theocratic regime, then consumed by the war with Iraq that had begun the previous September, concluded the Algiers Accords with the United States to end the hostage crisis. A key provision of the 1981 accords was a form of security assurance, based on the principle of state sovereignty, in which the United States pledged "it is and from now on will be the policy of the United States not to intervene, directly or indirectly, politically or militarily, in Iran's internal affairs."[80]

The State Department's designation of Iran as a state sponsor of terrorism in 1984 led to the imposition of additional U.S. economic sanctions. The Reagan administration's antipathy toward Iran's "outlaw government" produced a "tilt" toward Saddam's Iraq in its attritional war with Iran, even to the point of silence when Iraqi forces used chemical weapons against Iranian military forces. And yet, even as the administration sought to block arms sales to Iran through Operation Staunch, President Ronald Reagan approved a convoluted covert program to provide weapons via Israel to Iran in the mistaken belief that "moderates" within the Tehran regime were supportive of a rapprochement with the United States. The resulting Iran-Contra affair (so named because the proceeds of the arms sales were intended to fund the Contra guerrillas fighting to overthrow the pro-Moscow Sandinista regime in Nicaragua) nearly brought down the Reagan presidency.[81] In the wake of the scandal, bilateral relations further deteriorated when the United States extended naval protection to Kuwait shipping (as part of a strategy of coercive diplomacy to compel Iran to accept a UN cease-fire with Iraq) and the USS *Vincennes* accidentally shot down an Iranian civil airliner over the Persian Gulf.

In his 1989 inaugural address, President George H. W. Bush made a conciliatory gesture to Iran, declaring "good will begets good will."[82] Yet the competing pulls of Iranian domestic politics produced contradictory behavior: on his death, Ayatollah Ruhollah Khomeini was succeeded as supreme leader by an obscure hard-line cleric, Seyyed Ali Khamenei, who emphasized the centrality of anti-Americanism in the Islamic Republic's worldview, while Iranian president Rafsanjani, a perceived political pragmatist, expended political capital to win the release of U.S. hostages from Lebanon's pro-Iranian Hizbollah. In the wake of the 1991 Gulf War, the Bush administration's National Security Council examined U.S. policy options toward Iran, including consideration of "constructive engagement" through the selective lifting of economic sanctions. The policy review reportedly concluded that any gesture that "might be politically meaningful in Tehran ... would have been politically impossible" in Washington.[83]

The Clinton administration, ending the 1980s policy of alternately cultivating relations with Iraq or Iran to maintain a regional balance of power, adopted a strategy of "dual containment." When the term "rogue state" entered the official U.S. foreign policy lexicon, Iran was included in the Clinton administration's core group of countries so designated because of its active WMD programs and state-sponsored terrorism. In June 1996, an Iranian-backed group of Shiite Muslims bombed the Khobar Towers in Saudi Arabia, killing nineteen American military personnel. The Clinton administration considered direct retaliation against Iran but eventually demurred out of concern for the risk of military escalation and the lack of evidence directly linking the terrorist act to the Iranian regime's top leadership. Instead, the CIA's covert Operation Sapphire undertook targeted actions worldwide to disrupt the activities of Iran's Revolutionary Guards and intelligence service.[84]

In Iran's 1997 presidential election, the unexpected victory of the reformist candidate, Mohammed Khatami, over a virulently anti-American cleric, altered the political dynamic. In a conciliatory January 1998 interview on CNN, Khatami called for "a dialogue of civilizations," although he did not go so far as to advocate the normalization of "political relations" with the United States. But Khatami's overture came as the Clinton administration received conclusive evidence from Saudi law enforcement authorities implicating the Iranian Revolutionary Guard and the Lebanese Hizbollah in the 1996 Khobar bombing. In eschewing direct military action, the administration concluded that the best way to prevent future Iranian terrorism was to ensure that Khatami prevailed in the internal power struggle.

In an important March 2000 speech, Secretary of State Madeleine Albright announced the lifting of U.S. sanctions on Iran's nonoil exports and signaled the possibility of further trade liberalization if Iran ended its external conduct of concern. Addressing Iran's historical grievances impeding the normalization of relations, she acknowledged Washington's "significant role" in the 1953 coup and said that U.S. support of the Saddam Hussein regime during the Iran-Iraq War had been "shortsighted."[85] While praising the country's "trend toward democracy" under Khatami, Albright obliquely observed that key levers of state power, notably the military and the judiciary, remained in "unelected hands." In Tehran, Albright's conciliatory message was dismissed by Khamenei as "deceitful and belated." The supreme leader's rejection politically reined in Khatami and was a blunt rebuff to the Clinton administration's exploratory initiative to improve bilateral relations.[86]

The Bush and Obama Administrations

The Bush administration's attitude toward Iran was presaged by Condoleezza Rice, writing in *Foreign Affairs* in early 2000 as an adviser to the presidential candidate: "Changes in U.S. policy toward Iran would require changes in Iranian behavior.... Iran's motivation is not to disrupt simply the development of an international system based on markets and democracy, but to replace it with an alternative: fundamentalist Islam."[87] The persistent tension in U.S. policy during the Bush years was whether the desired changes in Iranian conduct would necessitate a change of regime.

Despite the failed Clinton effort to engage Iran, the Bush administration explored whether Iran, in the wake of the 9/11 terrorist attacks, a longtime supporter of Afghanistan's Northern Alliance, would cooperate in the unfolding U.S. military campaign to take down the Taliban regime, which was harboring Al Qaeda. The Iranians were hawkish supporters of U.S. military action against the Taliban but withheld overflight rights for U.S. aircraft out of political sensitivity to collaboration with Washington. After the fall of the Taliban regime in November 2001, Iran played a constructive role in the UN-sponsored process to establish a successor government. But at the UN General Assembly meeting, Khatami rejected Bush's "with us or with the terrorists" rhetoric, declaring that Hizbollah and Hamas were legitimate national resistance groups. In January 2002, the Israeli navy interdicted a ship, the *Karine A*, with Iranian arms bound for Yasir Arafat's Palestinian Authority. The Tehran regime's direct involvement in the *Karine A* episode dealt a "body blow" to the State Department's budding initiative to engage Iran.[88] In his 2002 State of the Union speech, Bush included Iran in the "axis of evil," along with Iraq and North Korea, and warned that these rogue states might transfer WMD to their "terrorist allies, [thereby] giving them the means to match their hatred."[89]

In May 2003, two months after the fall of Baghdad, the Bush White House received a document through the Swiss government that purported to be a wide-ranging proposal to normalize relations with Iran. The centerpiece of this so-called grand bargain was an Iranian offer to end con-

duct of concern with respect to proliferation and terrorism in return for a
U.S. assurance of regime security and the lifting of economic sanctions.[90]
Although the provenance of the document was ultimately discredited, the
question remains whether the United States missed an opportunity at its
point of maximum leverage—two years before the election of radical president Mahmoud Ahmadinejad and before Iran had an operational uranium
enrichment facility—to test Iran's intentions by offering the Tehran regime
a structured choice between the tangible benefits of behavior change and
the penalties for noncompliance.[91]

In mid-2003, after Iran's covert uranium enrichment program at Natanz
was exposed by the IAEA, the three major European Union (EU) governments—Britain, France, and Germany—launched the so-called EU-3
diplomatic initiative toward Iran. The effort, which in November 2004
yielded a temporary Iranian commitment to suspend uranium enrichment,
was motivated by the Europeans' strong desire, first, to avoid a replication
of the transatlantic breakdown that had occurred over Iraq and, second, to
demonstrate the efficacy of traditional diplomacy and nonmilitary instruments as an alternative to regime change in addressing nonproliferation
challenges. The United States belatedly joined the EU-3 diplomatic effort
as an indirect partner in early 2005, but the Bush administration's approach
remained stymied by an unwillingness to broadly engage on the nuclear
question.

The critical period between the end of the Iraq war and the election of
Ahmadinejad (who ended the EU-3's negotiated uranium enrichment suspension) presented the last opportunity to bind Iran's nuclear program. But
again, what proved politically possible in Washington (for example, dropping U.S. opposition to Iran's joining the World Trade Organization) was
politically insufficient to force a hard choice in Tehran. The package offered to Iran in June 2006 by the P5+1 (the permanent members of the UN
Security Council plus Germany) conspicuously omitted the one incentive
that only the United States could offer, a commitment of nonintervention.[92]
As Secretary of State Condoleezza Rice bluntly put it, "Security assurances
are not on the table."[93]

The Tehran regime's rebuff of the P5+1 and its flouting of the UN demand that Iran resume the suspension of its uranium enrichment activities
led to three Security Council resolutions in 2006–07 blocking Iranian arms
exports and nuclear commerce and calling on member states to inspect cargo
planes and ships entering or leaving Iran that were suspected of carrying
proscribed goods.[94] The Bush administration also used targeted sanctions

to punish, and thereby affect the decision-making calculus of, the clerical regime's core support groups. In 2007, the Bush administration designated Iran's elite Revolutionary Guards a terrorist organization and launched a quiet campaign by the State and Treasury Departments to lobby international banks and financial institutions to eschew dealings with Iran.[95]

The publication in November 2007 of the unclassified summary of the U.S. NIE on Iran recast the debate about the country's nuclear capabilities and intentions. According to the NIE, U.S. intelligence agencies concluded with "high confidence" that Iran "halted its nuclear weapons program" in 2003 "in response to increasing international scrutiny and pressure." Further, the agencies "do not know whether [Iran] currently intends to develop nuclear weapons."[96] This finding essentially reversed that of the previous NIE in 2005, which had said that Iran had an active clandestine weapons program. But while concluding that Iran had suspended work on that part of its covert military program relating to weapon design, the 2007 NIE also cited significant progress in Iran's declared "civil work" relating to uranium enrichment that "could be applied to producing [fissile material for] a nuclear weapon if a decision is made to do so": "Tehran at a minimum is keeping open the option to develop nuclear weapons."[97]

The 2007 NIE greatly complicated the Bush administration's effort to build international support for measures to curb Iran's nuclear program. Officials were pressed to explain why the development of a latent capability should necessitate urgent action. The NIE essentially removed the onus from Russia and China to support additional action by the Security Council to curb Iran's "civilian" program and thereby deny it a latent breakout capability.[98] The public release of the document triggered a political controversy in the United States. The administration's critics cited the new estimate as proof that the White House had been exaggerating the Iranian nuclear threat, just as it had exaggerated in the lead-up to the Iraq war. Hard-liners on Iran lambasted the NIE's methodology and charged that the intelligence community had inappropriately crossed the line into policy prescription. Even some IAEA officials privately voiced skepticism and concern that the U.S. assessment had been too "generous with Iran."[99] Amid widespread public speculation about the possibility of U.S. air strikes on Iran's nuclear infrastructure, the NIE finding that Iran had halted its weapons program essentially took the military option off the table during the Bush administration's final year.

The Obama administration's new approach toward adversarial states was evident in the president's precedent-setting message of March 2009 to the government and people of the Islamic Republic of Iran to mark the Iranian New Year (*Nowruz*). Obama called for "engagement that is honest and grounded in mutual respect."[100] The president reportedly reiterated that call for dialogue in a private letter to Supreme Leader Khamenei.[101] After Iran's disputed June presidential election, which returned Ahmadinejad to office, the Obama administration criticized the clerical regime's crackdown on the Green Movement but eschewed regime change rhetoric and maintained its willingness to engage diplomatically on the nuclear issue. At the G-20 meeting in late September, President Obama, French president Nicolas Sarkozy, and British prime minister Gordon Brown jointly revealed the existence of a covert uranium enrichment site near the holy city of Qom. After the revelation of the illicit site, negotiations between Iran and the P5+1 focused on an interim plan under which some three-quarters of Iran's low-enriched uranium would be shipped to Russia and France for reprocessing. At the technical meeting that followed in mid-October to discuss implementation of the plan, a midlevel Iranian official signaled acceptance, only to see the decision reversed in Tehran. The opposition reportedly came not only from hard-liners but also from Green Movement leaders, who wanted to deny Ahmadinejad the political credit for a nuclear agreement with the P5+1. The episode again highlighted the complex domestic politics of the nuclear question in Iran.

The Iranian Domestic Context

Regime Dynamics

Iran's dual identities—a cause or a nation—reflect the persisting schism in its postrevolutionary leadership. Just as revolutions begin more as causes than as concrete programs of action, so too are successful revolutions soon subject to the practical requirements of government. Consider the competing pulls of radicalism and pragmatism reflected in the Soviet shift from Leon Trotsky's "permanent revolution" to Stalin's "socialism in one country" (see Chapter 2). Iran's political landscape is commonly described in terms of vying factions—radical, conservative, and reformist. But these shorthand tags can obscure important differences within and between the groups, depending on the domestic or foreign policy issue.[102]

At the heart of Iran's identity crisis is a legitimacy crisis. The country's very name, the Islamic Republic of Iran, draws on both religious and secular sources of legitimacy. The revolution's elimination of the separation between mosque and state has created institutionalized systemic tensions. Driven by Khomeini's unique personal stature and charismatic leadership, Iran's 1979 constitution created an entirely new position, supreme leader (*velayat-i-faqih*), with paramount authority over all state institutions, including the military, internal security services, the judiciary, and broadcasting services, as well as over powerful "foundations" that are actually multibillion-dollar government-run conglomerates. The supreme leader's ultimate power is channeled through the Guardian Council, a body of senior Islamic jurists, which can veto legislation passed by the parliament (Majlis) and vets prospective electoral candidates. The Guardian Council certified Ahmadinejad's victory in the disputed presidential reelection of 2009. Relative to those of the supreme leader, the powers of the presidency, essentially Iran's highest secular office, are largely limited to running the government bureaucracy (particularly with respect to delivering social services and managing the economy). The structure is reminiscent of the Soviet system, where formal governmental institutions operated in tandem with a parallel ruling party structure that exercised controlling authority. Hence, the most powerful position in the Soviet Union was general secretary of the Communist Party, not the president. A similar pattern is evident in Iran, where Supreme Leader Khamenei has inserted "a vast network of 'clerical commissars' in major public institutions who are empowered to intervene in state matters to enforce his authority."[103]

Iran's fractured politics are a reflection of the breakup of the broad alliance that brought down the shah. The unlikely coalition ranged from secular technocrats, students, and urban poor to clerical moderates and antimodernists. Khomeini was able to manage the inherent policy tensions among these disparate interest groups because of his personal standing and charisma. By contrast, his successor, Khamenei, needed to establish his own social and political base. To do so, he cultivated the country's paramilitary forces—the Revolutionary Guards and Basij—and allowed them (contrary to Khomeini's stance) to assume an expanded political and economic role.[104] Khamenei's strategy brought the supreme leader into political competition with Ahmadinejad, who sought the support of the same hard-line groups to strengthen the powers of the presidency relative to his predecessors. In February 2010, the increased influence and prominence of the Revolutionary Guards prompted Secretary of State Hillary Clinton to warn, "We see that the government of Iran, the supreme leader, the president, the parliament, is being supplanted and that *Iran is moving toward a military dictatorship.*"[105]

The Green Movement emerged as a political opposition force in the wake of the June 2009 presidential election in which Ahmadinejad was certified the victor over the reformist standard bearer, former prime minister Mir Hossein Mousavi. Charges of a rigged election triggered mass demonstrations, which were brutally suppressed by the regime's security services and paramilitary forces, including the Basij and the Revolutionary Guards. The regime prosecuted prominent Green Movement activists and theorists, including Khatami's former vice president, Mohammad Ali Abtahi, in Soviet-style show trials complete with coerced confessions.[106] In autumn 2009, Green Movement demonstrations shifted from voter fraud to the legitimacy of the theocratic regime itself. Students chanted, "Khamenei is a murderer. His rule is null and void."[107] The Green Movement was divided between those who wished to work within the 1979 postrevolutionary constitution and those who advocated broad systemic change. Mousavi, characterizing the regime as "institutionalized corruption hiding behind a pretense of piety," called for constitutional reform but did not directly challenge Khamenei's legitimacy or the expansive concept of *velayat-i-faqih* on which the constitutional position of supreme leader was grounded.[108] The perpetuation of that unelected paramount position negates the possibility of ever separating mosque and state and is at the heart of the Islamic Republic's crisis of political legitimacy.

Khamenei provided decisive support to Ahmadinejad in 2009, but with the Green Movement in retreat, renewed competition broke out between the regime's contending conservative factions. Trying to stay above the fray and maintain a political balance, the supreme leader publicly reversed Ahmadinejad's unilateral dismissal of the intelligence minister.[109] What unites the conservative factions, whether radical or more pragmatic, is the core belief that the Islamic Republic's foreign policy is an important source of domestic legitimation. Yet from issue to issue, the factions may differ over the degree of tactical accommodation that the regime must prudently make to remain in power. International integration carries tangible economic benefits but risks political contagion. Khamenei dismissed the Obama administration's interest in diplomatic engagement as merely a tactical shift to achieve the U.S. objective of regime change through the fomentation of a "soft" or "velvet" revolution targeting Iranian civil society. Iran's nuclear challenge remains an embedded issue, a surrogate for the broader, persisting debate about Iran's relationship to the outside world.

Nuclear Capabilities and Intentions

Iran's nuclear motivations are not specific to the clerical regime. Indeed, then–CIA director George Tenet went so far as to assert during congressional testimony in February 2003, "No Iranian government, regardless of its ideological leanings, is likely to willingly abandon WMD programs that are seen as guaranteeing Iran's security."[110] This insight again highlights the key proliferation dynamic: the lead proliferation indicator is *regime intent*, whereas the U.S. perception of threat (particularly in the post-9/11 era) is linked to *regime character*.

Suspicions of Iran's nuclear intentions date to the shah's era. The initial components of Iran's nuclear infrastructure (a five-megawatt light-water research reactor and related laboratories at the Tehran Nuclear Research Center) were acquired through nuclear cooperation with the United States under the Atoms for Peace program. After acceding to the NPT in 1970, the shah launched an ambitious plan to develop civil nuclear energy, which envisioned not only reactor construction but also the acquisition of nuclear fuel-cycle technology (including uranium enrichment and reprocessing) to reduce the country's reliance on outside assistance. The Ford administration viewed nuclear cooperation with Iran as a tangible symbol of the U.S. bilateral relationship with a key regional ally as well as a potentially lucrative commercial opportunity for U.S. firms. Secretary of State Kissinger later acknowledged that proliferation concerns did not figure in the Ford administration's decision to permit the transfer of fuel-cycle technology.[111] Although "no evidence has emerged confirming that Iran actually began a dedicated nuclear weapons program under the Shah," concluded an IISS study, "… Iranian officials appreciated that the acquisition of enrichment and reprocessing facilities for Iran's civilian nuclear power program would inherently create a nuclear weapons option."[112]

Khomeini's opposition on theological grounds led to the suspension of Iran's nuclear program, including a halt to the construction of German-made reactors at Bushehr. In 1985, the clerical regime, facing a national security imperative at the height of the attritional Iran-Iraq War, revived the nuclear infrastructure inherited from the shah. On Khomeini's death in 1988, Iran looked to China and Russia as potential sources of nuclear technology. While Russia took over the Bushehr reactor project, Beijing provided components for a key uranium conversion facility in Esfahan. But the Clinton administration diplomatically pressed both countries to forgo nuclear commerce with Iran, making the cessation a condition for U.S.

civil nuclear exports to China and threatening the cutoff of U.S. aid to Russia to get the Kremlin to forgo the sale of fuel-cycle technology.

Details of Iran's extensive covert program to acquire sensitive nuclear technology surfaced after the IAEA's June 2003 report based on Iranian opposition sources, which had charged Iran with possessing undeclared nuclear facilities and pursuing activities outside the NPT safeguards system.[113] Of particular importance were essential design plans and components that A. Q. Khan, the Pakistani black marketer, provided for a pilot uranium enrichment plant at Natanz. By the late 1990s, at the height of Khatami's reformist presidency, Iran crossed the important technological threshold of self-sufficiency in centrifuge manufacturing.[114] American concern is that Iranian centrifuges capable of producing low-enriched uranium to run nuclear reactors that are not even on the drawing board can keep spinning to produce highly enriched uranium for bombs.[115]

The theocratic regime, dismissing suspicions of its nuclear intentions, has consistently maintained that the country is merely exercising its prerogative under Article IV of the NPT to develop civilian nuclear energy. Activities that Washington views as a violation of nonproliferation norms are defended in Tehran as a sovereign right. President Ahmadinejad accused the United States of plotting to keep Iran "backward" to maintain a system of "nuclear apartheid."[116] Standing up to U.S. "bullying" on the nuclear issue also taps the culture of victimization and sense of embattlement that the regime has cultivated within Iranian society to gain a freer hand in defining the country's security requirements. From secularists to religious fundamentalists, a broad domestic consensus exists on Iran's right to have civil nuclear energy, and the populace has been receptive to the clerics' critique of U.S. selective concern about nonproliferation norms. Yet this sentiment does not translate into across-the-board Iranian political support for a policy of acquiring nuclear weapons. The putative energy rationale for the program, let alone the case for nuclear weapons, has never been rigorously debated.[117]

Iran's nuclear program "has been marked by persistence and incrementalism, by determination rather than urgency."[118] It is not a crash program to acquire a weapon as quickly as possible in the face of an existential threat. The toppling of the Saddam Hussein regime undercut the immediate strategic rationale for nuclear weapons. But even before the 2003 war removed the Iraqi threat, the clerical regime focused on Israel as an all-purpose bogey to curry favor with the Arab states and to argue that the Israeli threat justifies Iran's long-range ballistic missile program.

"If, one day, the Islamic world is also equipped with weapons like those that Israel possesses now," former president Rafsanjani stated, "then the imperialists' strategy will reach a standstill because the use of even one nuclear bomb inside Israel will destroy everything."[119] This much-publicized speech by Rafsanjani in December 2001 was interpreted both ominously, as "rais[ing] the disquieting possibility that Iranians may see nuclear weapons as a means of pursuing an eliminationist solution to the Arab-Israel conflict," and benignly, as signaling the Iranian interest in a nuclear deterrent.[120]

The November 2007 NIE stated that the halt in Iran's nuclear weapons program in 2003 was "in response to increasing international scrutiny and pressure," without specifying the source of that pressure.[121] Bush admin-istration officials credited the cessation of Iran's weaponization effort in 2003 to the demonstration effect of Iraq. However, an alternative inter-pretation offered at the time was that the Iranians, having had their covert uranium enrichment program at Natanz exposed to the IAEA and thereby facing the prospect of punitive action, halted their weaponization activities to remove any immediate justification for a U.S. military strike. During the freeze on this component of its program, the Tehran regime acceler-ated work at the Natanz facility, now a declared civilian site under IAEA monitoring, to master the uranium enrichment process, thus providing the Iranian leadership with a breakout option to produce weapons-grade fissile material.

In January 2011, U.S. officials revised their estimate of when Iran could acquire nuclear weapons, citing technical setbacks that the program had encountered. Press reports attributed those problems to the Stuxnet com-puter worm, a destructive virus developed with the Israelis that had ren-dered inoperable an estimated one-fifth of Iran's nuclear centrifuges.[122] In February 2011, a new NIE on Iran's nuclear capabilities and intentions was completed and circulated within the U.S. government, but it was not (as with the 2007 estimate) made public. Director of National Intelligence James Clapper, providing an overview of the NIE in congressional testi-mony, stated that Iran's continued progress in mastering uranium enrich-ment "strengthens our assessment that Iran has the scientific, technical, and industrial capacity to eventually produce nuclear weapons."[123] The Febru-ary 2011 NIE concluded that the clerical regime had "resumed internal dis-cussions" and was "keeping open the option to develop nuclear weapons." The "central issue," according to Clapper, remains whether Iranian leaders have the will to build a bomb.[124]

Assessment and Implications

A 1974 NIE, "Prospects for Further Proliferation of Nuclear Weapons," offered a telling assessment of the shah's nuclear intentions: "If he is alive in
the mid-1980s, if Iran ... has all the facilities necessary for nuclear weapons, and if other countries [i.e., India] have proceeded with weapons development, we have no doubt that Iran will follow suit."[125] The United States
would likely have accommodated to a nuclear Iran under the shah, as it did
with Israel, India, and Pakistan (though none were NPT signatories). But
while Iran's nuclear intentions are not specific to the Islamic Republic, the
U.S. perception of the threat posed by the prospect of a nuclear Iran *is* specific to this regime. After 9/11, the link between threat and regime character
led to the Bush administration's emphasis on changing "rogue" regimes to
end the objectionable behavior that derives from their very character. The
dilemma is that the timelines—the "two clocks"—for regime change and
nuclear weapons acquisition are not in sync.[126] With regime change in Tehran not an immediate prospect, Washington's options in dealing with Iran's
nuclear challenge are limited.

Military action—air strikes on Iran's nuclear infrastructure—would
only set back the program for several years, not end it. Having mastered the
uranium enrichment process to acquire the requisite material for a weapon,
the program could be reconstituted. More fundamentally, in Tehran, military action would be viewed as the initiation of a regime-toppling war.
The envisioned scope of U.S. military action would reinforce that Iranian
perception: an air campaign would likely be of the magnitude of Operation
Desert Fox in Iraq, which spanned four days in late December 1998, rather
than a single mission like Israel's lightning air strike on the Iraqi Osirak
reactor in 1981. Because the prospect of a U.S. air strike on Iran's nuclear
infrastructure has been a matter of open speculation, Ayatollah Khamenei,
the supreme leader, has warned that such a strike would lead to Iranian
retaliation against U.S. interests worldwide.

The diplomatic alternative to military action is not more promising,
given the surrogate status of the nuclear issue for the broader foreign policy debate about Iran's relations with the outside world. The link between
the theocratic regime's external and internal policy agendas is subtle and
complex. For radicals, such as President Ahmadinejad, the Islamic Republic's external behavior (such as support for Palestinian groups that reject
negotiations with Israel) remains an integral source of domestic legitimacy.
Negotiating a pragmatic deal on Iran's external behavior (an acceptable

prospect to reformists and practical hard-liners in the country) would be staunchly opposed by Ahmadinejad's faction as a betrayal of the revolution. Indeed, to these hard-liners, the very notion of deeper integration into an international order in which the United States remains the predominant power is anathema. Moreover, the revenues deriving from relatively high oil prices insulate Ahmadinejad from his radical regime's own economic mismanagement and thereby dampen domestic pressures that would otherwise press the regime to reach an international accommodation.

The IAEA, which issued thirty reports between 2003 and 2010 detailing the Islamic Republic's covert nuclear activities, found Iran in noncompliance with the NPT in September 2005 for "failures and breaches of its obligations to comply" with its safeguards agreement and called on the Tehran regime to suspend uranium enrichment.[127] In terms of weaponization, however, a breakout or "sneak-out" option, using enriched uranium from its declared facility at Natanz, would be highly difficult to accomplish without international detection. The most likely breakout scenario would involve weapons-grade uranium produced at a clandestine facility. But an IISS study in 2010 concluded, "The likelihood that any dash by Iran for a bomb would be detected before it assembled a single weapon, much less the small arsenal that would be needed to make break-out worth the risk, allows time for a negotiated solution, should Iran's leaders decide to seek one."[128]

Iranian officials have cultivated ambiguity about the country's nuclear intentions. After Iran crossed the technological threshold of uranium enrichment, Ahmadinejad declared Iran to be a "nuclear state." The concern is that centrifuges that fabricate low-enriched uranium under the guise of a civil nuclear program can keep spinning to yield highly enriched uranium for weapons. In February 2010, as the Security Council was considering the imposition of additional sanctions on Iran, Ahmadinejad defiantly stated, "When we say that we don't build nuclear bombs, it means that we won't do that because we don't believe in having them.... [I]f one day we wanted to create an atomic bomb, we would announce it publicly and would create it."[129]

When asked about the possibility of a military option to resolve Iran's nuclear challenge, then–IAEA chief ElBaradei observed, "You cannot bomb knowledge"—a reference to Iran's demonstrated capability to enrich uranium.[130] Iran's ability to enrich uranium provides Tehran with an inherent hedge to produce a weapon. As long as the clerical regime retains power, that threat can be mitigated but not eliminated.

Living with Nuclear Outliers

Alternative Futures

For U.S. policy-makers, the nuclear challenges posed by North Korea and
Iran are embedded in the broader question of these outlier states' future
evolution. Concepts of societal change, which should be based on rigorous target state analysis, constitute key threshold assumptions for strategy
development (see Chapter 3). To return to a telling example, the 2002
assessment that North Korea was "teetering" undergirded the Bush administration's preferred strategy of pressuring the Kim Jong Il regime to
the point of collapse. Regime change would thereby eliminate the North
Korean threat, which arose from the character of the regime. For revolutionary and outlier states, societal change leading to reintegration into the
international community can be either externally imposed or internally
self-generated (see Chapter 2). External pathways—in which one state or
a coalition of states ousts the ruling regime of another state through war or
military intervention—are inherently controversial and, accordingly, rare,
because this agent of change runs contrary to the Westphalian principles
enshrining state sovereignty and noninterference in domestic affairs. Internally generated change typically occurs when intra-elite bargaining al-
ters a regime's calculus of decision and leads to a strategic departure from
past policies.

Externally induced change in either Iran or North Korea is unlikely under current circumstances. With Iran, despite the regime change rhetoric
of some Bush administration officials after the toppling of the Saddam
Hussein regime, the United States was severely constrained in replicat-
ing the Iraq model of coercive nonproliferation through a change of regime. Nor could Washington realistically aim to replicate in Iran the 2011
Libyan precedent of U.S.-assisted regime change: the opposition Green
Movement has itself ruled out armed rebellion against the clerical regime,
which, in any case, retains a monopoly on force within Iranian society and
would unhesitatingly crush an attempted counterrevolution. In the case of
North Korea, the nexus of power and proximity afford China unique influence. Yet China has refused to exercise that influence to promote change
in the Kim family's gulag state, evidently preferring the known challenge
of its erratic client in a divided Korea to the unknown potential of a unified Korea aligned to the United States. In short, China serves as North
Korea's "strategic umbrella," insulating the regime from the economic

consequences of its politico-military provocations and blocking international efforts to exert meaningful pressure on the Pyongyang regime to alter its behavior.[131]

If societal change is to come to North Korea and Iran, it is likely to originate from within. These outlier regimes have proved remarkably resilient, despite famine and economic contraction (North Korea) and attritional war (Iran). Yet both face profound domestic political challenges: in North Korea, uncertainty as to whether the Kim family system will survive another dynastic succession from Kim Jong Il to Kim Jong Un; in Iran, the ongoing political legitimacy crisis precipitated by the regime's suppression of Green Movement demonstrations after the contested 2009 election.

In North Korea, the only institution capable of challenging the Kim family's continued rule is the military, whose power and status as an interest group have increased under the regime's "military first" policy. With some 1 million men in active service, the Korean People's Army is the world's fourth-largest armed force. Overall, the military, which also encompasses a network of factories (the one functioning sector of the economy), accounts for approximately one-quarter of the country's gross domestic product. Kim Jong Il sought to ensure that the military would remain unswervingly dedicated to his regime's security through his personal vetting of the promotions of high-ranking officers, lavish rewards to the military elite from the court economy, and occasional purges of the military to preempt the possibility of a coup. (Unconfirmed reports exist of two attempts against the Kim family, in 1991 and 1995, and of dissident generals having fled to China.) Experts have speculated that a military coup would fall under one of two categories: a "reformist or progressive coup" to modernize the country and end its self-imposed international isolation, or a "conservative or reactionary coup" to maintain the status quo, prevent destabilizing change, and preserve the country's nuclear weapons program as both a deterrent and a source of bargaining leverage with outside powers.[132] In assessing the prospects for societal change driven by the military, a major unknown factor in the opaque North Korean system is the significance of the generational shift occurring within that key institution's leadership. Through a strategy combining the co-optation and coercion of the regime's core interest groups, Kim Jong Il effectively "coup-proofed" his regime, though whether that condition will hold during the political turbulence of a succession from the "Dear Leader" to his son is uncertain.[133]

In Iran, the policy tension created by the Islamic Republic's competing identities persists. Hopes that societal change could emerge from within through a moderation of the revolution were dashed in 1999, when the Khatami experiment ended with the suppression of reformists and, again, a decade later, with the suppression of the Green Movement. The disputed 2009 presidential election and violent crackdown on the Green Movement sharply undercut the Islamic Republic's domestic political legitimacy. Some observers perceive Iran as vulnerable to civil resistance from below, particularly as the Arab Awakening is shaking and toppling autocratic regimes across the Middle East. Yet optimistic assessments of the prospects for societal change must be tempered by a sobering reality: the clerical regime retains a monopoly on force and would use whatever means necessary to put down a domestic challenge to its paramount authority. As Iran expert Shaul Bakhash has observed, a symbiotic relationship exists between the supreme leader and the Revolutionary Guards: Khamenei has "facilitated the expanding role of the Guard commanders and the security agencies in the government. The Guards commanders need Khamenei to lend religious and constitutional legitimacy to the regime. They, in turn, protect the regime against the opposition—even if the opposition rises from within the ruling establishment's own ranks."[134] When necessary, the clerical regime has purged the officer corps to ensure political reliability, as after the 1997 election of Khatami, when it was reported that a significant percentage of the Revolutionary Guards had voted for the reformist candidate. An uprising from below could be successful only if supported by elements from within the military and security services, as happened in Romania in 1989, when the institutions on which Ceauşescu relied to stay in power turned on the regime. In Iran, however, the strong likelihood, given the symbiotic relationship between the supreme leader and the Revolutionary Guards, is that a civil uprising from below would be met with a brutal Tiananmen-style crackdown from above.

Containment 2.0

Given the formidable obstacles to societal change in North Korea or Iran, Washington's nonproliferation policies should not be premised on the assumption of near-term regime collapse. At the opposite end of the policy continuum to that of regime change, the Obama administration has pursued an alternative strategy of engaging adversaries, but it has not broken the diplomatic impasse over the countries' nuclear programs. The policy marked a departure from the approach of the Bush administration by offering Pyongyang and Tehran a structured choice incorporating tangible benefits for behavior change and penalties for noncompliance. By clarifying that the U.S. objective was a change of behavior, not a change of regime, the Obama administration sought to replicate the 2003 Libyan agreement, whose key provision was a tacit but clear assurance of regime security. In contrast to the Bush administration's persistent mixed message, the Obama administration clearly communicated that it would be willing "to take yes for an answer." But by early 2010, with North Korea and Iran rebuffing the Obama administration's diplomatic overture, conservative critics were asking whether Obama would be willing "to take no for an answer."[135]

Both Pyongyang and Tehran seized on NATO's 2011 intervention in Libya as proof that Qaddafi had been duped by the West when he dismantled his nuclear program. A North Korean official stated that the 2003 agreement had been "an invasion tactic to disarm the country," while Iran's supreme leader declared that U.S.-assisted regime change in Libya had validated Iran's decision not to "retreat [but] to increase [its] nuclear facilities year after year."[136] The Libyan intervention has stiffened resistance in Pyongyang and Tehran and made the already long odds of successful nuclear diplomacy longer still. For North Korea and Iran, that rationale that the Libyan military operation was undertaken as a "humanitarian intervention" rather than to achieve nonproliferation ends is an analytical distinction without a political difference. With its regime takedowns in Iraq (2003) and Libya (2011), Washington has essentially priced itself out of the security assurance market in Pyongyang and Tehran.

All options may remain on the table, but none is good. Regime change is not a near-term prospect; engagement has come to naught; and with respect to the nuclear issue, the military option is no silver bullet. In North Korea, there is no longer a target; Pyongyang separated and removed the plutonium from Yongbyon and now has a small arsenal. In Iran, bombing would, at best, set back but not end the nuclear program. Between regime change and engagement, the remaining alternative along the policy continuum (see Chapter 3) is a retooled version of the containment strategy that George Kennan advanced in the wake of World War II to address the far more ominous threat to international order posed by Stalin's Soviet Union. The three complementary elements of such an updated strategy are coercive diplomacy, deterrence, and the reassurance of allies.

Coercive Diplomacy

A U.S. diplomat with long experience negotiating with the Pyongyang regime once observed, "The North Koreans do not respond to pressure. But without pressure, they do not respond." The same can be said of the Iranians. Coercive diplomacy, a variant of Thomas Schelling's concept of compellence, seizes the initiative to bring these outlier states into compliance with their NPT obligations. Punitive measures, such as targeted sanctions on the core support groups on which the regimes rely to maintain power, are meant to compel changes in behavior by "sharpening the contradictions" (in the phrase of a former U.S. official). Coercive diplomacy, primarily using the stick of sanctions, can also be viewed as incorporating a carrot, to the extent that the lifting of sanctions should be an inducement for Pyongyang and Tehran to alter their behavior. Can such external pressure bring about a change in these regimes' calculus of decision?

With respect to Iran, Director of National Intelligence James Clapper stated in March 2011, "We continue to judge Iran's nuclear decision-making is guided by a cost-benefit approach, which offers the international community opportunities to influence Tehran."[137] North Korean decision-making evinces a similar inner logic. Both regimes view their nuclear programs, as well as the broader issue of their relationship to the outside world, through the prism of regime survival. Assessing the impact of sanctions on Iran, then–CIA director Leon Panetta stated, "I think the sanctions have some impact.... It could help weaken the regime. It could create some economic problems. Will it deter them from their ambitions with regard to nuclear capability? Probably not."[138] President Obama has similarly questioned whether the Iranian regime's "ideological commitment to nuclear weapons is such that they're not making a simple cost-benefit analysis on this issue."[139]

Certain factors influence the effectiveness of sanctions. In Iran, fluctuations in the price of oil affect revenues available to the clerical regime, including fuel and food subsidies to assuage popular discontent with its economic mismanagement. In North Korea, Chinese direct aid and trade relations make the Kim Jong Il regime less reliant on illicit activities and insulate Pyongyang from the consequences of sanctions. The U.S. ability to economically "squeeze" these regimes through coercive diplomacy using sanctions is contingent on factors outside Washington's control.

Iran claims that it does not seek nuclear weapons, though its mastery of uranium enrichment creates an inherent hedge option; North Korea oscillates between declaring its status as a nuclear power and its avowed interest in "denuclearization," Pyongyang's definition of which would require the United States, among other conditions, to renounce its extended nuclear deterrent commitment to South Korea and Japan. Yet the hard reality is that the window in which a rollback of Iran's and North Korea's nuclear capabilities was possible has closed. If that objective is no longer attainable, the plausible alternative would be to establish limits on their nuclear programs. Bounding the two countries' programs would entail curbing, through negotiations, their acquisition of additional fissile material.

With Iran, the objective would be to limit uranium enrichment to the pilot site at Natanz under the IAEA's additional protocol to prevent cheating. North Korea's cash-strapped regime is open to a deal; for example, Pyongyang reportedly offered to ship out 12,000 fresh fuel rods, sufficient to produce eight bombs' worth of plutonium, for compensation.[140] Perhaps the highest priority of negotiations with North Korea would be freezing its uranium enrichment program, which provides the Pyongyang regime an alternative route to nuclear weapons production. Arguing that a nuclear rollback in North Korea is no longer attainable, particularly in light of U.S.-led and U.S.-assisted regime changes in Iraq and Libya, North Korea expert Andrei Lankov concludes, "[T]he long-term solution of the talks will be some kind of arms restriction deal in which Pyongyang is forced to freeze its nuclear program and dismantle existing nuclear facilities for a hefty fee—with the implicit or explicit assumption that some fissile material and nuclear devices would remain hidden somewhere. This deal has its obvious shortcomings, but, given the alternatives, it's better than nothing."[141] By a similar strategic logic, Iran, whose determined and incremental nuclear program is not a crash effort to acquire a weapon, will want to retain a breakout option.

Deterrence and Reassurance

The U.S. characterization of Iran's decision-making as being "guided by a cost-benefit approach" is an important threshold assumption for strategy development, indicating as it does that the Islamic Republic is not an irrational, undeterrable state. Although Iran (as one would similarly argue of North Korea) is deterrable, deterrence can fail through miscalculation and misperception. Efforts to avoid deterrence failure should be viewed within the historical context of Washington's failed attempts to set and enforce red lines with Pyongyang and Tehran. Underscoring this problem, former State Department official Mitchell Reiss observed that the Bush administration "defined proliferation downward" by overlooking objectionable North Korean conduct in order to maintain a faltering diplomatic process.[142]

Although President Bush declared, after its October 2006 nuclear test, that "the transfer of nuclear weapons or material by North Korea to states or non-state entities would be considered a grave threat to the United States," Pyongyang crossed the red line of *state-to-state transfer* with its covert provision of a prototype nuclear reactor to Syria. Shortly after Israel bombed that facility in September 2007 while it was under construction, the arrival of a North Korean cargo ship in a Syrian port prompted Secretary of Defense Robert Gates to warn against DPRK nuclear exports: "If such an activity were taking place, it would be a matter of great concern because the president has put down a very strong marker with the North Koreans about further proliferation efforts, and obviously any effort by the Syrians to pursue weapons of mass destruction would be a concern."[143]

Interdiction through the Proliferation Security Initiative (PSI), a multinational effort launched by the Bush administration in May 2003, has been an important tool in preventing transfers of WMD technology and missile delivery systems to states of concern and nonstate actors. In late December 2010, for example, a North Korean ship suspected of carrying nuclear or ballistic missile technology bound for Burma was intercepted and (though not forcibly boarded) eventually turned back.[144] China argues that such interdiction activities constitute a violation of state sovereignty and has refused to join PSI. Accordingly, in April 2004, Beijing blocked the inclusion of PSI in Security Council Resolution 1540, which requires all states to implement measures to prevent terrorist groups from acquiring WMD and related technologies. For the foreseeable future, sovereignty concerns are likely to frustrate efforts to realize President Obama's call in his April 2009 Prague speech to transform PSI into a "durable international institution."

Through PSI's interdiction activities, the United States aims to achieve *deterrence by denial*. The vital complement is U.S. declaratory policy, a form of *deterrence by punishment* under which states are to be held fully accountable for their actions. A key issue, considered earlier, is whether the United States should maintain this current stance of calculated ambiguity. Or to deter a nuclear transfer from a state to a terrorist group, such as Al Qaeda, should it explicitly threaten a regime-changing response?

Washington's ability to provide reassurance to U.S. allies that is both militarily and politically credible is essential to prevent them from acquiring independent nuclear capabilities to counter North Korea and Iran. Indeed, so credible is the U.S. commitment of extended deterrence that North Korea's decision to cross the red line of nuclear testing in October 2006 did not precipitate a cascade of proliferation in northeast Asia. In its aftermath, neither Japan nor South Korea has fundamentally reconsidered its nonnuclear status. South Korea has long lived under the threat of North Korea's forward-deployed artillery holding Seoul hostage to the equivalent of a nuclear weapon. In the Middle East, Iran's regional ascendance is viewed as carrying a greater risk of catalytic proliferation if the Islamic Republic crosses the nuclear threshold. But given the possible regional reaction to an overt nuclear Iran, and in the absence of an urgent threat, Iran may choose to continue a nuclear hedge strategy indefinitely. The U.S. nuclear umbrella, which was a major factor constraining nuclear proliferation in Europe and Asia during the Cold War, will remain essential in the Middle East. In July 2009, Secretary of State Hillary Clinton, reiterating that extended nuclear deterrent commitment to U.S. allies in the Persian Gulf, stated that Iran would not be permitted to "intimidate and dominate" the region if it acquired nuclear weapons.[145] Proliferation dynamics in northeast Asia and the Persian Gulf also have important implications for the deployment of U.S. conventional forces as a tangible symbol of the U.S. security commitment to deter and, if necessary, counter North Korean and Iranian military adventurism.

The outlier states pose a frontal challenge to the global nuclear order whose cornerstone is the NPT. With both North Korea and Iran, a retooled strategy of containment—one combining coercive diplomacy, deterrence, and reassurance—would decouple the nuclear issue from the question of regime change and harness internal forces as the agent of societal change.

Conclusion

Outlaw. Pariah. Crazy. Backlash. Renegade. Rogue. Outlier. Policy-makers and analysts have used them all to describe a diverse set of states that flout established international norms. From the Cold War through the post-9/11 eras, the connotation of the terms, as examined in Chapter 1, has varied considerably across two dimensions.

The first is whether the conduct of concern violates *internal* or *external* behavioral norms. An important shift in emphasis from the former to the latter occurred around 1980. Before then, terms such as "outlaw," "pariah," and "rogue" referred to regimes, such as Idi Amin's Uganda and Pol Pot's Cambodia, that abused their own populace. After 1980, the "rogue state" moniker (with Saddam Hussein's Iraq as archetype) was linked to conduct that violated external behavioral norms with respect to weapons of mass destruction (WMD) proliferation and state sponsorship of terrorism. (Secretary of State Condoleezza Rice's term "outposts of tyranny"—which she named as "Cuba, Iran, North Korea, Zimbabwe, Burma, and Belarus"—encompassed *both* human rights pariahs and countries of proliferation concern.)[1] But whereas states that defy external behavioral norms invariably violate internal behavioral norms, the reverse is not always the case. Thus, whereas North Korea and Iran are states of proliferation concern that also violate the rights of their citizens, Zimbabwe and Burma are human rights pariahs that are neither pursuing nuclear weapons nor sponsoring terrorism.

The second key respect in which the use of terms such as "outlaw" or "pariah" state has varied relates to the *character* of a ruling regime. After 9/11, President George W. Bush declared that the threatening conduct of rogue states was but a reflection of their "true nature." The Bush administration, viewing Saddam Hussein's Iraq and other rogue states through the

177

"prism of 9/11," controversially argued that durable changes in behavior could be achieved only through changes of regime; the rehabilitation and reintegration of irredeemable rogue regimes into the "community of nations" was not possible—and the administration was not prepared to run that risk. In eschewing the "rogue" rubric and introducing the term "outlier," President Barack Obama was reportedly sending a deliberate message: a "pathway" back into the international community was open to those states whose ruling regimes made the "choice" to no longer defy the "rules-based international system."

Yet that rules-based international order from which the outliers stand apart is in flux. In his classic work *The Twenty Years' Crisis*, E. H. Carr elucidated how international norms are a manifestation of the international system's hierarchy of power; a redistribution of power among major states (particularly when a rising power challenges the status quo) can trigger instability and potentially conflict.[2] The current rise of the so-called BRICs (Brazil, Russia, India, and China) heralds just such a possible redistribution. The paramount question is whether these power shifts will undermine what, since the end of the Cold War, has been the defining feature of international relations: the lower risk of major conflict among the great powers. That decreased risk reflects Russia's and China's societal evolution from revolutionary states into orthodox (albeit still nondemocratic) great powers. Although both states vigorously assert their interests on their geographic peripheries (witness Russia's incursion into Georgia's and China's naval deployments in the South China Sea), neither is advancing an alternative vision to the current "liberal international order." That order is based largely on Western norms that were in the political DNA of the modern state system as it expanded globally from its European origins. With "the rise of the rest," however, the BRICs and other states will seek to influence the defining and enforcing of international norms commensurate with the new distribution of systemic power. Increasingly, the norms that allow reference to the international system as a "community" or a "society" will be contested. Hence, the Chinese government bluntly rejected the U.S. State Department's criticism of its human rights record by invoking an alternative definition that focuses not on individual rights (as in the Western tradition) but on collective rights (relating to the social safety net).

Social scientist Samuel Huntington's term "uni-multipolar" captures the hybrid character of an international system in transition—unipolar militarily, multipolar politically and economically.[3] For the United States, the "unipolar moment" (in conservative commentator Charles Krauthammer's phrase) is over.[4] Although America is no longer a "hyperpower" that can unilaterally determine outcomes, it remains the leading power (primus inter pares) in international relations. As Henry Kissinger observed in a November 2008 essay titled "An End of Hubris," America "will remain the most powerful country, but not retain the position of self-proclaimed tutor"; Washington should learn "the limits of hegemony" by moving "beyond largely American conceptions" when working with the BRICs to address global challenges.[5]

The key to America's success after World War II, according to political scientist John Ikenberry, was the embedding of U.S. military and economic power in multilateral institutions, which made it more legitimate and less threatening to others.[6] But with the redefinition of threat after 9/11, President Bush declared that the United States would no longer be bound by (and would not "seek a permission slip" from) the United Nations to defend itself. This departure underlay the decision to launch a preventive war against Iraq in 2003 without the legitimizing imprimatur of the UN Security Council. Under Barack Obama, the pendulum has swung back from unilateralism to multilateralism. Consistent with that shift, the challenge posed by outliers has been recast in terms of noncompliance with international norms instead of fitting the unilateral American rogue model.

In sum, the policy dilemmas arising from definitional issues associated with terms such as "pariah" and "outlier" state may be exacerbated by the ongoing redistribution of power in the international system and its uncertain implications for the United States. Central to this interconnected set of issues is the cornerstone principle of international relations: sovereignty.

The setting and enforcement of norms will remain a dilemma in an international system that lacks a supranational authority and relies on states to consensually opt into international law (through treaty or custom). The question is particularly thorny with respect to internal behavioral norms, given the Westphalian protection of the state against intervention by other states in their domestic affairs. The founders of the United Nations after World War II briefly considered barring rogue states from membership but ultimately decided that it was better to have the worst of the worst inside the institution and subject to its pressures rather than in some outside "lawless zone."

The inherently contentious nature of challenges to national sovereignty was evident in the U.S.-led and U.S.-assisted military interventions in Iraq and Libya, respectively. In 2003, with Iraq, President George W. Bush was unable to obtain the Security Council's authorization of military intervention because the administration maintained that bringing Saddam Hussein into compliance with the Security Council's disarmament resolutions would require the negation of Iraqi sovereignty through an externally imposed regime change. By contrast, in 1990, President George H. W. Bush readily received Security Council authorization to reverse Iraq's brazen 1930s-style interstate aggression against Kuwait. In 2011, with Libya, though the Security Council resolution approving the use of force made no mention of regime change, U.S. and North Atlantic Treaty Organization officials did not conceal their intent to oust Muammar Qaddafi from power under a "responsibility to protect" rubric. In the aftermath of the regime change in Tripoli, the Russian government asserted that the UN-approved mission in Libya set no precedent for Syria, which was then experiencing widespread civil unrest against the Assad regime.

The international community is broadly resistant on sovereignty grounds to externally induced changes of regime, even when undertaken to prevent gross violations of human rights. The Iraq and Libya interventions in the decade after 9/11 were not unlike Tanzania's incursion into Uganda and Vietnam's invasion of Cambodia in the late 1970s. Although the intervening parties claimed humanitarian justifications in both the Ugandan and Libyan cases, hard calculations of strategic interest also underlay their decision-making. The international community largely acquiesced to the regime changes, with no acrimonious debates in the Security Council, because no major power saw its interests affected by the oustings of Idi Amin and Qaddafi. Those conditions did not pertain in the cases of Cambodia and Iraq. Vietnam's invasion of Cambodia to topple the "auto-genocidal" Pol Pot regime was viewed by the superpowers from the perspective of their Cold War interests and ultimately condemned by the Security Council. The U.S. invasion of Iraq was similarly viewed by the major powers through a strategic prism and was launched after a rancorous debate split the Security Council's permanent members.

A major challenge for policy-makers is how to address an outlier state's threatening external behavior (with respect to proliferation and terrorism) while not turning a blind eye to egregious internal behavior (with respect to human rights). The functional issue of concern—most notably, the North Korean and Iranian nuclear programs—is embedded in the broader question of those states' societal evolution. As discussed in Chapter 3, strategies—whether to contain, engage, or change—are premised on concepts of societal change that should flow from a rigorous analysis of the outlier state's strategic culture (or "political personality," in George

Kennan's phrase).[7] Key threshold assumptions about societal change are frequently unarticulated or reflect an ideological predilection—or even a vain hope. For example, a 2002 assessment by a senior George W. Bush official that North Korea was "teetering" buttressed the administration's preferred squeeze strategy to bring about regime change in Pyongyang through regime collapse. The link between strategies and concepts of societal change is similarly evident in the ongoing debate about Iran's nuclear program, in which some argue that a military strike on Iran's nuclear infrastructure could trigger a civil society uprising against the clerical regime. America's foreign policy debacles of the past half-century—Vietnam and Iraq—have stemmed from flawed strategies based on faulty target state analysis. Although each case is highly context dependent, the development of a specific strategy toward a particular outlier state should be informed by what political scientist Alexander George called "conditional generalizations," derived from the structured comparison of a range of historical cases. (Thus, the analysis of historical pathways in Chapter 2 illuminated the development of targeted strategies toward the outlier states described in Chapters 3 and 4.)

What were the concepts of societal change in the two "rogue states"—Iraq and Libya—that were the targets of external intervention to bring about regime change?

Iraq: The underlying assumption of the George H. W. Bush administration in the wake of the 1991 war was that Saddam Hussein would not survive the humiliation of military defeat by the coalition forces and that elements of his own regime would move against him in a coup. When that did not occur, comprehensive sanctions imposed by the Security Council were viewed as the instrument whose punishing effect would generate popular pressure for regime change. The administration and subsequent administrations failed to anticipate Saddam's political durability, made possible through the brutal efficiency of his internal security services and elite military units. By the time George W. Bush assumed office, with international sanctions eroding, no internal pathway to regime change was evident. Against that backdrop, President Bush decided that the exigencies of the post-9/11 era—the "nexus" of proliferation and terrorism—called for a preventive war to topple the Saddam regime. In her memoir, former secretary of state Condoleezza Rice writes, "The fact is, we invaded Iraq because we believed we had run out of other options. The sanctions were not working, the [UN weapons] inspections were unsatisfactory, and we could not get Saddam to leave by other means."[8] The administration never seriously considered the alternative option of continued containment and deterrence, as advocated by former national security adviser Brent Scowcroft, among others. George W. Bush also made the critical decision to expand the mission in Iraq from decapitating the Saddam regime to bringing democracy. But the administration, whose officials often likened Saddam's regime to the Nazis, embarked on a Germany-style transformation without a Germany-sized occupying force. The toppling of Saddam's statue in central Baghdad was accompanied by widespread looting that (along with the deep de-Baathification program and the disbanding of the Iraqi army) set the occupation on a downward trajectory. As discussed in Chapter 2, the conditions that set the Federal Republic of Germany on a pathway into the community of nations (through democratization and reintegration) were present neither within Iraq nor among its neighboring states.

Libya: The surprise December 2003 announcement of Libya's accession to verified WMD disarmament completed the strategic turnabout that Qaddafi initiated in the late 1990s to end the country's international pariah status. Central to Libya's disarmament was a tacit but clear assurance of regime security from the Bush administration to Qaddafi if he relinquished his unconventional arsenal.[9] With the WMD agreement and the settlement of the Pan Am 103 terrorist bombing, the Qaddafi regime ended the external behavior that had led to Libya's designation as a "rogue state." But the agreements did not address Qaddafi's atrocious human rights record. The implicit concept of societal change underlying U.S. strategy toward Libya after 2003 was that Libya's increased integration into the global economy would empower technocrats and an entrepreneurial middle class to press for economic reform. The expansion of economic links with the outside world and the creation of domestic constituencies for economic reform would promote the development of Libya's civil society. Despite that hopeful scenario in which economic change would drive political change, Qaddafi was able to tangibly benefit from Libya's rehabilitation while inoculating his regime from the political contagion that might occur through increased economic integration. Significantly, the United States and other Western states attached no political conditionality to their expanded economic relations with the Qaddafi regime. Such conditionality has been an important instrument for the European Union to bring candidate member states in Eastern Europe into increased compliance with internal behavioral norms. Yet the sobering reality is that such success has been difficult to replicate beyond Europe. A comparative study of transitions from autocracy found that "even where political conditionality was applied, autocrats frequently enjoyed considerable room to maneuver [and] often got away with minimal reforms that fell short of democracy."[10]

The United States will, with reason, continue to focus primarily on threatening conduct that violates *external* behavioral norms. But along with a forthright declaratory policy that sheds light on human rights abuses by outlier states, a push to extend the rule of law to the expansion of economic relations (a tacit form of political conditionality) could help to promote improved compliance with *internal* behavioral norms.

The ongoing nuclear crises with North Korea and Iran are unfolding against the political backdrop of the precedents set in Iraq and Libya. With both North Korea and Iran, the prospect of an externally induced change of regime is remote. The Iraq precedent of a Germany-style invasion and occupation by the United States is not applicable, under foreseeable circumstances, to these cases. Even the replication of the Libya precedent, where the precipitants of change were indigenous and organic, would be highly problematic. Neither Iran nor North Korea is Libya, where a state with a small population clustered in coastal cities was susceptible to outside military intervention in support of a popular uprising whose magnitude eclipsed the Qaddafi regime's coercive capabilities.

In responding to questions and criticism about the inconsistency of U.S. policy—why Libya and not Syria or Iran—Secretary of State Hillary Clinton stated, "The answer starts with a very practical point: Situations vary dramatically from country to country. It would be foolish to take a one-size-fits-all approach and barrel forward regardless of circumstances on the ground. Sometimes, as in Libya, we can bring dozens of countries together to protect civilians and help people liberate their country without a single American life lost. In other cases, to achieve that same goal, we would have to act alone, at a much greater cost, with far greater risks, and perhaps even with troops on the ground."[11]

In the case of North Korea, the only plausible pathway of externally induced regime change would be of the kind undertaken by regional neighbors, such as the Tanzanian intervention in Uganda and the Vietnamese invasion of Cambodia to oust tyrannical regimes. Although China has the proximity and power to bring about a regime change in Pyonyang—a development that would be embraced by the international community, notwithstanding its breach of sovereignty—Beijing remains unlikely to do so. It has provided the necessary subventions to maintain the Kim family regime's political power through disastrous economic circumstances that could have otherwise threatened regime stability. If, however, the post–

Conclusion

Kim Jong Il succession were to create a regime crisis—for example, a violent factional struggle—it might well precipitate overt Chinese action in North Korea.[12]

If externally induced change is severely constrained in North Korea and Iran (both on sovereignty grounds and conditions within the target states), what are the potential pathways and prospects for internally induced change?

With North Korea, Secretary of State Clinton's assessment of Qaddafi— he "spent forty-two years hollowing out every part of his government not connected ... to keeping him in power"—would appear to hold true of the Kim family.[13] With a totalitarian grip that Ceauşescu envied, the North Korean regime is unlikely to be challenged by a civil society uprising. One possible pathway would be a Ceauşescu-style coup against the Kim family by the regime's core support groups: the military and the security services. After the death of Kim Jong Il, is yet another dynastic succession from Kim father to Kim son possible? The Kim family cult is central to regime legitimacy. That Kim Jong Il was no Kim Il Sung holds doubly true for Kim Jong Un. The succession becomes the occasion for intra-elite bargaining, with an indeterminate outcome. Outside powers—China far above all others—have the ability to influence this process.

With Iran, the ascension of the reformist president Mohammed Khatami in the late 1990s created hopes of regime change through political evolution, as had occurred in the Soviet Union. This potential pathway was captured in the characterization of Khatami by admirers as "Ayatollah Gorbachev." Ultimately, however, Khatami was unwilling to challenge the key tenet of the regime of which he was part: the role of the supreme leader. The rightward shift in Iranian politics, symbolized by election of the hard-line president Mahmoud Ahmadinejad in 2005, ended speculation about reform from within. The Green Movement emerged in 2009 as an indigenous movement, but it too has sought the reform, not the overthrow, of the Islamic Republic's ruling regime.

The nuclear issue is a surrogate for the broader debate about Iran's role in the world. That is why the Iranian regime rejected a Libyan-type deal to bring its nuclear program into nuclear Nonproliferation Treaty compliance. A senior Iranian national security official, Hassan Rouhani, tellingly observed that the Libyan model "does not [just] mean that they would only assemble all centrifuges and put them on a ship and send them to Washington. The Libyan model means following the path of recognizing Israel, means [cutting] off relations with liberation movements in the world."[14]

Integration with the outside world is thus viewed as a slippery slope that potentially threatens regime survival. The United States should be willing to offer a straightforward assurance of nonintervention and nonbelligerence if an outlier state comes into compliance with its nuclear Nonproliferation Treaty obligations. But Washington neither can nor should offer to insulate an outlier regime from the political consequences of its increased integration into the international system.

Although outside pressure can raise the costs of Iranian noncompliance, Russia and China have been resistant. Moscow and Beijing often seem more intent on blocking U.S. diplomacy than on generating meaningful pressure to prevent the rise of another nuclear weapons state on their periphery. After the International Atomic Energy Agency reported in November 2011 that Iran had resumed work on nuclear weaponization, the Russian Foreign Ministry rejected the imposition of additional sanctions on the Tehran regime, asserting that such punitive measures would "be seen in the international community as an instrument for regime change in Iran."[15] Even as the United States and its European allies have imposed tough sanctions targeting the Iranian regime's core interest groups, President Obama has hypothesized, "It may be that [the Iranian regime's] ideological commitment to nuclear weapons is such that they're not making a simple cost-benefit analysis on this issue."[16] Or Washington may simply not comprehend the Tehran regime's calculus of decision—that is, how it weighs its interests and values.

So here we are then. The Obama administration assumed office having no good option to deal with the North Korean and Iranian nuclear challenges. Every option carries risk. In neither country is a complete nuclear rollback possible. What level of risk are U.S. policy-makers prepared to run? Though North Korea has the more advanced nuclear program, it is an impoverished, insular state whose besieged regime is simply seeking to survive. By contrast, Iran, with its oil wealth and radical activism, remains the more dynamic threat. Kissinger's question—does Iran see itself as a nation or a cause?—persists. Iran retains the use of terrorism as an instrument of policy even as state sponsorship of terrorism has dramatically declined since 9/11. That outlier mentality and conduct reflect the extent to which the Iranian regime views its radical foreign policy as a source of domestic legitimation. Thus, Ahmadinejad has called for the creation of a "new world order" that would relegate Iran's enemies to the "graveyard."[17] The regime's execrable rhetoric ("Death to Israel"), Holocaust denial, and conspiracy theories (including the grotesque charge that the U.S. government carried out the 9/11 terrorist attacks to create a pretext to attack the Muslim world) reinforce the world's sense of urgency about the Iranian nuclear program. The case for a military strike on Iran's nuclear program rests on an assessment of the theocratic regime as undeterrable and apocalyptic. But that depiction of Iran as an irrational state runs contrary to National Intelligence Estimates that have characterized the clerical regime's decision-making as being "guided by a cost-benefit approach." When asked whether the Iranian regime was messianic or rational, President Obama stated, "I do think ... that as we look at how they operate and the decisions they've made over the past three decades, that they care about the regime's survival."[18]

In the wake of the November 2011 International Atomic Energy Agency report, which triggered renewed speculation about a U.S. (or Israeli) military strike on Iran's nuclear sites, Secretary of Defense Leon Panetta stated that such an action would delay the Iranian program by only three years and could have "unintended consequences."[19] A decision to bomb Iran's nuclear infrastructure is synonymous with a decision to go to war with Iran. In downplaying the military option, Panetta called for "the toughest sanctions—economic, diplomatic pressures—on Iran to change their behavior."[20] Such pressure to affect Iranian decision-making was applied through the "crippling sanctions" imposed by the United States and the European Union that, according to President Obama in a March 2012 interview, were "virtually grinding the Iranian economy to a halt."[21]

Iran's ability to enrich uranium gives it an inherent hedge option for a nuclear weapon. U.S. intelligence analysts maintain that Iran has not yet decided to cross the threshold from a potential capability to an actual weapon.[22] Indeed, as discussed in Chapter 4, the strategic ambiguity of a hedge—of going so far but no further, at least not yet—might well serve Iranian interests. With Iran under the pressure of sanctions, President Obama has observed that the Tehran regime has the opportunity to "make a strategic calculation that, at minimum, pushes [off] much further ... whatever potential breakout capacity they may have.... [F]or them to prove to the international community that their intentions are peaceful and that they are, in fact, not pursuing weapons, is not inconsistent with what they've said. So it doesn't require them to knuckle under to us."[23] But critics of the administration assert that, given the character of the Iranian regime, allowing Iran to retain even a latent capability to acquire nuclear weapons constitutes an unacceptable threat.

"I do not have a policy of containment; I have a policy to prevent Iran from obtaining a nuclear weapon," said President Obama in a speech to the American Israel Public Affairs Committee in March 2012.[24] His eschewal of "containment" is a reflection of the political optic through which the term has come to be viewed in the contemporary debate—acquiescing to Iran's successful development of nuclear weapons and then deterring their use through the retaliatory threat of U.S. nuclear weapons. This connotation is a departure from Kennan's concept of containment—keeping regimes in check until they collapsed of their own internal weakness—which Kennan advanced as a strategic alternative to détente and regime rollback to counter the threat of Joseph Stalin's Soviet Union.

A former U.S. senior official once quipped that "problems have solutions; dilemmas have horns." In the case of both Iran and North Korea, the nuclear question is a surrogate for the broader issue of their relationship with the outside world. President Obama, clarifying the Bush administration's mixed message about the objective of U.S. policy (regime change versus behavior change) offered the Iranian and North Korean regimes a "choice" and a "pathway" to rejoin the "community of nations." Yet that is the crux of the problem with the outliers: *the very process of integration, which the Obama administration depicts as a tangible reward for coming into compliance with international norms, is perceived in Tehran and Pyongyang as a threat to regime survival.*

Washington should remain pragmatically open to negotiations, but with the expectation, given the tortured history that has gotten us to where we are now, that such talks can realistically aim to bound, not roll back, the nuclear programs in both countries. But if engagement is problematic, the military option is no silver bullet: North Korea now has a small nuclear arsenal at unknown sites with which it could retaliate against an attack, and Iran has mastered the uranium enrichment process and could reconstitute its nuclear program after an attack. How then to straddle the horns of the dilemma? Between the poles of engagement and military action lies a third option on the policy continuum, which I support on the basis of this study's analysis: *a retooled, updated version of Kennan's strategy of containment that would decouple the nuclear issue from the question of regime change and rely on internal forces as the agent of societal change.*

The Obama administration's shift in nomenclature from "rogue" to "outlier" state is emblematic of its broader approach to foreign policy—an approach that defies easy labeling as an "Obama Doctrine." U.S. foreign policy is typically characterized in terms of the competing pulls of liberalism and realism—Wilson versus Kissinger, so to speak. In addition to those traditional two, President Obama's policy has tapped a third school of American thought: pragmatism. Pragmatism has deep and strong American roots, and America will do well not to lose sight of them in the enduring challenge of balancing its values and its interests.

Appendix

Excerpts from National Security Strategy Documents of September 2002 and May 2010

The following are excerpts of two key texts—the National Security Strategy documents of the George W. Bush and Barack Obama administrations, published in 2002 and 2010, respectively—that embody the shifting terms of U.S. strategy toward "rogue" and "outlier" states.

President George W. Bush's National Security Strategy, September 2002

… The nature of the Cold War threat required the United States—with our allies and friends—to emphasize deterrence of the enemy's use of force, producing a grim strategy of mutual assured destruction. With the collapse of the Soviet Union and the end of the Cold War, our security environment has undergone profound transformation.

Having moved from confrontation to cooperation as the hallmark of our relationship with Russia, the dividends are evident: an end to the balance of terror that divided us; an historic reduction in the nuclear arsenals on both sides; and cooperation in areas such as counterterrorism and missile defense that until recently were inconceivable.

But new deadly challenges have emerged from rogue states and terrorists. None of these contemporary threats rival the sheer destructive power that was arrayed against us by the Soviet Union. However, the nature and motivations of these new adversaries, their determination to obtain destructive powers hitherto available only to the world's strongest states, and the greater likelihood that they will use weapons of mass destruction against us, make today's security environment more complex and dangerous.

In the 1990s we witnessed the emergence of a small number of rogue states that, while different in important ways, share a number of attributes. These states:

- brutalize their own people and squander their national resources for the personal gain of the rulers;
- display no regard for international law, threaten their neighbors, and callously violate international treaties to which they are party;
- are determined to acquire weapons of mass destruction, along with other advanced military technology, to be used as threats or offensively to achieve the aggressive designs of these regimes;
- sponsor terrorism around the globe; and
- reject basic human values and hate the United States and everything for which it stands.

At the time of the Gulf War, we acquired irrefutable proof that Iraq's designs were not limited to the chemical weapons it had used against Iran and its own people, but also extended to the acquisition of nuclear weapons and biological agents. In the past decade North Korea has become the world's principal purveyor of ballistic missiles, and has tested increasingly capable missiles while developing its own WMD arsenal. Other rogue regimes seek nuclear, biological, and chemical weapons as well. These states' pursuit of, and global trade in, such weapons has become a looming threat to all nations.

We must be prepared to stop rogue states and their terrorist clients before they are able to threaten or use weapons of mass destruction against the United States and our allies and friends. Our response must take full advantage of strengthened alliances, the establishment of new partnerships with former adversaries, innovation in the use of military forces, modern technologies, including the development of an effective missile defense system, and increased emphasis on intelligence collection and analysis.

...

It has taken almost a decade for us to comprehend the true nature of this new threat. Given the goals of rogue states and terrorists, the United States can no longer solely rely on a reactive posture as we have in the past. The inability to deter a potential attacker, the immediacy of today's threats, and the magnitude of potential harm that could be caused by our adversaries' choice of weapons, do not permit that option. We cannot let our enemies strike first.

In the Cold War, especially following the Cuban missile crisis, we faced a generally status quo, risk-averse adversary. Deterrence was an effective defense. But deterrence based only upon the threat of retaliation is less likely to work against leaders of rogue states more willing to take risks, gambling with the lives of their people, and the wealth of their nations.

- In the Cold War, weapons of mass destruction were considered weapons of last resort whose use risked the destruction of those who used them. Today, our enemies see weapons of mass destruction as weapons of choice. For rogue states these weapons are tools of intimidation and military aggression against their neighbors. These weapons may also allow these states to attempt to blackmail the United States and our allies to prevent us from deterring or repelling the aggressive behavior of rogue states. Such states also see these weapons as their best means of overcoming the conventional superiority of the United States.
- Traditional concepts of deterrence will not work against a terrorist enemy whose avowed tactics are wanton destruction and the targeting of innocents; whose so-called soldiers seek martyrdom in death and whose most potent protection is statelessness. The overlap between states that sponsor terror and those that pursue WMD compels us to action.

For centuries, international law recognized that nations need not suffer an attack before they can lawfully take action to defend themselves against forces that present an imminent danger of attack. Legal scholars and international jurists often conditioned the legitimacy of preemption on the existence of an imminent threat—most often a visible mobilization of armies, navies, and air forces preparing to attack.

We must adapt the concept of imminent threat to the capabilities and objectives of today's adversaries. Rogue states and terrorists do not seek to attack us using conventional means. They know such attacks would fail. Instead, they rely on acts of terror and, potentially, the use of weapons of mass destruction—weapons that can be easily concealed, delivered covertly, and used without warning.

The targets of these attacks are our military forces and our civilian population, in direct violation of one of the principal norms of the law of warfare. As was demonstrated by the losses on September 11, 2001, mass civilian casualties is the specific objective of terrorists and these losses would be exponentially more severe if terrorists acquired and used weapons of mass destruction.

The United States has long maintained the option of preemptive actions to counter a sufficient threat to our national security. The greater the threat, the greater is the risk of inaction—and the more compelling the case for taking anticipatory action to defend ourselves, even if uncertainty remains as to the time and place of the enemy's attack. To forestall or prevent such hostile acts by our adversaries, the United States will, if necessary, act preemptively.

The United States will not use force in all cases to preempt emerging threats, nor should nations use preemption as a pretext for aggression. Yet in an age where the enemies of civilization openly and actively seek the world's most destructive technologies, the United States cannot remain idle while dangers gather....

Source: Full Text: "Bush's National Security Strategy," *New York Times*, September 20, 2002, http://www.nytimes.com/2002/09/20/politics/20STEXT _FULL.html?pagewanted=all.

President Barack Obama's National Security Strategy, May 2010

Pursuing Comprehensive Engagement

… Engagement is the active participation of the United States in relationships beyond our borders. It is, quite simply, the opposite of a self-imposed isolation that denies us the ability to shape outcomes. Indeed, America has never succeeded through isolationism. As the nation that helped to build our international system after World War II and to bring about the globalization that came with the end of the Cold War, we must reengage the world on a comprehensive and sustained basis.

Engagement begins with our closest friends and allies—from Europe to Asia; from North America to the Middle East. These nations share a common history of struggle on behalf of security, prosperity, and democracy. They share common values and a common commitment to international norms that recognize both the rights and responsibilities of all sovereign nations. America's national security depends on these vibrant alliances, and we must engage them as active partners in addressing global and regional security priorities and harnessing new opportunities to advance common interests. For instance, we pursue close and regular collaboration with our close allies the United Kingdom, France, and Germany on issues of mutual and global concern.

We will continue to deepen our cooperation with other 21st century centers of influence—including China, India, and Russia—on the basis of mutual interests and mutual respect. We will also pursue diplomacy and development that supports the emergence of new and successful partners, from the Americas to Africa; from the Middle East to Southeast Asia. Our ability to advance constructive cooperation is essential to the security and prosperity of specific regions, and to facilitating global cooperation on issues ranging from violent extremism and nuclear proliferation, to climate change, and global economic instability—issues that challenge all nations, but that no one nation alone can meet.

To adversarial governments, we offer a clear choice: abide by international norms, and achieve the political and economic benefits that come with greater integration with the international community; or refuse to accept this pathway, and bear the consequences of that decision, including greater isolation. Through engagement, we can create opportunities to resolve differences, strengthen the international community's support for our actions, learn about the intentions and nature of closed regimes, and plainly demonstrate to the publics within those nations that their governments are to blame for their isolation.

Successful engagement will depend upon the effective use and integration of different elements of American power. Our diplomacy and development capabilities must help prevent conflict, spur economic growth, strengthen weak and failing states, lift people out of poverty, combat climate change and epidemic disease, and strengthen institutions of democratic governance. Our military will continue strengthening its capacity to partner with foreign counterparts, train and assist security forces, and pursue military-to-military ties with a broad range of governments. We will continue to foster economic and financial transactions to advance our shared prosperity. And our intelligence and law enforcement agencies must cooperate effectively with foreign governments to anticipate events, respond to crises, and provide safety and security.

...

Promoting a Just and Sustainable International Order

Our engagement will underpin a just and sustainable international order— just, because it advances mutual interests, protects the rights of all, and holds accountable those who refuse to meet their responsibilities; sustainable because it is based on broadly shared norms and fosters collective action to address common challenges.

This engagement will pursue an international order that recognizes the rights and responsibilities of all nations. As we did after World War II, we must pursue a rules-based international system that can advance our own interests by serving mutual interests. International institutions must be more effective and representative of the diffusion of influence in the 21st century. Nations must have incentives to behave responsibly, or be isolated when they do not. The test of this international order must be the cooperation it facilitates and the results it generates—the ability of nations to come together to confront common challenges like violent extremism, nuclear proliferation, climate change, and a changing global economy.

That is precisely the reason we should strengthen enforcement of international law and our commitment to engage and modernize international institutions and frameworks. Those nations that refuse to meet their responsibilities will forsake the opportunities that come with international cooperation. Credible and effective alternatives to military action—from sanctions to isolation—must be strong enough to change behavior, just as we must reinforce our alliances and our military capabilities. And if nations challenge or undermine an international order that is based upon rights and responsibilities, they must find themselves isolated.

We succeeded in the post–World War II era by pursuing our interests within multilateral forums like the United Nations—not outside of them. We recognized that institutions that aggregated the national interests of many nations would never be perfect; but we also saw that they were an indispensable vehicle for pooling international resources and enforcing international norms. Indeed, the basis for international cooperation since World War II has been an architecture of international institutions, organizations, regimes, and standards that establishes certain rights and responsibilities for all sovereign nations.

In recent years America's frustration with international institutions has led us at times to engage the United Nations system on an ad hoc basis. But in a world of transnational challenges, the United States will need to invest in strengthening the international system, working from inside international institutions and frameworks to face their imperfections head on and to mobilize transnational cooperation.

We must be clear-eyed about the factors that have impeded effectiveness in the past. In order for collective action to be mobilized, the polarization that persists across region, race, and religion will need to be replaced by a galvanizing sense of shared interest. Swift and effective international action often turns on the political will of coalitions of countries that comprise regional or international institutions. New and emerging powers who seek greater voice and representation will need to accept greater responsibility for meeting global challenges. When nations breach agreed international norms, the countries who espouse those norms must be convinced to band together to enforce them.

We will expand our support to modernizing institutions and arrangements such as the evolution of the G-8 to the G-20 to reflect the realities of today's international environment. Working with the institutions and the countries that comprise them, we will enhance international capacity to prevent conflict, spur economic growth, improve security, combat climate change, and address the challenges posed by weak and failing states. And we will challenge and assist international institutions and frameworks to reform when they fail to live up to their promise. Strengthening the legitimacy and authority of international law and institutions, especially the U.N., will require a constant struggle to improve performance.

…

Reverse the Spread of Nuclear and Biological Weapons and Secure Nuclear Materials

The American people face no greater or more urgent danger than a terrorist attack with a nuclear weapon. And international peace and security is threatened by proliferation that could lead to a nuclear exchange. Indeed, since the end of the Cold War, the risk of a nuclear attack has increased. Excessive Cold War stockpiles remain. More nations have acquired nuclear weapons. Testing has continued. Black markets trade in nuclear secrets and materials. Terrorists are determined to buy, build, or steal a nuclear weapon. Our efforts to contain these dangers are centered in a global nonproliferation regime that has frayed as more people and nations break the rules.

That is why reversing the spread of nuclear weapons is a top priority. Success depends upon broad consensus and concerted action, we will move forward strategically on a number of fronts through our example, our partnerships, and a reinvigorated international regime. The United States will:

Pursue the Goal of a World Without Nuclear Weapons: While this goal will not be reached during this Administration, its active pursuit and eventual achievement will increase global security, keep our commitment under the NPT, build our cooperation with Russia and other states, and increase our credibility to hold others accountable for their obligations. As long as any nuclear weapons exist, the United States will sustain a safe, secure, and effective nuclear arsenal, both to deter potential adversaries and to assure U.S. allies and other security partners that they can count on America's security commitments. But we have signed and seek to ratify a landmark New START Treaty with Russia to substantially limit our deployed nuclear warheads and strategic delivery vehicles, while assuring a comprehensive monitoring regime. We are reducing the role of nuclear weapons in our national security approach, extending a negative security assurance not to use or threaten to use nuclear weapons against those nonnuclear nations that are in compliance with the NPT and their nuclear nonproliferation obligations, and investing in the modernization of a safe, secure, and effective stockpile without the production of new nuclear weapons. We will pursue ratification of the Comprehensive Test Ban Treaty. And we will seek a new treaty that verifiably ends the production of fissile materials intended for use in nuclear weapons.

Strengthen the Nuclear Non-Proliferation Treaty: The basic bargain of the NPT is sound: countries with nuclear weapons will move toward disarmament; countries without nuclear weapons will forsake them; and all countries can access peaceful nuclear energy. To strengthen the NPT, we will seek more resources and authority for international inspections. We will develop a new framework for civil nuclear cooperation. As members of the Global Nuclear Energy Partnership have agreed, one important element of an enhanced framework could be cradle-to-grave nuclear fuel management. We will pursue a broad, international consensus to insist that all nations meet their obligations. And we will also pursue meaningful consequences for countries that fail to meet their obligations under the NPT or to meet the requirements for withdrawing from it.

Present a Clear Choice to Iran and North Korea: The United States will pursue the denuclearization of the Korean peninsula and work to prevent Iran from developing a nuclear weapon. This is not about singling out nations—it is about the responsibilities of all nations and the success of the nonproliferation regime. Both nations face a clear choice. If North Korea eliminates its nuclear weapons program, and Iran meets its international obligations on its nuclear program, they will be able to proceed on a path to greater political and economic integration with the international community. If they ignore their international obligations, we will pursue multiple means to increase their isolation and bring them into compliance with international nonproliferation norms.

...

Advance Peace, Security, and Opportunity in the Greater Middle East

...

Promote a Responsible Iran: For decades, the Islamic Republic of Iran has endangered the security of the region and the United States and failed to live up to its international responsibilities. In addition to its illicit nuclear program, it continues to support terrorism, undermine peace between Israelis and Palestinians, and deny its people their universal rights. Many years of refusing to engage Iran failed to reverse these trends; on the contrary, Iran's behavior became more threatening. Engagement is something we pursue without illusion. It can offer Iran a pathway to a better future, provided Iran's leaders are prepared to take it. But that better pathway can only be achieved if Iran's leaders change course, act to restore the confidence of the international community, and fulfill their obligations. The United States seeks a future in which Iran meets its international responsibilities, takes its rightful place in the community of nations, and enjoys the political and economic opportunities that its people deserve. Yet if the Iranian Government continues to refuse to live up to its international obligations, it will face greater isolation.

...

Values

...

Practicing Principled Engagement with Non-Democratic Regimes: Even when we are focused on interests such as counterterrorism, nonproliferation, or enhancing economic ties, we will always seek in parallel to expand individual rights and opportunities through our bilateral engagement. The United States is pursuing a dual-track approach in which we seek to improve government-to-government relations and use this dialogue to advance human rights, while engaging civil society and peaceful political opposition, and encouraging U.S. nongovernmental actors to do the same. More substantive government-to-government relations can create permissive conditions for civil society to operate and for more extensive people-to-people exchanges. But when our overtures are rebuffed, we must lead the international community in using public and private diplomacy, and drawing on incentives and disincentives, in an effort to change repressive behavior....

Source: White House, "National Security Strategy," May 2010, http:// www.whitehouse.gov/sites/default/files/rss_viewer/national_security_ strategy.pdf.

Notes

Introduction

1. David E. Sanger and Thom Shanker, "Obama's Nuclear Strategy Intended as a Message," *New York Times*, April 7, 2010, A6, http://www.nytimes.com/2010/04/07/world/07arms.html?scp=9&sq=David+E.+Sanger&st=nyt.

2. Letter from National Security Adviser Sandy Berger to the author, February 21, 2000.

3. White House, "President Barack Obama's Inaugural Address," January 20, 2009, http://www.whitehouse.gov/blog/inaugural-address/.

4. White House, "Remarks by the President at the Acceptance of the Nobel Peace Prize," December 10, 2009, http://www.whitehouse.gov/the-press-office/remarks-president-acceptance-nobel-peace-prize.

5. White House, "National Security Strategy 2010," May 2010, http://www.whitehouse.gov/sites/default/files/rss_viewer/national_security_strategy.pdf.

6. Ibid., 11.

7. George F. Kennan ("X"), "The Sources of Soviet Conduct," *Foreign Affairs* 25, no. 4 (July 1947): 566–82, http://www.historyguide.org/europe/kennan.html.

8. Ibid.

1 Outlier States and International Society

1. White House, "National Security Strategy 2010," May 2010, 40, http://www.whitehouse.gov/sites/default/files/rss_viewer/national_security_strategy.pdf.

2. Ibid., 11, 12.

3. Hedley Bull, *The Anarchical Society: A Study of Order in World Politics*, 3rd ed. (New York: Palgrave, 2002; originally 1977), 9–10.

4. Ibid., 13.

5. An early example is Thomas Jefferson's letter to James Monroe on March 22, 1822, in which Jefferson states that the United States should be "the first to receive and welcome [newly independent South American republics] into the family of nations."

See Thomas Jefferson, *The Writings of Thomas Jefferson*, vol. 10 (Charleston, SC: BiblioBazaar, 2008), 208.

6. Senator Barack Obama's speech at Woodrow Wilson International Center, Washington, DC, August 1, 2007 (emphasis added), http://www.cfr.org/publication/13974/obamas_speech_at_woodrow_wilson_center.html.

7. White House, "National Security Strategy 2002," September 17, 2002, 13–14, http://georgewbush-whitehouse.archives.gov/nsc/nss/2002/.

8. Ibid., transmittal letter.

9. George W. Bush, "Address before a Joint Session of the Congress on the State of the Union," in *Weekly Compilation of Presidential Documents* 38, no. 5 (2002): 133–39, http://frwebgate.access.gpo.gov/cgi-bin/getdoc.cgi?dbname=2002_presidential_documents&docid=pd04fe02_txt-11.pdf.

10. James Mann, *The Rise of the Vulcans: The History of Bush's War Cabinet* (New York: Viking, 2004), 92–93.

11. George W. Bush, "Second Inaugural Address," January 20, 2005, http://www.bartleby.com/124/pres67.html.

12. Robert Jervis, "The Remaking of a Unipolar World," *Washington Quarterly* 29, no. 3 (Summer 2006): 7–8, 13.

13. Elaine Sciolino, "Clinton Steps In and the World Looks On," *New York Times*, January 24, 1993, sec. 4, p. 1.

14. Steve Schifferes, "Rumsfeld Brushes aside WMD Fears," *BBC News Online*, July 9, 2003, http://news.bbc.co.uk/2/hi/americas/3054423.stm.

15. David E. Sanger, "Viewing the War as a Lesson to the World," *New York Times*, April 6, 2003, B1.

16. Richard W. Stevenson and Felicity Barringer, "A Nation at War: Recovery; Bush Urging U.N. to Lift Sanctions Imposed on Iraq," *New York Times*, April 17, 2003, http://www.nytimes.com/2003/04/17/world/a-nation-at-war-recovery-bush-urging-un-to-lift-sanctions-imposed-on-iraq.html?scp=1&sq=redefined+war&st=nyt&pagewanted=print.

17. Sonni Efron, "War with Iraq/Diplomacy: Looking Past Baghdad to the Next Challenge," *Los Angeles Times*, April 6, 2003, 10.

18. Vice President Dick Cheney, as quoted in Glenn Kessler, "Cheney Wields Power with Few Fingerprints," *Washington Post*, October 5, 2004, A1.

19. Quoted in Robert McMahon, "Negotiating with Hostile States," Council on Foreign Relations Backgrounder, June 2, 2008 (emphasis added), http://www.cfr.org/publication/16402/negotiating_with_hostile_states.html.

20. Tahman Bradley, "Kissinger Backs Direct Talks 'Without Conditions' with Iran," September 15, 2008, http://blogs.abcnews.com/politicalradar/2008/09/kissinger-backs.html.

21. Lydia Saad, "Americans Favor President Meeting with U.S. Enemies," June 2, 2008, http://www.gallup.com/poll/107617/Americans-Favor-President-Meeting-US-Enemies.aspx.

22. White House, "President Barack Obama's Inaugural Address," January 20, 2009, http://www.whitehouse.gov/blog/inaugural-address/.

23. George H. W. Bush, "Inaugural Address," January 20, 1989, http://www.bartleby.com/124/pres63.html. Like Obama, Bush used the fist imagery: "The 'offered hand' is a reluctant fist."

24. Alexander George, "The Role of Knowledge in Policymaking," in *Bridging the Gap: Theory and Practice in Foreign Policy* (Washington, DC: United States Institute of Peace Press, 1993), 19–30.

25. U.S. Department of State, "Secretary of State Hillary Rodham Clinton Interview with David Sanger and Mark Landler of the *New York Times*," August 6, 2010, http://www.state.gov/secretary/rm/2010/08/145784.htm.

26. As quoted in Glenn Kessler, "Protests Loom in London for Visit by Bush," *Washington Post*, November 17, 2003, A1.

27. George's contribution is assessed in Jack S. Levy, "Deterrence and Coercive Diplomacy: The Contributions of Alexander George," *Political Psychology*, vol. 29, no. 4 (August 2008): 537–51.

28. "National Security Strategy 2010," 11.

29. Ibid., 24.

30. Clinton, "Interview with David Sanger and Mark Landler of the *New York Times*."

31. Ibid.

32. As quoted in David E. Sanger, "U.S. Seeks to Offer a Balm to Iran for Sanctions' Sting," *New York Times*, August 8, 2010, A10, http://www.nytimes.com/2010/08/08/world/middleeast/08sanctions.html?scp=17&sq=&st=nyt.

33. Geir Lundestad, *The American "Empire,"* (Oxford: Oxford University Press, 1991), 54–62.

34. G. John Ikenberry, *After Victory: Institutions, Strategic Restraint, and the Rebuilding of Order after Major Wars* (Princeton, NJ: Princeton University Press, 2001), 246–56.

35. George W. Bush, "State of the Union Address" January 20, 2004, http://millercenter.org/president/speeches/detail/4542.

36. John Lewis Gaddis, *Surprise, Security, and the American Experience* (Cambridge, MA: Harvard University Press, 2004), 101.

37. On unipolarity versus unilateralism, see Robert S. Litwak, "The Overuse of American Power," in *History and Neorealism*, ed. Ernest R. May, Richard Rosecrance, and Zara Steiner (Cambridge: Cambridge University Press, 2010), 246–66.

38. White House, Office of the Press Secretary, "Remarks by the President in Address to the Nation on the End of Combat Operations in Iraq," August 31, 2010, http://www.whitehouse.gov/the-press-office/2010/08/31/remarks-president-address-nation-end-combat-operations-iraq.

39. The term "unipolar moment" was coined by Charles Krauthammer in an influential *Foreign Affairs* article of that title in the *America and the World* 1990–91 edition, *Foreign Affairs* 70, no. 1 (1990–91): 23–33. After 9/11, he updated his analysis in "The Unipolar Moment Revisited," *National Interest* 70 (Winter 2002): 5–17.

40. CNN/USA Today/Gallup poll cited in CNN, "Poll: Sending Troops to Iraq a Mistake," June 25, 2004, http://www.cnn.com/2004/ALLPOLITICS/06/24/poll.iraq/.

41. John Mueller, "The Iraq Syndrome," *Foreign Affairs* 84, no. 6 (November–December 2005): 44–54.

42. Meg Bortin, "Survey Finds Deep Discontent with American Foreign Policy," *New York Times*, November 18, 2005, A12.

43. Gerald F. Seib, "Deficit Balloons into National-Security Threat," *Wall Street Journal*, February 2, 2010, A4.

44. The phrase "rogue capitalism" was coined in Britain during the 2010 parliamentary elections and cited in John F. Burns, "Brown and His Party Show Signs of Life," *New York Times*, March 28, 2010, A10, http://www.nytimes.com/2010/03/28/world/europe/28britain.html?_r=1.

45. Fareed Zakaria, "The Rise of the Rest," *Newsweek*, May 3, 2008, http://www.newsweek.com/2008/05/03/the-rise-of-the-rest.html. The acronym BRIC was coined by Goldman Sachs chief economist Jim O'Neill in 2001.

46. World Bank, World Development Indicators database, July 1, 2010, http://siteresources.worldbank.org/DATASTATISTICS/Resources/GDP.pdf; David Barboza, "China Passes Japan as Second-Largest Economy," *New York Times*, August 16, 2010, B1, http://www.nytimes.com/2010/08/16/business/global/16yuan.html?_r=1&scp=2&sq=China%20economy&st=cse. Yet China's per capita GDP of $3,600 (compared with $46,000 for the United States) puts it on a par with Algeria and Albania.

47. National Intelligence Council (NIC), Office of the Director of National Intelligence, *Global Trends 2025: A Transformed World* (Washington, DC: US Government Printing Office, 2008), vi, http://www.dni.gov/nic/PDF_2025/2025_Global_Trends_Final_Report.pdf.

48. Stockholm International Peace Research Institute, SIPRI Military Expenditure Database (2009), http://www.sipri.org/databases/milex/.

49. Samuel P. Huntington, "The Lonely Superpower," *Foreign Affairs* 78, no. 2 (March–April 1999): 35–49, http://www.foreignaffairs.com/articles/54797/samuel-p-huntington/the-lonely-superpower.

50. NIC, *Global Trends 2025*, 1.

51. Ibid., x.

52. See Stanley Hoffman's foreword in Bull, *The Anarchical Society*, xxviii.

53. Henry A. Kissinger, *A World Restored: The Politics of Conservatism in a Revolutionary Era* (Boston: Houghton Mifflin, 1957), 1–2 (emphasis added).

54. Bull, *The Anarchical Society*, 171.

55. Jack E. Goldsmith and Eric Posner, *The Limits of International Law* (Oxford: Oxford University Press, 2005), 23.

56. Ibid.

57. Stephen Krasner, *Sovereignty: Organized Hypocrisy* (Princeton, NJ: Princeton University Press, 1999), 52.

58. Gerry Simpson, *Great Powers and Outlaw States: Unequal Sovereigns in the International Legal Order* (Cambridge: Cambridge University Press, 2004), 16, n. 39.

59. Bardo Fassbender, *UN Security Council Reform and the Right of Veto: A Constitutional Perspective* (The Hague: Kluwer Law International), 13.

60. Raymond Aron, *The Imperial Republic: The United States and the World, 1945–1973* (Englewood Cliffs, NJ: Prentice-Hall, 1974).

61. "Rogue Regime" (editorial), *Washington Post*, April 3, 1979, A18.

62. Pursuant to the Export Administration Act of 1979, the secretary of state annually designates those states that are determined to be sponsors of terrorism.

63. From a speech to the American Bar Association in July 1985 in *Public Papers of the Presidents: Ronald Reagan, 1985* (Washington, DC: U.S. Government Printing Office, 1986), 879.

64. Bruce Jentleson, *With Friends Like These: Reagan, Bush, and Saddam, 1982–1990* (New York: W.W. Norton, 1994), 77.

65. Anthony Lake, "Confronting Backlash States," *Foreign Affairs* 73, no. 2 (March–April 1994): 45–46, 55.

66. Michael J. Glennon, *Limits of Law, Prerogatives of Power after Kosovo* (New York: Palgrave, 2001), 120.

67. ICISS, *The Responsibility to Protect* (Ottawa: International Development Research Centre, 2001), 15, http://responsibilitytoprotect.org/ICISS%20Report.pdf.

68. Ibid., 71.

69. Office of the Secretary-General, United Nations, *A More Secure World: Our Shared Responsibility; Report of the High-Level Panel on Threats, Challenges, and Change*, December 2, 2004, http://www.un.org/secureworld/report.pdf.

70. Adam Roberts, "Why and How Intervene? *Jus ad bellum* and *jus in bello* in the New Context," remarks at a colloquium sponsored by Centre d'Études et de Recherches Internationales, Paris, January 15–16, 2004.

71. Ian Johnson, "China Rights Report Cites Improvements, but Also Failings," *New York Times*, September 27, 2010, A7, http://www.nytimes.com/2010/09/27/world/asia/27china.html?_r=1&scp=3&sq=China%20and%20human%20rights&st=cse.

72. Ibid.

73. John Lewis Gaddis, *The Long Peace: Inquiries into the History of the Cold War* (Oxford: Oxford University Press, 1987).

74. NIC, *Global Trends 2025*, 1.

75. Miroslav Nincic, *Renegade Regimes: Confronting Deviant Behavior in International Politics* (New York: Columbia University Press, 2005), 52.

76. Harold Hongju Koh, "Why Do Nations Obey International Law," *Yale Law Journal* 106, no. 8 (June 1997): 2599–659.

77. Nincic, *Renegade Regimes*, 52.

78. Simpson, *Great Powers and Outlaw States*, 282, 312.

79. Articles 2.1 and 2.7, "Charter of the United Nations," adopted June 26, 1945, http://www.un.org/en/documents/charter/.

80. Francis Fukuyama, "Has History Restarted Since September 11?" John Bonython Lecture, Centre for Independent Studies, Melbourne, Australia, August 8, 2002, as cited in Amitai Etzioni, *From Empire to Community* (New York: Palgrave Macmillan, 2004), 198.

81. Marlise Simons, "International Court May Define Aggression as Crime," *New York Times*, May 31, 2010, A7, http://www.nytimes.com/2010/05/31/world/31icc.html?_r=1&scp=5&sq=Harold%20Koh&st=cse.

82. Kal Raustiala and Anne-Marie Slaughter, "International Law, International Relations and Compliance," in *Handbook of International Relations*, ed. Walter Carlsnaes, Thomas Risse, and Beth A. Simmons (London: Sage, 2002), 539.

83. G. John Ikenberry and Charles A. Kupchan, "Socialization and Hegemonic Power," *International Organization* 44, no. 3 (Summer 1990): 286.

84. Kalevi Holsti, *Peace and War: Armed Conflict and International Order 1648–1989* (Cambridge: Cambridge University Press, 1991), 338.

85. Michael J. Glennon, *The Fog of Law: Pragmatism, Security, and International Law* (Washington, DC: Stanford University Press, 2010), 53.

86. Krasner, *Sovereignty*, 52.

87. Richard Haass, "The Case for 'Integration,'" *National Interest* 81 (Fall 2005): 22–29, http://nationalinterest.org/article/the-case-for-integration-577.

2 Pathways into the "Community of Nations"

1. White House, Office of the Press Secretary, "Remarks by President Barack Obama, Prague, Czech Republic," April 5, 2009, http://www.whitehouse.gov/the_press_office/Remarks-By-President-Barack-Obama-In-Prague-As-Delivered/.

2. See, for example, Richard Haass, "The Case for 'Integration,'" *National Interest* 81 (Fall 2005), 22–29, http://nationalinterest.org/article/the-case-for-integration-577.

3. Jeffrey W. Legro, "Purpose Transitions: China's Rise and the American Response," in *China's Ascent: Power, Security, and the Future of International Politics*, ed. Robert S. Ross and Zhu Feng (Ithaca, NY: Cornell University Press), 165.

4. White House, "National Security Strategy 2010," May 2010, 11, http://www.whitehouse.gov/sites/default/files/rss_viewer/national_security_strategy.pdf.

5. This qualitative methodology was developed by political scientist Alexander George; see his "Case Studies: The Method of 'Structured, Focused Comparison,'" in *Diplomacy: New Approaches in History, Theory and Policy*, ed. Paul Gordon Lauren (New York: Free Press, 1979), 43–68.

6. For an excellent discussion of the postwar settlement of 1945 see G. John Ikenberry, *After Victory: Institutions, Strategic Restraint, and the Rebuilding of Order after Major Wars* (Princeton, NJ: Princeton University Press, 2001), 50–79.

7. Konrad H. Jarausch, *After Hitler: Recivilizing Germans, 1945–1995* (Oxford: Oxford University Press, 2006), 115.

8. Gregg O. Kvistad, "Building Democracy and Changing Institutions: The Professional Civil Service and Political Parties in the Federal Republic of Germany," in *The Postwar Transformation of Germany: Democracy, Prosperity, and Nationhood*, ed. John S. Brady, Beverly Crawford, and Sarah Elise Wiliarty (Ann Arbor: University of Michigan Press, 1999), 68.

9. As historian Norman Naimark observes, "The Soviets and the SED [Socialist Unity Party of Germany] did not create the Stasi as an afterthought for securing the East German state structure and protecting its accomplishments. Rather, from the very beginning, security concerns within the German communist party and the Soviet military government helped create an East German state that was inseparable from its internal police functions." See his *To Know Everything and to Report Everything Worth Knowing: Building the East German Police State, 1945–1949*, Cold War International History Project Working Paper no. 10 (Washington, DC: Woodrow Wilson International Center for Scholars, May 1996), 3, http://www.wilsoncenter.org/topics/pubs/ACFB6F.PDF.

10. "Germany" in James Dobbins, John G. McGinn, Keith Crane, Seth G. Jones, Rollie Lal, Andrew Rathmell, Rachel M. Swanger, and Anga R. Timilsina, *America's Role in Nation-Building: From Germany to Iraq* (Santa Monica, CA: RAND Corporation, 2003), 19.

11. Ibid., 11–12.

12. Ruud Van Dijk, *The 1952 Stalin Note Debate: Myth or Missed Opportunity for German Unification?* Cold War International History Project Working Paper no. 14 (Washington, DC: Woodrow Wilson International Center for Scholars, May 1996), 35, http://www.wilsoncenter.org/topics/pubs/ACFB54.pdf.

13. Christian F. Ostermann, ed., *Uprising in East Germany, 1953: The Cold War, the German Question, and the First Major Upheaval behind the Iron Curtain* (Washington, DC: National Security Archive, 2001).

14. John Gaddis, *We Now Know: Rethinking Cold War History* (New York: Oxford University Press, 1997), 115, as cited in Dobbins et al., *America's Role in Nation-Building*, 22.

15. Hope M. Harrison, *Driving the Soviets Up the Wall: Soviet-East German Relations, 1953–1961* (Princeton, NJ: Princeton University Press, 2003), 54.

16. Ibid., 9.

17. Mary Fulbrook, *History of Germany, 1918–2000: The Divided Nation* (Oxford: Blackwell, 2004), 170.

18. For a detailed account and analysis of the diplomacy leading to German unification see Robert L. Hutchings, *American Diplomacy and the End of the Cold War: An Insider's Account of U. S. Policy in Europe, 1989–1992* (Washington, DC: Wilson Center Press, 1997), 90–142.

19. Ibid., 93.

20. Ibid., 138.

21. U.S. Diplomatic Mission to Germany, "A Europe Whole and Free: Remarks of President George H. W. Bush in Mainz, Federal Republic of Germany," May 31, 1989, http://usa.usembassy.de/etexts/ga6-890531.htm.

22. George F. Kennan ("X"), "The Sources of Soviet Conduct," *Foreign Affairs* 25, no. 4 (July 1947): 566–82, http://www.historyguide.org/europe/kennan.html.

23. George F. Kennan, "Just Another Great Power," *New York Times*, April 9, 1989; Kennan's statement to the Senate Foreign Relations Committee on April 4, 1989, http://www.nytimes.com/1989/04/09/opinion/just-another-great-power.html?scp=6&sq=George+Kennan&st=nyt.

24. Klaus Larres, *Churchill's Cold War: The Politics of Personal Diplomacy* (New Haven, CT: Yale University Press, 2002), 38.

25. George F. Kennan, *Soviet-American Relations, 1917–1920* (Princeton, NJ: Princeton University Press, 1956), 85.

26. Discussed in Sheila Fitzpatrick, The Russian Revolution (Oxford, Oxford University Press, 2008), 115.

27. Kennan, "Just Another Great Power."

28. Robert C. Tucker, *Stalin in Power: The Revolution from Above, 1928–1941* (New York: Norton, 1992), xiv.

29. John Lewis Gaddis, *Strategies of Containment: A Critical Appraisal of Postwar American National Security* (Oxford: Oxford University Press, 2005), 15.

30. Ibid., 9.

31. Ibid.

32. Ibid., 20.

33. Vladislav Zubok and Constantine Pleshakov, *Inside the Kremlin's Cold War: From Stalin to Khrushchev* (Cambridge, MA: Harvard University Press, 1996), 36.

34. William Taubman, *Khrushchev: The Man and His Era* (New York: Norton, 2003), xx.

35. Robert S. Litwak, *Détente and the Nixon Doctrine: American Foreign Policy and the Pursuit of Stability, 1969–1976* (Cambridge: Cambridge University Press, 1984), 191.

36. This discussion draws on Robert S. Litwak, "Détente," in *The Oxford Companion to Politics of the World*, ed. Joel Krieger (Oxford: Oxford University Press, 2001), 214–15.

37. Jack Snyder, *Myths of Empire: Domestic Politics and International Ambition* (Ithaca, NY: Cornell University Press, 1991), 46.

38. Ibid.

39. Paul Dibb, *The Soviet Union: The Incomplete Superpower* (New York: Palgrave Macmillan, 1986).

40. Jeffrey W. Legro, *Rethinking the World: Great Power Strategies and International Order* (Ithaca, NY: Cornell University), 146.

41. Ibid.

42. Shoon Murray, *Anchors against Change: American Opinion Leaders' Beliefs after the Cold War* (Ann Arbor, MI: University of Michigan Press, 2002), 16.

43. George H. W. Bush and Brent Scowcroft, *A World Transformed* (New York: Alfred A. Knopf, 1998), 282–83, as cited in Deborah Welch Larson and Alexei Shevchenko, "Redrawing the Soviet Power Line," in *History and Neorealism*, ed. Ernest R. May, Richard Rosecrance, and Zara Steiner (Cambridge: Cambridge University Press, 2010), 304.

44. Philip Zelikow and Condoleezza Rice, *Germany Unified and Europe Transformed: A Study in Statecraft* (Cambridge MA: Harvard University Press, 1995), 137.

45. Legro, *Rethinking the World*, 152; Larson and Shevchenko, "Redrawing the Soviet Power Line," 280.

46. Larson and Shevchenko, "Redrawing the Soviet Power Line," 274.

47. Kennan, "The Sources of Soviet Conduct."

48. Freedom House, *Freedom in the World—Russia* (2010 edition), http://67.192.63.63/template.cfm?page=22&country=7904&year=2010.

49. Erin E. Arvedlund, "Russia Told It Understates Dependence on Oil Sales," *New York Times*, February 19, 2004, http://query.nytimes.com/gst/fullpage.html?res=9C02E ED6123DF93AA25751C0A9629C8B63.

50. Transparency International, *Corruption Perceptions Index* (2010), http://www.transparency.org/policy_research/surveys_indices/cpi/2010/results.

51. Fox News, "Russia Could Become 'Criminal' State in 10 Years, Top Judge Claims," December 10, 2010, http://www.myfoxdc.com/dpp/news/russia-could-become-criminal-state-in-10-years-top-judge-claims-ncxdc-121010.

52. Kennan, "Just Another Great Power."

53. White House, Office of the Press Secretary, "Remarks by President Obama and President Hu of the People's Republic of China at Official Arrival Ceremony," January 19, 2011, http://www.whitehouse.gov/the-press-office/2011/01/19/remarks-president-obama-and-president-hu-peoples-republic-china-official.

54. White House, "National Security Strategy 2010," 43.

55. Richard M. Nixon, "Asia after Viet Nam," *Foreign Affairs* 46, no. 1 (October 1967): 111–25.

56. Pew Research Center for the People and the Press, "U.S. Seen as Less Important, China as More Powerful," December 3, 2009, http://people-press.org/report/569/americas-place-in-the-world.

57. The term "responsible stakeholder" was coined by Deputy Secretary of State Robert B. Zoellick in a speech titled "Whither China: From Membership to Responsibility?" to the National Committee on U.S.-China Relations, September 21, 2005, http://www.ncuscr.org/files/2005Gala_RobertZoellick_Whither_China1.pdf.

58. "Peer competitor" is defined as a state with "the power and motivation to confront the United States on a global scale in a sustained way and to a sufficient level

where the ultimate outcome of a conflict is in doubt." The term gained currency in the U.S. Department of Defense in the post–Cold War era to characterize the potential challenge posed by the rise of China as a major power. See Thomas S. Szayna, Daniel Byman, Steven C. Bankes, Derek Eaton, Seth G. Jones, Robert Mullins, Ian O. Lesser, and William Rosenau, *Peer Competitors: A Framework for Analysis* (Santa Monica, CA: RAND Corporation, 2001), 7, http://www.rand.org/pubs/monograph_reports/MR1346 .html.

59. Chen Jian, "Tiananmen and the Fall of the Berlin Wall: China's Path toward 1989 and Beyond," in *The Fall of the Berlin Wall: The Revolutionary Legacy of 1989*, ed. Jeffrey A. Engel (Oxford: Oxford University Press, 2009), 99. This chapter provides an outstanding historical analysis of the events leading up to the 1989 crackdown and its aftermath based on available Chinese sources.

60. R. Keith Schoppa, *The Columbia Guide to Modern Chinese History* (New York: Columbia University Press, 2000), 115. Roderick MacFarquhar, *The Origins of the Cultural Revolution: Volume II, the Great Leap Forward* (New York: Columbia University Press, 1983), 330, provides a range of estimated deaths: 16.4 million to 29.5 million people.

61. See William Burr and Jeffrey T. Richelson, "Whether to 'Strangle the Baby in the Cradle': The United States and the Chinese Nuclear Program, 1960–64," *International Security* 25, no. 3 (Winter 2000–01): 54–99, which is based on oral history interviews with former U.S. officials and declassified documents.

62. Ibid., 76–77.

63. Chen Jian, "China and the Cold War after Mao," in *The Cambridge History of the Cold War, Volume III, Endings*, ed. Melvyn P. Leffler and Odd Arne Westad (Cambridge: Cambridge University Press, 2010), 181–82.

64. Yang Kuisong, "The Sino-Soviet Border Clash of 1969: From Zhenbao Island to Sino-American Rapprochement," *Cold War History* 1, no. 1 (August 2000): 36.

65. Ibid., 49.

66. Chen Jian, "China and the Cold War after Mao," 184.

67. Chen Jian, "Tiananmen and the Fall of the Berlin Wall," 102–103.

68. Ibid., 110–13.

69. Ibid., 113.

70. Ibid., 122.

71. Ibid., 125–26.

72. Margaret M. Pearson, "China's Integration into the International Trade and Investment Regime," in *China Joins the World: Progress and Prospects*, ed. Elizabeth Economy and Michel Oksenberg (New York: Council on Foreign Relations Press, 1999), 166.

73. Pitman Potter, as cited in Ann Kent, "China's Changing Attitude to the Norms of International Law and Its Global Impact," in *China's "New" Diplomacy: Tactical or Fundamental Change*, ed. Pauline Kerr, Stuart Harris, and Qin Yaqing (New York: Palgrave Macmillan, 2008), 61.

74. Robert S. Sutter, *Chinese Foreign Relations: Power and Policy since the Cold War* (Plymouth, U.K.: Rowman and Littlefield, 2008), 73.

75. Michael D. Swaine and Alastair Ian Johnston, "China and Arms Control Institutions," in *China Joins the World*, ed. Elizabeth Economy and Michel Oksenberg, 100.

76. Alastair Iain Johnston, *Social States: China in International Institutions, 1980–2000* (Princeton, NJ: Princeton University Press, 2008), 41.

77. Swaine and Johnston, "China and Arms Control Institutions," 118.

78. Yong Deng, *China's Struggle for Status: The Realignment of International Relations* (Cambridge: Cambridge University Press, 2008), 41.

79. Ibid.

80. Office of the Secretary of Defense, *FY04 Report on PRC Military pursuant to the FY 2000 National Defense Authorization Act: Annual Report on the Military Power of the People's Republic of China*, 37, http://www.defense.gov/pubs/d20040528PRC. pdf; Office of the Secretary of Defense, *Annual Report to Congress: Military and Security Developments Involving the People's Republic of China 2010*, 35, http://www .defense.gov/pubs/pdfs/2010_CMPR_Final.pdf.

81. Zhang Yunling and Tang Shiping, "China's Regional Strategy," in *Power Shift: China and Asia's New Dynamics*, ed. David Shambaugh (Berkeley: University of California Press, 2005), 53.

82. Ibid.

83. Ashley J. Tellis, "Domestic Politics and Grand Strategy in Asia," in *Domestic Political Change and Grand Strategy: Strategic Asia 2007–2008*, ed. Ashley J. Tellis and Michael Wills (Seattle, WA: National Bureau of Asian Research, 2007), 12.

84. Quoted in Office of the Secretary of Defense, *Annual Report to Congress: Military and Security Developments Involving the People's Republic of China 2010*, 56.

85. For historical background, see David Chandler, *A History of Cambodia*, 4th ed. (Boulder, CO: Westview, 2008), Chapters 12 and 13.

86. This estimate by Amnesty International is widely accepted; cited in Nicholas J. Wheeler, *Saving Strangers: Humanitarian Intervention in International Society* (Oxford: Oxford University Press, 2000), 78. Yale University's Cambodian Genocide Program estimates the number of deaths at approximately 1.7 million, http://www.yale .edu/cgp/.

87. The term, which was used solely in the case of Cambodia, has dropped from use since the 1980s and is controversial within genocide studies in academia. Its coinage was "an uncomfortable acknowledgment of the fact that the events in Cambodia seemed to match the enormity of ethnic genocide, yet did not fit the conventional interpretation of the UN definition." Robert Cribb, "Political Genocides in Postcolonial Asia," in *Oxford Handbook of Genocide Studies*, ed. Donald Bloxham and A. Dirk Moses (Oxford: Oxford University Press, 2010), 43.

88. Henry Kamm, "Cambodian Refugees Tell of Revolutionary Upheaval," *New York Times*, July 15, 1975, "The Week in Review," 69.

89. Evan Gottesman, *Cambodia after the Khmer Rouge: Inside the Politics of Nation Building* (New Haven, CT: Yale University Press, 2003), 43.

90. "Hanoi on the March" (editorial), *New York Times*, January 6, 1979, 18.

91. Mats Berdal and Michael Leifer, "Cambodia," in *United Nations Interventionism, 1991–2004*, ed. Mats Berdal and Spyros Economides (Cambridge: Cambridge University, 1996), 37.

92. Kenton Clymer, *The United States and Cambodia, 1969–2000: A Troubled Relationship* (New York: Routledge Curzon, 2004), 119.

93. Gottesman, *Cambodia after the Khmer Rouge*, 42–43.

94. Clymer, *The United States and Cambodia*, 120.

95. Berdal and Leifer, "Cambodia," 38.

96. U.S. Department of State, Bureau of East Asian and Pacific Affairs, "Background Note: Cambodia," July 23, 2010, http://www.state.gov/r/pa/ei/bgn/2732.htm.

97. "Amin's Legacy in Uganda," *Economist*, August 21, 2003, http://www.economist.com/node/2010135.

98. Library of Congress, Country Studies, *Uganda*, December 1990, http://memory.loc.gov/frd/cs/ugtoc.html. The OAU is now the African Union.

99. Memorandum from the President's Assistant for National Security Affairs (Kissinger) to President Nixon, "The Situation in Uganda," November 1, 1972, in Department of State, Office of the Historian, *Foreign Relations of the United States, vol. E-5, Documents on Sub-Saharan Africa, 1969–1972*, document 261, http://history.state.gov/historicaldocuments/frus1969-76ve05p1/d261.

100. BBC News, "Idi Amin Dies," August 16, 2003, http://news.bbc.co.uk/2/hi/3155925.stm.

101. "Amin: The Wild Man of Africa," *Time*, March 7, 1977, http://www.time.com/time/printout/0,8816,918762,00.html.

102. Ibid.

103. Tore Nyhamar, "How Do Norms Work? A Theoretical and Empirical Analysis of African International Relations," *International Journal of Peace Studies* 5, no. 2 (Autumn–Winter 2000), http://www.gmu.edu/programs/icar/ijps/vol5_2/nyhamar.htm.

104. Sean D. Murphy, *Humanitarian Intervention: The United Nations in an Evolving World Order* (Philadelphia: University of Pennsylvania Press, 1996), 105.

105. Freedom House, *Freedom in the World—Uganda* (2010 edition), http://67.192.63.63/template.cfm?page=22&country=7940&year=2010.

106. Peter Siani-Davies, "Romanian Revolution or Coup d'État?" *Communist and Post-Communist Studies* 29, no. 4 (1996): 453–65.

107. Ralph Blumenthal, "The Ceausescus: 24 Years of Fierce Repression, Isolation, and Independence," *New York Times*, December 26, 1989, http://query.nytimes.com/gst/fullpage.html?res=950DE5DA1431F935A15751C1A96F948260&scp=5&sq=Nicolae+Ceausescu+obituary&st=nyt.

108. Vladimir Tismăneanu, *Stalinism for All Seasons: A Political History of Romanian Communism* (Berkeley: University of California Press, 2003), 27.

109. Daniel Chirot, *Modern Tyrants: The Power and Prevalence of Evil in Our Age* (Princeton, NJ: Princeton University Press, 1994), 240.

110. Colin Woodward, "Romanian Scholars Rebuild Their Universities," *Chronicle of Higher Education* 41 (July 1995), A37.

111. David Binder, "The Cult of Ceausescu," *New York Times Magazine*, November 30, 1986, 1.

112. Tismăneanu, *Stalinism for All Seasons*, 21, 189.

113. Binder, "The Cult of Ceausescu."

114. Tismăneanu, *Stalinism for All Seasons*, 189.

115. "Document 67: Record of Third Conversation between Mikhail Gorbachev and Helmut Kohl, June 14, 1989," in *Masterpieces of History: The Peaceful End of the Cold War in Europe, 1989*, ed. Svetlana Savranskaya, Thomas Blanton, and Vladislav Zubok (Budapest: Central European Press, 2010), 478.

116. Tismăneanu, *Stalinism for All Seasons*, 89–90.

117. Dennis Deletant, *Ceaușescu and the Securitate, 1965–1989* (Armonk, NY: M.E. Sharpe, 1996), 238.

118. Daniel N. Nelson, "Romanian Security," in *Romania since 1989: Politics, Economics, and Society*, ed. Henry F. Carey (Lanham, MD: Lexington Books, 2004), 462.

119. Milada Anna Vachudova, *Europe Undivided: Democracy, Leverage, and Integration after Communism* (New York: Oxford University Press, 2005), 50, 152.

120. To strengthen its bid for NATO membership, Romania was a staunch supporter of U.S. policy after 9/11, including through the deployment of a token force to Afghanistan. As one Romanian officer stated, "Romania's road to NATO runs through Kandahar." Quoted in Rebecca R. Moore, *NATO's New Mission: Projecting Stability in a Post–Cold War World* (Westport, CT: Praeger, 2007), 84.

121. See, for example, Stephen Castle, "E.U. Scolds Romania for Faltering on Reforms," *New York Times*, July 20, 2010, http://www.nytimes.com/2010/07/21/world/europe/21iht-union.html.

122. Princeton N. Lyman, *Partner to History: The U.S. Role in South Africa's Transition to Democracy* (Washington, DC: United States Institute of Peace, 2002), 9.

123. Marina Ottaway, *South Africa: The Struggle for a New Order* (Washington, DC: Brookings Institution Press, 1993), 10.

124. Ibid., 9–10.

125. Lyman, *Partner to History*, 25.

126. For a superb treatment of the South African nuclear weapons program, see Mitchell Reiss, "South Africa: 'Castles in the Air,'" in *Bridled Ambition: Why Countries Constrain Their Nuclear Capabilities* (Washington, DC: Woodrow Wilson Center Press, 1995), 7–44. In 1991, with the end of apartheid, the South African nuclear program was dismantled, and the country joined the nuclear Nonproliferation Treaty (as discussed in Chapter 4).

127. T. R. H. Davenport and Christopher Saunders, *South Africa: A Modern History* (New York: St. Martin's Press, 2000), 535.

128. Pauline H. Baker, "The United States and South Africa: Persuasion and Coercion," in *Honey and Vinegar: Incentives, Sanctions, and Foreign Policy*, ed. Richard N. Haass and Meghan L. O'Sullivan (Washington, DC: Brookings Institution Press, 2000), 100.

129. Ibid., 103.

130. Patti Waldmeir, *Anatomy of a Miracle: The End of Apartheid and the Birth of a New South Africa* (New Brunswick, NJ: Rutgers University Press, 1997), 105.

131. Allister Sparks, *Tomorrow Is Another Country: The Inside Story of South Africa's Road to Change* (Chicago: University of Chicago Press, 1995), 88.

132. "South Africa's New Era: Transcript of de Klerk's News Session on Mandela," *New York Times*, February 11, 1990 (emphasis added), http://www.nytimes.com/1990/02/11/world/south-africa-s-new-era-transcript-of-de-klerk-s-news-session-on-mandela.html?scp=11&sq=De+Klerk&st=nyt.

133. Christopher S. Wren, "Turnout Heavy as South Africans Vote on Change," *New York Times*, March 18, 1992, http://www.nytimes.com/1992/03/18/world/turnout-heavy-as-south-africans-vote-on-change.html?pagewanted=all&src=pm.

134. Hermann Giliomee, *The Afrikaners: Biography of a People* (Charlottesville: University of Virginia Press, 2003), 598.

135. David M. Malone, ed., *The UN Security Council: From the Cold War to the 21st Century* (New York: Lynne Rienner for the International Peace Academy, 2004), 41.

136. Group of 77, "Declaration of the South Summit," April 10–14, 2000, http://www.g77.org/summit/Declaration_G77Summit.htm.

137. As quoted in Dan Bilefsky, "World Court Rules Kosovo Declaration Was Legal," *New York Times*, July 23, 2010, A4, http://www.nytimes.com/2010/07/23/world/

europe/23kosovo.html?scp=1&sq=International%20Court%20of%20Justice%20
and%20Kosovo&st=cse.

138. Giliomee, *The Afrikaners*, 598.

139. See Alexander George, *Bridging the Gap: Theory and Practice in Foreign Policy* (Washington, DC: United States Institute of Peace Press, 1993), 50–51ff.

3 Strategies to Contain, Engage, or Change

1. George F. Kennan ("X"), "The Sources of Soviet Conduct," *Foreign Affairs* 25, no. 4 (July 1947): 566–82, http://www.historyguide.org/europe/kennan.html.

2. Thanks to Blair Ruble, director of the Kennan Institute for Advanced Russian Studies at the Woodrow Wilson Center, for this discussion of Kennan's role.

3. Robert Jervis, *Why Intelligence Fails: Lessons from the Iranian Revolution and the Iraq War* (Ithaca, NY: Cornell University Press), 24.

4. Caroline F. Ziemke, Philippe Loustaunau, and Amy Alrich, *Strategic Personality and the Effectiveness of Nuclear Deterrence* (Alexandria, VA: Institute for Defense Analyses, 2000), p. ES-1 (emphasis added). An outstanding study using this approach was Jack Snyder, *The Soviet Strategic Culture: Limited Nuclear Operations* (Santa Monica, CA: RAND Corporation, 1977).

5. Alastair Ian Johnston, "Thinking about Strategic Culture," *International Security* 19, no. 4 (Spring 1995): 63–64.

6. Office of Public Affairs, Central Intelligence Agency, "Jeremiah News Conference," June 2, 1998, http://www.fas.org/irp/cia/product/jeremiah.html.

7. At the press conference describing the findings of his review panel, Admiral Jeremiah stated, "You begin to fall into a pattern. You operate the way you expect things to happen and you have to recognize that when there is a difference and you could argue that you need to have a contrarian view that might be part of our warning process, ought to include some diversion thinkers who look at the same evidence and come to a different conclusion and then you test that different set of conclusions against other evidence to see if it could be valid." See ibid.

8. Alexander George, *Bridging the Gap: Theory and Practice in Foreign Policy* (Washington, DC: United States Institute of Peace Press, 1993), 126–28.

9. This section on target state analysis is a revised and updated discussion of this qualitative method from Robert S. Litwak, "Strategies for a Change of Regime—or for Change within a Regime?," in *Regime Change: U.S. Strategy through the Prism of 9/11* (Washington, DC: Woodrow Wilson Center Press; Baltimore: Johns Hopkins University Press, 2007), 87–122.

10. Central Intelligence Agency, "Transmittal Message," *Comprehensive Report of the Special Advisor to the DCI on Iraq's WMD* (hereinafter *Duelfer Report*), September 30, 2004, vol. 1, p. 3 (emphasis added), http://www.gpoaccess.gov/duelfer/.

11. George, *Bridging the Gap*, 131.

12. Alexander George made this comment at a Woodrow Wilson Center workshop on "U.S. Strategies toward 'Rogue States': Strategies, Instruments, and Objectives," on May 13, 1997. This section draws heavily on his analysis in "Reforming Outlaw States and Rogue Leaders," in *Bridging the Gap*, 45–60.

13. An engagement-only option toward outlier states is not considered because that strategy would be neither analytically appropriate nor politically feasible.

14. This discussion of the rollback strategy articulated in NSC-158 is drawn from Christian F. Ostermann, "Operationalizing Roll-back: NSC 158," *American Historians of Foreign Relations Newsletter* 26, no. 3 (September 1996), 1–7.

15. See Fareed Zakaria, "The Reagan Strategy of Containment," *Political Science Quarterly* 105, no. 3 (1990): 373–95, and Bruce W. Jentleson, "The Reagan Administration and Coercive Diplomacy: Restraining More Than Remaking Governments," *Political Science Quarterly* 106, no. 1 (1991): 57–82.

16. Richard N. Haass, "Sanctioning Madness," *Foreign Affairs* 76, no. 6 (November–December 1997): 78.

17. Bruce W. Jentleson and Christopher A. Whytock, "Who 'Won' Libya? The Force-Diplomacy Debate and Its Implications for Theory and Policy," *International Security* 30, no. 3 (Winter 2005–06): 55. See also Bruce W. Jentleson, "Economic Sanctions and Post–Cold War Conflicts: Challenges for Theory and Policy," in *International Conflict Resolution after the Cold War*, ed. Paul C. Stern and Daniel Druckman (Washington, DC: National Academy Press, 2000), 135–37. Miroslav Nincic, in *Renegade Regimes: Confronting Deviant Behavior in World Politics* (New York: Columbia University Press, 2005), 25, argues: "The key ... to understanding renegade regimes is to fathom how their behavior is connected to expected consequences for their domestic security, asking how this may be affected by decisions to embrace or defy core international norms."

18. For an excellent discussion of coercive mechanisms to affect regime behavior, see Daniel Byman and Matthew Waxman, "Coercive Mechanisms," in *The Dynamics of Coercion: American Foreign Policy and the Limits of Military Might* (New York: Cambridge University Press, 2002), 48–86.

19. Richard N. Haass and Meghan L. O'Sullivan, "Engaging Problem Countries," Brookings Institution Policy Brief no. 61 (2000), http://www.brookings.edu/~/media/Files/rc/papers/2000/06sanctions_haass/pb61.pdf.

20. Richard N. Haass and Meghan L. O'Sullivan, eds., *Honey and Vinegar: Incentives, Sanctions, and Foreign Policy* (Washington, DC: Brookings Institution Press), 4.

21. George, *Bridging the Gap*, 50–51ff.

22. Ibid., 55–56. See David Cortright, "Incentives Strategies for Preventing Conflict," in *The Price of Peace: Incentives and International Conflict Prevention*, ed. David Cortright (New York: Rowman & Littlefield, 1997), 267–301.

23. Victor Cha, "What North Korea Really Wants," *Washington Post*, June 14, 2009, http://www.washingtonpost.com/wp-dyn/content/article/2009/06/12/AR2009061202685.html.

24. Steve Schifferes, "Rumsfeld Brushes Aside WMD Fears," *BBC News Online*, July 9, 2003, http://news.bbc.co.uk/2/hi/americas/3054423.stm.

25. "Obama Addresses Involvement in Iraq" (transcript by CQ Wire), *Washington Post*, February 27, 2009, http://www.washingtonpost.com/wp-dyn/content/article/2009/02/27/AR2009022701511.html.

26. Bruce Jentleson, *With Friends Like These: Reagan, Bush, and Saddam, 1982–1990* (New York: W.W. Norton, 1994), 52–53.

27. Ibid., 77.

28. As cited in George, *Bridging the Gap*, 45–47.

29. Ibid., 38.

30. Former president George H. W. Bush and National Security Adviser Brent Scowcroft, writing in their joint memoir, *A World Transformed* (New York: Knopf, 1998), 488.

31. Robin Wright, "U.S. Suggests Aid to Any Iraqi 'Successor Regime,'" *Los Angeles Times*, March 27, 1997, http://articles.latimes.com/1997-03-27/news/mn -42683_1_western-aid.

32. As cited in E. J. Dionne, "Who's Got the Wrong Values Now?" *Washington Post*, July 13, 2004, A15.

33. *Duelfer Report*, 33.

34. Bob Woodward, *Plan of Attack* (New York: Simon & Schuster, 2004), 137–38.

35. White House, Office of the Press Secretary, "Remarks by the President in Address to the Nation," March 17, 2003, http://www.whitehouse.gov/news/releases/ 2003/03/20030317-7.html.

36. Powell quoted in Elaine Sciolino, "Clinton Steps In and the World Looks On," *New York Times*, January 24, 1993, sec. 4, p. 1.

37. Jervis, *Why Intelligence Fails*, 123.

38. The text of "Key Judgments from the National Intelligence Estimate on Iraq's Continuing Programs for Weapons of Mass Destruction, October 2002" is an appendix in Joseph Cirincione, Jessica T. Matthews, and George Perkovich with Alexis Orton, *WMD in Iraq: Evidence and Implications* (Washington, DC: Carnegie Endowment for International Peace, 2004), 63–67, http://www.carnegieendowment.org/files/Iraq3 FullText.pdf. The NIE's characterization of the aluminum tubes was disputed by the State Department's Bureau of Intelligence and Research: "The activities we have detected do not … add up to a compelling case that Iraq is currently pursuing what INR would consider to be an integrated and comprehensive approach to acquire nuclear weapons."

39. Todd S. Purdum, *A Time of Our Choosing: America's War in Iraq* (New York: Times Books/Henry Holt, 2004), 58.

40. Eric Schmitt, "Rumsfeld Says U.S. Has 'Bulletproof' Evidence of Iraq's Links to Al Qaeda," *New York Times*, September 28, 2002, A9.

41. White House, Office of the Press Secretary, "Address on Iraq," Remarks in Cincinnati, OH, October, 7, 2002 (emphasis added), http://www.whitehouse.gov/news/ releases/2002/10/20021007-8.html. Deputy Secretary of Defense Paul Wolfowitz similarly asserted, "Disarming Iraq and the war on terror are not merely related. Disarming Iraq of its chemical and biological weapons and dismantling its nuclear weapons program is a crucial part of winning the war on terror." As quoted in Barton Gellman and Walter Pincus, "Iraq's Nuclear File: Depiction of Threat Outgrew Supporting Evidence," *Washington Post*, August 10, 2003, A9.

42. National Commission on Terrorist Attacks upon the United States, *The 9/11 Commission Report* (New York: W.W. Norton, 2004) 66, 228.

43. Commission on the Intelligence Capabilities of the United States Regarding Weapons of Mass Destruction, *Report to the President of the United States, March 31, 2005* (Washington, DC: U.S. Government Printing Office, 2005), letter of transmittal (emphasis added), http://www.gpoaccess.gov/wmd/pdf/full_wmd_report.pdf.

44. Douglas Jehl, "Senators Assail CIA Judgments on Iraq's Arms as Deeply Flawed," *New York Times*, July 9, 2004, A1.

45. Jervis, *Why Intelligence Fails*, 124.

46. *Duelfer Report*, vol. 1, 9.

47. Ibid., vol. 1, 34–35.

48. Michael R. Gordon and Bernard E. Trainor, *Cobra II: The Inside Story of the Invasion and Occupation of Iraq* (New York: Pantheon Books, 2006), 65; Michael R.

Gordon and Bernard E. Trainor, "Hussein Saw Iraqi Unrest as Top Threat," *New York Times*, March 12, 2006, A1.

49. Tim Arango and Michael S. Schmidt, "U.S. Scales Back Diplomacy in Iraq Amid Fiscal and Security Concerns," *New York Times*, October 23, 2011, A6, http://www.nytimes.com/2011/10/23/world/middleeast/us-scales-back-diplomacy-in-iraq-amid-fiscal-and-security-concerns.html?scp=2&sq=Christopher%20Hill&st=cse.

50. Richard N. Haass, *War of Necessity, War of Choice* (New York: Simon & Schuster, 2009), 253–54

51. Ibid., 257.

52. James Dobbins, Seth G. Jones, Benjamin Runkle, and Siddharth Mohandas, *Occupying Iraq: A History of the Coalition Provisional Authority* (Santa Monica, CA; RAND Corporation, 2009), xix, http://www.rand.org/pubs/monographs/MG847.html.

53. The CPA succeeded the short-lived Office for Reconstruction and Humanitarian Assistance under General Jay Gardner. Gardner was reportedly dismissed because of his opposition to deep de-Baathification.

54. Rajiv Chandrasekaran, *Imperial Life in the Emerald City: Inside Iraq's Green Zone* (New York: Vintage Books, 2007), 80.

55. Ibid., 81.

56. Ibid., 109.

57. Steven Simon, "The Price of the Surge," *Foreign Affairs* 87, no. 3 (May–June 2008), 57–76, http://www.foreignaffairs.com/articles/63398/steven-simon/the-price-of-the-surge.

58. BBC News, "Maliki Returns Fire at U.S. Critics," August 26, 2007, http://news.bbc.co.uk/2/hi/middle_east/6964677.stm.

59. Frederic Wehrey, Dalia Dassa Kaye, Jessica Watkins, Jeffrey Martini, and Robert A. Guffey, *The Iraq Effect: The Middle East after the Iraq War* (Santa Monica, CA: RAND Corporation, 2010), 13, http://www.rand.org/pubs/monographs/2010/RAND_MG892.pdf.

60. Ibid., 3.

61. Meghan L. O'Sullivan, "Limiting Libya," in *Shrewd Sanctions: Statecraft and State Sponsors of Terrorism* (Washington, DC: Brookings Institution Press, 2003), 173–232.

62. "Kaddafi—The Most Dangerous Man in the World?" *Newsweek*, July 20, 1981, cover page.

63. Bob Woodward, "CIA Anti-Qaddafi Plan Backed: Reagan Authorizes Covert Operation to Undermine Libyan Regime," *Washington Post*, November 3, 1985, A1; IIE chronology.

64. "Reagan Lists Terms for Lifting Libyan Sanctions," *New York Times*, January 12, 1986, sec. 1, p. 12.

65. Daniel Byman and Matthew Waxman, *The Dynamics of Coercion: American Foreign Policy and the Limits of Military Might* (Cambridge: Cambridge University Press, 2002), 93–94.

66. Alexander L. George, *Forceful Persuasion: Coercive Diplomacy as an Alternative to War* (Washington, DC: United States Institute of Peace, 1991), 58. In announcing the retaliatory air strikes, President Reagan declared, "If necessary, we shall do it again."

67. Byman and Waxman, *The Dynamics of Coercion*, 94–95.

68. Patrick E. Tyler, "Libyan Stagnation a Big Factor in Qaddafi Surprise," *New York Times*, January 8, 2004, A3.

69. O'Sullivan, *Shrewd Sanctions*, 204. Chapter 5 ("Limiting Libya"), 173–232, provides an excellent comprehensive assessment of the impact of sanctions on Libya.

70. Ray Takeyh, "The Rogue Who Came in from the Cold," *Foreign Affairs* 80, no. 3 (May–June 2001): 65.

71. As quoted in ibid., 66.

72. Yehudit Ronen, "Qadhafi and Militant Islamism: Unprecedented Conflict," *Middle Eastern Studies* 38, no. 4 (October 2002): 11.

73. As quoted in Robin Gedye, "UN Should Fight for Rights, Says Berlusconi," *Daily Telegraph* (London), September 4, 2003, http://www.telegraph.co.uk/news/worldnews/europe/italy/1440562/UN-should-fight-for-rights-says-Berlusconi.html.

74. Fox News, "U.S.: Al-Qaddafi Eager to End Weapons Programs," December 21, 2003, http://www.foxnews.com/story/0,2933,106323,00.html.

75. As quoted in Carla Ann Robbins, "In Giving Up Arms, Libya Hopes to Gain New Economic Life," *Wall Street Journal*, February 12, 2004, A10.

76. Sharon A. Squassoni, "Disarming Libya: Weapons of Mass Destruction," CRS Report for Congress no. RS21823, Congressional Research Service, Library of Congress, Washington, DC, 2004, 4–5, http://fpc.state.gov/documents/organization/32007.pdf.

77. David E. Sanger, "U.S. Lifts Bans on Libyan Trade, but Limits on Diplomacy Remain," *New York Times*, April 24, 2004, http://www.nytimes.com/2004/04/24/world/us-lifts-bans-on-libyan-trade-but-limits-on-diplomacy-remain.html?scp=2&sq=Libya&st=nyt.

78. Michele Dunne, "Libya: Security Is Not Enough," Policy Brief 32, Carnegie Endowment for International Peace, Washington, DC, 2004, 7.

79. Andrew Solomon, "Circle of Fire," *New Yorker*, May 8, 2006, 60–61.

80. BBC News, "Rice in Talks with Libya's Qaddafi," September 5, 2008, http://news.bbc.co.uk/2/hi/7599199.stm.

81. Neil MacFarquhar, "Libyan Leader Delivers a Scolding in U.N. Debate," *New York Times*, September 24, 2009, A15, http://www.nytimes.com/2009/09/24/world/24nations.html.

82. Kareem Fahim and David D. Kirkpatrick, "Qaddafi's Grip on the Capital Tightens as Revolt Grows," *New York Times*, February 23, 2011, A1, http://www.nytimes.com/2011/02/23/world/africa/23libya.html?scp=93&sq=Libya&st=nyt.

83. Helene Cooper and Mark Lander, "U.S. Imposes Sanctions on Libya in Wake of Crackdown," *New York Times*, February 26, 2011, A1, http://www.nytimes.com/2011/02/26/world/middleeast/26diplomacy.html?scp=156&sq=Libya&st=nyt.

84. David D. Kirkpatrick and Kareem Fahmi, "Rebels in Libya Gain Power and Defectors," *New York Times*, February 28, 2011, A1, http://www.nytimes.com/2011/02/28/world/africa/28unrest.html?scp=192&sq=Libya&st=nyt#.

85. Frank Gardner, "Who Is Propping Up Qaddafi," *BBC News Online*, March 2, 2011, http://www.bbc.co.uk/news/mobile/world-africa-12558066.

86. Thom Shanker, "Gates Ratchets Up His Campaign of Candor," *New York Times*, March 5, 2011, A4, http://www.nytimes.com/2011/03/05/world/05gates.html?scp=272&sq=Libya&st=nyt.

87. See, for example, Richard N. Haass, "The U.S. Should Keep Out of Libya," *Wall Street Journal*, March 8, 2011, http://online.wsj.com/article/SB10001424052748703386704576186371889744638.html, and Anne-Marie Slaughter, "Fiddling While Libya Burns," *New York Times*, March 14, 2011, A25, http://www.nytimes.com/2011/03/14/opinion/14slaughter.html.

88. Eliott Abrams, "Our Bargain with the New Gadhafi," *Wall Street Journal*, February 25, 2011, http://www.cfr.org/libya/our-bargain-new-gadhafi/p24250.

89. Helene Cooper and David E. Sanger, "Target in Libya Is Clear, Intent Is Not," *New York Times*, March 21, 2011, A1, http://www.nytimes.com/2011/03/21/world/africa/21assess.html?scp=507&sq=Libya&st=nyt.

90. "Text of Obama's Remarks on Libya," *New York Times*, March 28, 2011, http://www.nytimes.com/2011/03/29/us/politics/29prexy-text.html?ref=africa.

91. Barack Obama, David Cameron, and Nicolas Sarkozy, "Libya's Pathway to Peace," *New York Times*, April 14, 2011, http://www.nytimes.com/2011/04/15/opinion/15iht-edlibya15.html.

92. Steven Lee Meyers, "Allies Renew Demand for Qaddafi to Give Up Power," *New York Times*, March 29, 2011, http://www.nytimes.com/2011/03/30/world/africa/30london.html?scp=23&sq=Libya&st=nyt.

93. "Beijing Signals Acceptance of Regime Change in Libya," *China Economic Review*, August 23, 2011, http://www.chinaeconomicreview.com/content/beijing-signals-acceptance-regime-change-libya.

94. Simon Denyer and Leila Fadel, " Gaddafi Accepts African Union's Road Map for Peace," *Washington Post*, April 10, 2011, http://www.washingtonpost.com/world/african-leaders-arrive-in-libya-in-attempt-to-broker-cease-fire-gaddafi-hopes-for-sympathy/2011/04/10/AF0VH6ED_story.html.

95. "Early Military Lessons from Libya," *IISS Strategic Comments* 17, no. 34 (September 2011), International Institute for Strategic Studies, London.

96. Ibid.

97. Reuters, "Libyan Chemical Weapons Stockpiles Intact, Say Inspectors," *Guardian* (U.K.), November 4, 2011, http://www.guardian.co.uk/world/2011/nov/04/libya-chemical-weapons-stockpiles-intact.

98. State Department Legal Adviser Harold Koh, "International Law in a Post-9/11 World," Gerber Lecture, University of Maryland Law School, October 6, 2011.

99. G. John Ikenberry, *After Victory: Institutions, Strategic Restraint, and the Rebuilding of Order after Major Wars* (Princeton, NJ: Princeton University Press, 2001), 246–56.

100. David E. Sanger, "Viewing the War as a Lesson to the World," *New York Times*, April 6, 2003, B1.

101. Jentleson and Whytock, "Who 'Won' Libya?," 55.

102. Before the 2003 war, John W. Dower dismissed any comparison with the U.S. post–World War II occupation of Japan: "The problem is that few if any of the ingredients that made this success possible are present—or would be present—in the case of Iraq. The lessons we can draw from the occupation of Japan all become warnings where Iraq is concerned." The quote is from "A Warning from History: Don't Expect Democracy in Iraq," *Boston Review* (February–March 2003), http://bostonreview.net/BR28.1/dower.html.

4   Nuclear Outliers

1. David E. Sanger and Peter Baker, "Obama Limits When U.S. Would Use Nuclear Arms," *New York Times*, April 6, 2010, A1, http://www.nytimes.com/2010/04/06/world/06arms.html.

2. Kurt M. Campbell, Robert Einhorn, and Mitchell B. Reiss, eds., *The Nuclear Tipping Point* (Washington, DC: Brookings Institution Press, 2004).

3. BBC News, "Bush Names Pakistan 'Major Ally,'" June 17, 2004, http://news .bbc.co.uk/2/hi/3814013.stm.

4. David E. Sanger and Thom Shanker, "Obama's Nuclear Strategy Intended as a Message," *New York Times*, April 7, 2010, A6, http://www.nytimes.com/2010/04/07/ world/07arms.html.

5. White House, Office of the Press Secretary, "Remarks by President Barack Obama, Prague, Czech Republic," April 5, 2009, http://www.whitehouse.gov/ the_press_office/Remarks-By-President-Barack-Obama-In-Prague-As-Delivered.

6. This section draws on and extends my analysis in "Strategies for a Change of Regime—or for Change within a Regime?," in Robert S. Litwak, *Regime Change: U.S. Strategy through the Prism of 9/11* (Washington, DC: Woodrow Wilson Center Press; Baltimore: Johns Hopkins University Press, 2007), 87–122.

7. For example, the Gilpatric Committee report of 1965, written in the aftermath of China's 1964 nuclear test, concluded, "The world is fast approaching a point of no return in the prospects of controlling the spread of nuclear weapons." The declassified document can be accessed at http://www.gwu.edu/~nsarchiv/NSAEBB/NSAEBB1/ nhch7_3.htm.

8. For a comprehensive review of the academic literature, see Scott D. Sagan, "The Causes of Weapons Proliferation," *Annual Review of Political Science* 14 (2011): 227. See also Mitchell Reiss, *Bridled Ambition: Why Countries Constrain Their Nuclear Capabilities* (Washington, DC: Wilson Center Press; Baltimore: Johns Hopkins University Press, 1995), and Maria Rost Rublee, *Nonproliferation Norms: Why States Chose Nuclear Restraint* (Athens, GA: University of Georgia Press, 2009).

9. Etel Solingen, *Nuclear Logics: Contrasting Paths in East Asia and the Middle East* (Princeton, NJ: Princeton University Press, 2007), 5.

10. According to Caroline F. Ziemke, Philippe Loustaunau, and Amy Alrich, strategic personality "focuses on broad historical and cultural patterns that evolve over the whole course of a state's history (its historical plot) and identifies the fundamental consistencies in its long-term strategic conduct in order to shed light on how they might shape its current and future strategic decisions. The methodology is not deterministic and, hence, not precisely predictive." See Caroline F. Ziemke, Philippe Loustaunau, and Amy Alrich, *Strategic Personality and the Effectiveness of Nuclear Deterrence* (Alexandria, VA: Institute for Defense Analyses, November 2000), ES-1.

11. Bush's State of the Union address on January 29, 2002, contained the reference to the "axis of evil." See Chapter 1.

12. As cited in Bruce Hoffman, *Inside Terrorism*, rev. ed. (New York, Columbia University Press, 2006), 269

13. A third potential pathway is *indigenous production*. This route receives much attention because of the widely held view that the primary constraint on a nonstate actor's ability to construct a nuclear weapon is mere access to the requisite nuclear material. But as nuclear physicist and former weapons designer Stephen Younger authoritatively writes in *The Bomb: A Short History* (New York: HarperCollins, 2009), 146, "[N]uclear weapons development still requires the resources of a nation-state." Nuclear terrorism is more likely to take the form of so-called dirty bombs (also referred to as radiation dispersal devices, or RDDs). The immediate casualties from such an attack would result from the blast effect of the device's conventional explosive rather than its

radioactive core. RDDs have been called "weapons of mass disruption" because their impact would be primarily economic, social, and psychological.

14. Director of Central Intelligence, National Intelligence Estimate, *Iraq's Continuing Programs for Weapons of Mass Destruction*, October 2002, http://www.gwu.edu/~nsarchiv/NSAEBB/NSAEBB80/wmd15.pdf.

15. See David Albright, Paul Brannan, Robert Kelley, and Andrea Scheel Stricker, "Burma: A Nuclear Wannabe, Suspicious Links to North Korea, and High-Tech Procurements and Enigmatic Facilities," *ISIS Reports*, January 28, 2010, http://isis-online.org/isis-reports/detail/burma-a-nuclear-wanabee-suspicious-links-to-north-korea-high-tech-procureme/.

16. "Nuclear Proliferation in South Asia: The Power of Nightmares," *Economist*, June 24, 2010, http://www.economist.com/node/16426072.

17. Whether the Pakistani government was complicit remains a matter of contention. Nonproliferation scholar Matthew Kroenig argues that the activities of the Khan network were "state-sponsored by any reasonable definition of the term." Cited in Sagan, "The Causes of Weapons Proliferation," 231.

18. Graham Allison, *Nuclear Terrorism: The Ultimate Preventable Catastrophe* (New York: Times Books and Henry Holt, 2004), 20–23.

19. Transcript of "President Obama's 100th-Day Press Briefing," *New York Times*, April 29, 2009, http://www.nytimes.com/2009/04/29/us/politics/29text-obama.html?_r=1&pagewanted=print.

20. Testimony of Stephen P. Cohen to the Senate Committee on Homeland Security and Government Affairs, "The U.S.-Pakistan Strategic Relationship and Nuclear Safety/Security," June 12, 2008 (110th Cong., 2nd sess.), http://www.brookings.edu/testimony/2008/0612_pakistan_cohen.aspx.

21. The two variants of deterrence were developed in Glenn H. Snyder, *Deterrence by Denial and Punishment*, Research Monograph no. 1 (Princeton, NJ: Princeton University, Center for International Studies, January 1959).

22. David E. Sanger, "2 Nuclear Weapons Challenges, 2 Different Strategies," *New York Times*, June 21, 2003, http://www.nytimes.com/2003/06/21/world/2-nuclear-weapons-challenges-2-different-strategies.html?scp=16&sq=David+E.+Sanger&st=nyt.

23. David E. Sanger, *The Inheritance: The World Obama Confronts and the Challenges to American Power* (New York: Harmony, 2009), 327 (emphasis added).

24. See White House, Office of the Press Secretary, "Remarks by the National Security Adviser, Stephen Hadley, to Center for International Security and Cooperation," Stanford University, Stanford, CA, February 8, 2008 (emphasis added), http://georgewbush-whitehouse.archives.gov/news/releases/2008/02/20080211-6.html.

25. Department of Defense, *Nuclear Posture Review Report* (Washington, DC: Department of Defense, April 2010), vii, http://www.defense.gov/npr/.

26. David E. Sanger and Thom Shanker, "White House Is Rethinking Nuclear Policy," *New York Times*, March 1, 2010, A1, http://www.nytimes.com/2010/03/01/us/politics/01nuke.html.

27. Department of Homeland Security, "National Technical Nuclear Forensics Center," updated March 8, 2011 (emphasis added), http://www.dhs.gov/xabout/structure/gc_1298646190060.shtm.

28. Robert L. Gallucci, "Averting Nuclear Catastrophe: Contemplating Extreme Responses to U.S. Vulnerability," *Harvard International Review* 26, no. 4 (Winter 2005): 83–84.

29. Michael A. Levi, *Deterring State Sponsorship of Nuclear Terrorism*, Council Special Report no. 29 (New York: Council on Foreign Relations Press, 2008), 4, as cited in Debra K. Decker, *Before the First Bomb Goes Off: Developing Nuclear Attribution Standards and Policies* (Harvard Kennedy School, Belfer Center for Science and International Affairs, April 2011), 34–35.

30. David E. Sanger, "Obama's Worst Pakistan Nightmare," *New York Times Magazine*, January 11, 2009, MM32, http://www.nytimes.com/2009/01/11/magazine/11pakistan-t.html.

31. "PM Regrets US Unilateral Action; Warns of Retaliation if Strategic Assets Attacked," *Pakistan Times*, May 2, 2011 (emphasis added), http://pakistantimes.net/pt/detail.php?newsId=21444.

32. For a more detailed analysis of U.S. policy before the Obama administration, see my earlier work on this case: Robert Litwak, "North Korea: Proliferation in a Failed State" in *Regime Change*, 245–91.

33. Andrew Ward, "Kim's Game Takes the World by Surprise," *Financial Times*, October 19, 2002, 10.

34. This early Cold War history is discussed in Don Oberdorfer, "Where the Wild Birds Sing," in *The Two Koreas: A Contemporary History*, 2nd ed. (Reading, MA: Addison Wesley, 2001), 1–26.

35. For documentary evidence from the former Soviet archives on Kim Il Sung's primary role vis-à-vis Stalin in the initiation of the Korean War, see Kathryn Weathersby, "New Findings on the Korean War," *Cold War International History Project Bulletin* 3, Woodrow Wilson International Center for Scholars, Washington, DC, 1993, 1, 14–18.

36. The Truman quote is from his press conference on November 30, 1950; as quoted in William Burr, "'Consultation Is Presidential Business': Secret Understandings on the Use of Nuclear Weapons, 1950–1974," in *National Security Archive Electronic Briefing Book*, no. 159 (Washington, DC: National Security Archive, July 1, 2005), http://www.gwu.edu/~nsarchiv/NSAEBB/NSAEBB159/index.htm.

37. Henry Kissinger, then Nixon's national security adviser, later concluded, "Military options … suffered from the disability that those that seemed safe were inadequate to the provocation, while those that seemed equal to the challenge appeared too risky in terms of the fear of a two-front war.… In retrospect it is clear that we vastly overestimated North Korea's readiness to engage in tit-for-tat." *White House Years* (Boston: Little, Brown, 1979), 318.

38. For a detailed history of Soviet–North Korean nuclear cooperation, see James Clay Moltz and Alexandre Y. Mansourov, eds., *The North Korea Nuclear Program: Security, Strategy, and New Perspectives from Russia* (New York: Routledge, 2000).

39. Joel S. Wit, Daniel B. Poneman, and Robert L. Gallucci, *Going Critical: The First North Korean Nuclear Crisis* (Washington, DC: Brookings Institution Press, 2004), xiv.

40. Stephen Engelberg with Michael R. Gordon, "Intelligence Study Says North Korea Has Nuclear Bomb," *New York Times*, December 26, 1993, sec. 1, p. 1.

41. Reiss, *Bridled Ambition*, 268.

42. As cited in Bradley Martin, *Under the Loving Care of the Fatherly Leader: North Korea and the Kim Dynasty* (New York: St. Martin's Press, 2004), 676.

43. Leon V. Sigal, *Disarming Strangers: Nuclear Diplomacy with North Korea* (Princeton, NJ: Princeton University Press, 1998), 158–59.

44. Former ambassador Robert Gallucci spoke at a meeting on "North Korea in U.S.-Japan Relations" at the Woodrow Wilson Center, Washington, DC, on January 15, 1999.

45. Jane Perlez, "Albright Heading to North Korea to Pave Way for Clinton," *New York Times*, October 22, 2000, sec. 1, p. 8.

46. Michael R. Gordon, "How Politics Sank Accord on Missiles with North Korea," *New York Times*, March 6, 2001, A1.

47. Fred Kaplan, "Rolling Blunder: How the Bush Administration Let North Korea Get Nukes," *Washington Monthly*, May 2004, http://www.washingtonmonthly.com/features/2004/0405.kaplan.html.

48. As cited in Jack Pritchard, "What I Saw in North Korea," *New York Times*, January 21, 2004, A27. Pritchard was a senior State Department official responsible for North Korea who resigned over differences with the Bush administration.

49. Howard W. French, "Officials Say U.S. Will Reposition Its Troops in South Korea," *New York Times*, June 3, 2003, A6.

50. Peter Slevin, "What to Say to North Korea? Officials Divided over How to Move Nation off 'Axis of Evil,'" *Washington Post*, June 3, 2002, A12.

51. UN Security Resolution 1718, October 14, 2006, http://www.un.org/News/Press/docs/2006/sc8853.doc.htm.

52. Helene Cooper, "U.S. Declares North Korea off Terror List," *New York Times*, October 12, 2008, http://www.nytimes.com/2008/10/13/world/asia/13terror.html.

53. White House, Office of the Press Secretary, "Statement of the President," May 25, 2009, http://www.whitehouse.gov/the_press_office/Statement-from-the-President-Regarding-North-Korea/.

54. Glenn Kessler, "Analysis: North Korea Tests U.S. Policy of 'Strategic Patience,'" *Washington Post*, May 27, 2010, http://www.washingtonpost.com/wp-dyn/content/article/2010/05/26/AR2010052605047.html?sid=ST2010052502499.

55. Associated Press, "Life Expectancy Plummets, North Korea Says," May 16, 2001.

56. Oberdorfer, *The Two Koreas*, 297.

57. Kongdan Oh and Ralph Hasig, *North Korea: Through the Looking Glass* (Washington, DC: Brookings Institution Press, 2000), 66.

58. BBC News, "U.S. Says N. Korea a 'Criminal Regime,'" December 7, 2005, http://news.bbc.co.uk/2/hi/asia-pacific/4505960.stm.

59. Raphael F. Perl, "Drug Trafficking and North Korea: Issues for U.S. Policy," CRS Report for Congress no. RL32167 Congressional Research Service, Library of Congress, Washington, DC, November 7, 2006, 5–8, http://www.au.af.mil/au/awc/awcgate/crs/rl32167.pdf.

60. Foreign Policy, "The Failed States Index 2011," http://www.foreignpolicy.com/articles/2011/06/17/2011_failed_states_index_interactive_map_and_rankings.

61. International Institute for Strategic Studies (IISS), *North Korea's Weapon Programmes: A Net Assessment* (London: IISS, 2004), 24.

62. The documents cited here are from the collection compiled by the North Korea International Documentation Project of the Woodrow Wilson Center and can be accessed at http://www.wilsoncenter.org/nkidp.

63. Jonathan D. Pollack, *No Exit: North Korea, Nuclear Weapons and International Security* (London: Routledge for the International Institute for Strategic Studies, 2011), 141.

64. Ibid., 143.

65. Ibid. (emphasis added).

66. Oberdorfer, *The Two Koreas*, 420.

67. French, "Officials Say U.S. Will Reposition Its Troops in South Korea."

68. Marcus Noland, *Korea after Kim Jong-il*, Policy Analysis in International Economics no. 71 (Washington, DC: Institute for International Economics, January 2004), 13.

69. Pollack, *No Exit*, 179.

70. U.S. Department of State, Secretary of State Hillary Clinton, "Remarks at the United States Institute of Peace," October 11, 2009, http://www.state.gov/secretary/rm/2009a/10/130806.htm.

71. Mark McDonald, "North Koreans Struggle, and Party Keeps Its Grip," *New York Times*, February 27, 2011, A8, http://www.nytimes.com/2011/02/27/world/asia/27northkorea.html.

72. IISS, *North Korean Security Challenges: A Net Assessment* ("Strategic Dossier" launch statement summary), July 21, 2011, 4.

73. Elisabeth Bumiller and David E. Sanger, "Gates Warns of North Korea Missile Threat to U.S.," *New York Times*, January 12, 2011, A8, http://www.nytimes.com/2011/01/12/world/asia/12military.html.

74. For a more detailed analysis of U.S. policy before the Obama administration, see my earlier work on this case: "Iran: Revolutionary State or Ordinary Country?" in Litwak, *Regime Change*, 200–44.

75. Quoted in David Ignatius, "Talk Boldly with Iran," *Washington Post*, June 23, 2006, A25.

76. Iran TV, August 23 1994, BBC, ME/2085SI/8, cited in Shahram Chubin, *Whither Iran? Reform, Domestic Politics and National Security*, Adelphi Paper no. 342 (London: Oxford for the International Institute for Strategic Studies, 2002), 123.

77. For a comprehensive listing, see Jason Starr, "The U.N. Resolutions," in *The Iran Primer: Power, Politics, and U.S. Policy*, ed. Robin Wright (Washington, DC: United States Institute of Peace, 2010) 119–23, http://iranprimer.usip.org/resource/un-resolutions.

78. The 2011 NIE findings are reported in Greg Miller and Joby Warrick, "U.S. Report Finds Debate in Iran on Building Nuclear Bomb," *Washington Post*, February 19, 2011, http://www.washingtonpost.com/wp-dyn/content/article/2011/02/18/AR2011021807152.html.

79. Shahram Chubin, *Iran's Nuclear Ambitions* (Washington, DC: Carnegie Endowment for Peace, 2006), 123.

80. Algiers Accords, January 19, 1981, http://www.parstimes.com/history/algiers_accords.pdf.

81. Geoffrey Kemp, "The Reagan Administration," in *The Iran Primer*, ed. Robin Wright, 133–35.

82. George H. W. Bush, *Public Papers of the Presidents of the United States: George Bush, 1989*, vol. 1 (Washington, DC: U.S. Government Printing Office, 1990), 1–4.

83. Elaine Sciolino, "After a Fresh Look, U.S. Decides to Steer Clear of Iran," *New York Times*, June 7, 1992, as cited in George, *Bridging the Gap*, 60.

84. Bruce O. Reidel, "The Clinton Administration," in *The Iran Primer*, ed. Robin Wright, 139–41.

85. Madeleine K. Albright, "Remarks before the American-Iranian Council," Department of State, March 17, 2000, http://secretary.state.gov/www/statements/2000/000317.html.

86. BBC News, "Khamenei Rejects US Overtures," March 25, 2000, http://news.bbc.co.uk/1/hi/world/middle_east/690551.stm.

87. Condoleezza Rice, "Promoting the National Interest," *Foreign Affairs* 79, no. 1 (January–February 2000): 61.

88. Alan Sipress, "Bush's Speech Shuts Door on Tenuous Opening to Iran," *Washington Post*, February 4, 2002, A10.

89. CNN, "Bush State of the Union Address," January 29, 2002, http://articles.cnn.com/2002-01-29/politics/bush.speech.txt_1_firefighter-returns-terrorist-training-camps-interim-leader?_s=PM:ALLPOLITICS.

90. Guy Dinmore, "U.S. Stalls over Iran's Offer of Reform Deal," *Financial Times*, March 17, 2004, 1. A former U.S. official confirmed the *Financial Times* reporting to the author. Also discussed in Barbara Slavin, *Bitter Friends, Bosom Enemies: Iran, the U.S., and the Twisted Path to Confrontation* (New York: St. Martin's Press, 2007), 204–6; 229–31 is an appendix with the text of the document.

91. Three years later, Secretary Rice argued that the United States had not missed an opportunity in 2003: "[W]hat the Iranians wanted … was to be one-on-one with the United States so that this could be about the United States and Iran. Now … Iran has to answer to the international community. I think that's the strongest possible position to be in." Interview on National Public Radio, Vienna, Austria, June 2, 2006, http://merln.ndu.edu/archivepdf/iran/State/67391.pdf.

92. The P5+1 proposal is detailed in Kenneth Katzman, "Iran: U.S. Concerns and Policy Responses," CRS Report for Congress no. RL32048 Congressional Research Service, Library of Congress, Washington, DC, August 6, 2007, 17–18, http://www.fas.org/sgp/crs/mideast/RL32048.pdf.

93. Secretary Condoleezza Rice interview on *Fox News Sunday with Chris Wallace*, May 21, 2006, http://www.foxnews.com/story/0,2933,196364,00.html.

94. BBC News, "UN Sanctions against Iran," July 26, 2010, http://www.bbc.co.uk/news/world-middle-east-10768146.

95. Robin Wright, "Iranian Unit to be Labeled 'Terrorist,'" *Washington Post*, August 15, 2007, http://www.washingtonpost.com/wp-dyn/content/article/2007/08/14/AR2007081401662.html.

96. National Intelligence Council, "National Intelligence Estimate; Iran: Nuclear Intentions and Capabilities," November 2007, http://www.dni.gov/press_releases/20071203_release.pdf.

97. Ibid.

98. For a discussion of latency, see Mark Fitzpatrick, "Can Iran's Nuclear Capability Be Kept Latent," *Survival* 49, no. 1 (Spring 2007): 33–57.

99. Elaine Sciolino, "Monitoring Agency Praises U.S. Report, but Keeps Wary Eye on Iran," *New York Times*, December 5, 2007, A13.

100. John Limbert, "The Obama Administration," in *The Iran Primer*, ed. Robin Wright, 146–50.

101. Christiane Amanpour, "Obama Sent Letter to Iran Leader before Election, Sources Say," CNN, June 24, 2009, http://articles.cnn.com/2009-06-24/politics/iran.obama.letter_1_iranian-leader-tehran-university-iranian-government?_s=PM:POLITICS.

102. C. Christine Fair, "Iran: What Future for the Islamic State?" in Angel M. Rabasa, Cheryl Benard, Peter Chalk, C. Christine Fair, Theodore Karasik, Rollie Lal, Ian Lesser, and David Thaler, *The Muslim World after 9/11* (Santa Monica, CA: RAND, 2004), 218–24.

103. Karim Sadjapour, "The Supreme Leader," in *The Iran Primer*, ed. Robin Wright, 11–14.

104. Abbas Milani, "The Green Movement," in *The Iran Primer*, ed. Robin Wright, 41–44.

105. Mark Landler, "Clinton Raises U.S. Concern of Military Power in Iran," *New York Times*, February 16, 2010, A1 (emphasis added), http://www.nytimes.com/2010/02/16/world/middleeast/16diplo.html.

106. Laura Secor, "The Iran Show," *New Yorker*, August 31, 2009, http://www.newyorker.com/talk/comment/2009/08/31/090831taco_talk_secor.

107. Milani, "The Green Movement," 42.

108. Ibid.

109. Thomas Erdbrink, "Iran's Ahmadinejad Affirms Khamenei Decision, Tensions Remain," *Washington Post*, May 8, 2011, http://www.washingtonpost.com/world/middle-east/irans-ahmadinejad-affirms-khamenei-decision-tensions-remain/2011/05/08/AFpK82QG_story.html.

110. Testimony of George Tenet to the Senate Committee on Intelligence, "The Worldwide Threat in 2003: Evolving Dangers in a Complex World," February 11, 2003 (108th Cong., 1st sess.), http://www.iraqwatch.org/government/US/CIA/cia-tenet-threats-021103.htm.

111. Dafna Linzer, "Past Arguments Don't Square with Current Iran Policy," *Washington Post*, March 27, 2005, A15.

112. International Institute for Strategic Studies (IISS), *Iran's Strategic Weapons Programmes: A Net Assessment* (London: Routledge for IISS, 2005), 11.

113. The precipitant of the IAEA investigation of Iran's uranium enrichment program was charges made by a dissident group, the National Council of Resistance of Iran, in August 2002. Also revealed was the existence of a heavy-water plant at Arak, which could support a heavy-water moderated reactor, which would produce plutonium. The United States viewed the Arak facility as indicative of the Iranian intention to pursue both the highly enriched uranium and the plutonium routes to nuclear weapons.

114. Joby Warrick, "Nuclear Program in Iran Tied to Pakistan," *Washington Post*, December 21, 2003, A1.

115. Centrifuges are essential equipment for uranium enrichment, the multistage industrial process in which natural uranium is converted into special material capable of sustaining a nuclear chain reaction. Natural uranium occurs in two forms: U-238, making up 99 percent of the element, and the lighter U-235, accounting for less than 1 percent. The latter, however, is a fissionable isotope that emits energy when split. Uranium ore is crushed into a powder, refined, and then reconstituted into a solid form, known as "yellow cake." The yellow cake is then superheated and transformed into a gas, uranium hexafluoride. That gas is passed through a centrifuge and spun at high speed, with the U-238 drawn to the periphery and extracted, while the lighter U-235 clusters in the center and is collected. The collected U-235 material is passed through a series of centrifuges, known as a "cascade," with each successive pass-through increasing the percentage of U-235. Uranium for a nuclear reactor should be enriched to contain ap-

proximately 3 percent U-235, whereas weapons-grade uranium should ideally contain at least 90 percent.

116. Mahmoud Ahmadinejad, UN General Assembly address, September 17, 2005, http://www.un.org/webcast/ga/60/statements/iran050917eng.pdf.

117. This discussion of the internal debate on Iran's nuclear program draws on Shahram Chubin and Robert S. Litwak, "Debating Iran's Nuclear Aspirations," *Washington Quarterly* 26, no. 4 (August 2003): 99–114.

118. Chubin, *Iran's Nuclear Ambitions*, 7.

119. Akbar Hashemi Rafsanjani, Qods Day Speech (Jerusalem Day), December 14, 2001, http://www.globalsecurity.org/wmd/library/news/iran/2001/011214-text.html.

120. Michael Eisenstadt, "Delay, Deter and Contain, Roll-Back: Toward a Strategy for Dealing with Iran's Nuclear Ambitions," in Geoffrey Kemp, *Iran's Bomb: American and Iranian Perspectives* (Washington, DC: Nixon Center, 2004), 25.

121. National Intelligence Council, "National Intelligence Estimate; Iran: Nuclear Intentions and Capabilities."

122. William J. Broad, John Markoff, and David E. Sanger, "Israeli Test on Worm Called Crucial in Iran Nuclear Delay," *New York Times*, January 16, 2011, A1, http://www.nytimes.com/2011/01/16/world/middleeast/16stuxnet.html?_r=1&ref=stuxnet.

123. Mark Hosenball, "U.S. Intelligence: Iran Leaders Reopened Nuke Debate," *Reuters*, February 17, 2011, http://www.reuters.com/article/2011/02/17/us-iran-usa-nuclear-idUSTRE71G7YO20110217.

124. Ibid.

125. Director of Central Intelligence, *Special National Intelligence Estimate: Prospects for Further Proliferation of Nuclear Weapons*, August 23, 1974, http://www.gwu.edu/~nsarchiv/NSAEBB/NSAEBB240/snie.pdf.

126. Kenneth M. Pollack, *The Persian Puzzle: The Conflict between Iran and America* (New York: Random House, 2004), 390.

127. Michael Adler, "Iran and the IAEA," in *The Iran Primer*, ed. Robin Wright, 89–94.

128. Mark Fitzpatrick, "Executive Summary," in *Iran's Nuclear, Chemical and Biological Capabilities: A Net Assessment* (London: International Institute for Strategic Studies, 2011), 4.

129. Thomas Erdbrink and Glenn Kessler, "Ahmadinejad Makes Nuclear Claims, Stifles Protests on Revolution's Anniversary," *Washington Post*, February 12, 2010, http://www.washingtonpost.com/wp-dyn/content/article/2010/02/11/AR2010021100456.html.

130. Jerry Guo, "You Can't Bomb Knowledge: An Interview with Mohamed ElBaradei," *Newsweek*, December 10, 2009.

131. Sukhee Han, "The Limits of Humanitarian Intervention in North Korea," in *Conflict Management, Security, and Intervention in East Asia: Third Party Mediation in Regional Conflict*, ed. Jacob Berkovich, Kwei-Bo Huang, and Chung-Chian Teng (New York: Routledge, 2008), 139.

132. Yoel Sano, "North Korea: Military Holds the Key," *Asia Times*, February 18, 2005, http://www.atimes.com/atimes/Korea/GB18Dg02.html.

133. Daniel Byman and Jennifer Lind, "Keeping Kim: How North Korea's Regime Stays in Power," Policy Brief, Belfer Center for Science and International Affairs, Harvard Kennedy School, Cambridge, MA, July 2010, http://belfercenter.ksg.harvard.edu/publication/20269/keeping_kim.html.

134. Shaul Bakhash, "A Revolution's Anniversary: Iran's Creeping Military Rule," *Iran Primer* (blog), http://iranprimer.usip.org/blog/2011/feb/09/revolution%E2%80%99s-anniversary-iran%E2%80%99s-creeping-military-rule.

135. See, for example, Danielle Pletka, "Iran Sanctions Are Failing: What Next?" *Wall Street Journal*, March 31, 2010, http://www.aei.org/article/101858.

136. Mark McDonald, "North Korea Suggests Libya Should Have Kept Nuclear Program," *New York Times*, March 25, 2011, A12, http://www.nytimes.com/2011/03/25/world/asia/25korea.html; Howard LaFranchi, "Libya Fallout: Why Iran, North Korea Now Less Likely to Drop Nuclear Ambitions," *Christian Science Monitor*, April 1, 2011, http://www.csmonitor.com/USA/Foreign-Policy/2011/0401/Libya-fallout-Why-Iran-North-Korea-now-less-likely-to-drop-nuclear-ambitions.

137. As quoted in Jeffrey Lewis, "Clapper on Iran NIE," *Arms Control Wonk*, March 19, 2011, http://lewis.armscontrolwonk.com/archive/3703/clapper-on-iran-nie.

138. Cited in Patrick Clawson, "The Red Line: How to Assess Progress in U.S. Iran Policy," Washington Institute Strategic Report, Washington Institute for Near East Policy, Washington, DC, 2010, 11, http://www.washingtoninstitute.org/pubPDFs/StrategicReport05.pdf.

139. David E. Sanger, "U.S. Seeks to Offer a Balm to Iran for Sanctions' Sting," *New York Times*, August 7, 2010, http://www.nytimes.com/2010/08/08/world/middleeast/08sanctions.html?scp=17&sq=&st=nyt.

140. Joel Wit, "How to Talk to a North Korean," *Foreign Policy*, April 20, 2011, http://www.foreignpolicy.com/articles/2011/04/20/how_to_talk_to_a_north_korean?page=0,1.

141. Andrei Lankov, "Pyongyang Looks for the Next Payoff: The Lesson North Korean Leaders Learned from Libya Is That There Is No Security without Nuclear Weapons," *Wall Street Journal*, September 27, 2011.

142. Mitchell B. Reiss, "Hard Containment," *American Interest* (January–February 2010): 75.

143. Mark Mazzetti and Helene Cooper, "Israeli Nuclear Suspicions Linked to Raid in Syria," *New York Times*, September 18, 2007, http://www.nytimes.com/2007/09/18/world/asia/18korea.html.

144. David E. Sanger, "U.S. Said to Turn Back North Korea Missile Shipment," *New York Times*, January 13, 2011, A4, http://www.nytimes.com/2011/06/13/world/asia/13missile.html?_r=1&scp=1&sq=North%20Korea%20and%20Burma&st=cse.

145. Mark Landler and David E. Sanger, "Clinton Speaks of Shielding Mideast from Iran," *New York Times*, July 23, 2009, A1, http://www.nytimes.com/2009/07/23/world/asia/23diplo.html.

Conclusion

1. BBC News, "Rice Names 'Outposts of Tyranny,'" January 19, 2005, http://news.bbc.co.uk/2/hi/americas/4186241.stm.

2. E. H. Carr, *The Twenty Years' Crisis, 1919–1939: An Introduction to the Study of International Relations* (New York: Palgrave, 2001).

3. Samuel P. Huntington, "The Lonely Superpower," *Foreign Affairs* 78, no. 2 (March–April 1999): 35–49, http://www.foreignaffairs.com/articles/54797/samuel-p-huntington/the-lonely-superpower.

4. Charles Krauthammer, "The Unipolar Moment," *Foreign Affairs* 70, no. 1 (1990–91): 23–33.

5. Henry Kissinger, "An End of Hubris," *Economist* ("The World in 2009" edition), November 19, 2008, http://www.economist.com/node/12574180.

6. G. John Ikenberry, *After Victory: Institutions, Strategic Restraint, and the Rebuilding of Order after Major Wars* (Princeton, NJ: Princeton University Press, 2001).

7. George F. Kennan ("X"), "The Sources of Soviet Conduct," *Foreign Affairs* 25, no. 4 (July 1947): 566–82, http://www.historyguide.org/europe/kennan.html.

8. Condoleezza Rice, *No Higher Honor: A Memoir of My Years in Washington* (New York: Crown, 2011), 187.

9. Robert G. Joseph, in *Countering WMD: The Libyan Experience* (Fairfax, VA: National Institute Press, 2009), denies that the United States and Britain made any concessions or provided a quid pro quo in return for Libya's abandonment of its WMD and long-range missiles. But, he writes, "they also made it clear that Libya would remove a major obstacle to improved relations and greater economic benefits for the Libyan people." A willingness to improve relations meant, by definition, that the Bush administration would not pursue an Iraqi-style regime change strategy toward Libya—in essence, a tacit security assurance.

10. Steven Levitsky and Lucan A. Way, *Competitive Authoritarianism: Hybrid Regimes after the Cold War* (Cambridge: Cambridge University Press, 2010), 43.

11. Department of State, "Keynote Address by Secretary of State Hillary Rodham Clinton at the National Democratic Institute's 2011 Democracy Awards Dinner," Washington, DC, November 7, 2011, http://www.state.gov/secretary/rm/2011/11/176750.htm.

12. Center for U.S.-Korea Policy, Asia Foundation, "North Korea Contingency Planning and U.S.-ROK Cooperation," September 2009, 5, http://asiafoundation.org/resources/pdfs/DPRKContingencyCUSKP0908.pdf.

13. Department of State, "Keynote Address by Secretary of State Hillary Rodham Clinton."

14. As cited in Shahram Chubin, *Iran's Nuclear Ambitions* (Washington, DC: Carnegie Endowment for Peace, 2006), 76.

15. BBC News, "Russia Rules Out New Iran Sanctions over Nuclear Report," November 9, 2011, http://www.bbc.co.uk/news/world-middle-east-15659311.

16. David E. Sanger, "U.S. Seeks to Offer a Balm to Iran for Sanctions' Sting," *New York Times*, August 8, 2010, A10, http://www.nytimes.com/2010/08/08/world/middleeast/08sanctions.html?scp=17&sq=&st=nyt.

17. Al Akbar Dareini, "Iran, Venezuela Leader Seek 'New World Order,'" Associated Press, October 21, 2010, http://www.foxnews.com/world/2010/10/20/iran-venezuela-leader-seek-new-world-order/.

18. Jeffrey Goldberg, "Obama to Iran and Israel: 'As President of the United States, I Don't Bluff,'" *The Atlantic*, March 2, 2012, http://www.theatlantic.com/international/archive/2012/03/obama-to-iran-and-israel-as-president-of-the-united-states-i-dont-bluff/253875/.

19. BBC News, "US Defence Chief Panetta Warns Against Iran Strike," November 10, 2011, http://www.bbc.co.uk/news/world-middle-east-15688042.

20. Ibid.

21. Goldberg, "Obama to Iran and Israel."

22. James Risen and Mark Mazzetti, "U.S. Agencies See No Move by Iran to Build a Bomb," *New York Times*, February 25, 2012, A1, http://www.nytimes.com/2012/02/25/world/middleeast/us-agencies-see-no-move-by-iran-to-build-a-bomb.html?_r=1&ref=nuclearprogram.

23. Goldberg, "Obama to Iran and Israel."

24. White House, Office of the Press Secretary, "Remarks by the President at AIPAC Policy Conference," March 4, 2012, http://www.whitehouse.gov/the-press-office/2012/03/04/remarks-president-aipac-policy-conference-0.

Index